禪宗師承圖

丙辰立春　梁溪居士擬訂

佛紀二五二〇年　訂于蕉舍

（禪宗初祖）達摩 —慧可（二祖）487-593 —僧璨（三祖）-606 —道信（四祖）580-651 —弘忍（五祖）602-675

五祖弘忍（602-675）
六祖慧能（638-713）
神秀（弟子）-706　京兆普寂（651-739）高福（631-739）

智詵（609-702）—慧寂（665-731）—無相（684-762）—無住（714-774）

青原行思（-740）—石頭希遷（700-790）

玄覺（665-713）永嘉

南陽慧忠（-775）

南嶽懷讓（677-744）—馬祖道一（709-788）

荷澤神會（670-762）

禪宗師承圖（臨濟宗）

第二圖

〔錫� 印〕

臨濟 義玄（－866）
興化 存獎（830－888）
南院 慧顒
風穴 延沼（896－973）
首山 省念（925－993）

廣慧元璉（951－1036）　＋　華嚴道隆

南臺契瞳
　龍華曉愚
　　常熟軍珍　＋　金山惠洵

福聖善瑀
　天聖皓泰　＋　永慶文

黃檗重巒
　法華全舉　＋　永慶文

承天智嵩
　石霜法永　＋　福嚴保宗
　　　　　　　　承天智曩（－1085）
　　　　　　　　華嚴義然

智門遍覈
　芭蕉谷泉
　瑯瑘慧覺
　　泐潭曉月　＋　上藍慶晉
　　蔣山贊元（－1086）＋雪竇法雅
　　　　　　　　光孝普印　＋　東林常總
　　　　　　　　龍游清韻
　　　　　　　　石門永興

汾陽善昭（947－1024）
　石霜楚圓（987－1040）
　　黃龍慧南（1002－1069）（見另圖）
　　大寧道寬　＋　兜率惠證
　　楊岐方會（992－1049）（見另圖）
　　　定慧超信　＋　寫隆祖圓（1036－1246）
　　　　　　　　　　雙溪如珪

仁王處評
　龍潭智圓（976－1022）
　大愚守芝（－1037）
　　雲峯文悅（997－1062）＋壽寧齊曉
　　翠巖可真（－1064）＋大溈慕喆
　　　　　　　　　　　　（－1095）

首山懷志

谷隱蘊聰（965－1032）
　金山曇穎（989－1060）
　　瑞竹仲和
　　西余拱辰
　　普慧崇珍
　　廣教繼賢
　　金山懷賢
　　洞夏慧月
　　鷹天世珍
　　承天世珍
　　瑞光嵩

神鼎洪諲　＋　妙智光雲

葉縣歸省（991－1067）＋浮山法遠（991－1067）
　淨因道臻（1014－1093）＋長慶慧遷
　樓勝繼超

泐潭景祥
智海道平　＋　淨因繼成
　　　　　　　廬山法真
光孝慧蘭
　鴻福椿昇　＋　鄱州甘露常
　　瑞巖如勝
　　治父道川
廣教從原
開福崇哲
遠輪彥教

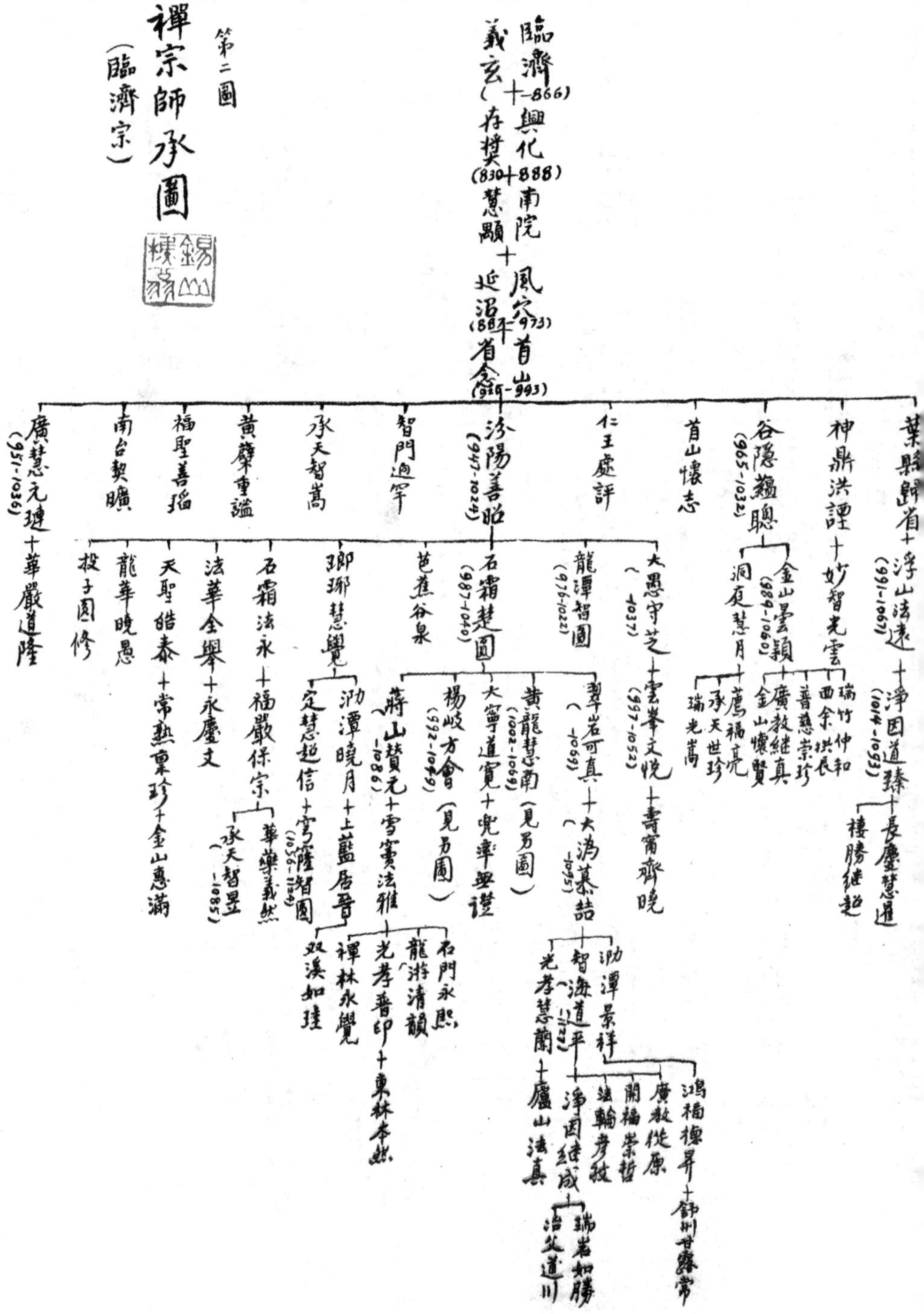

第三圖　禪宗師承圖（臨濟宗）（黃龍宗）

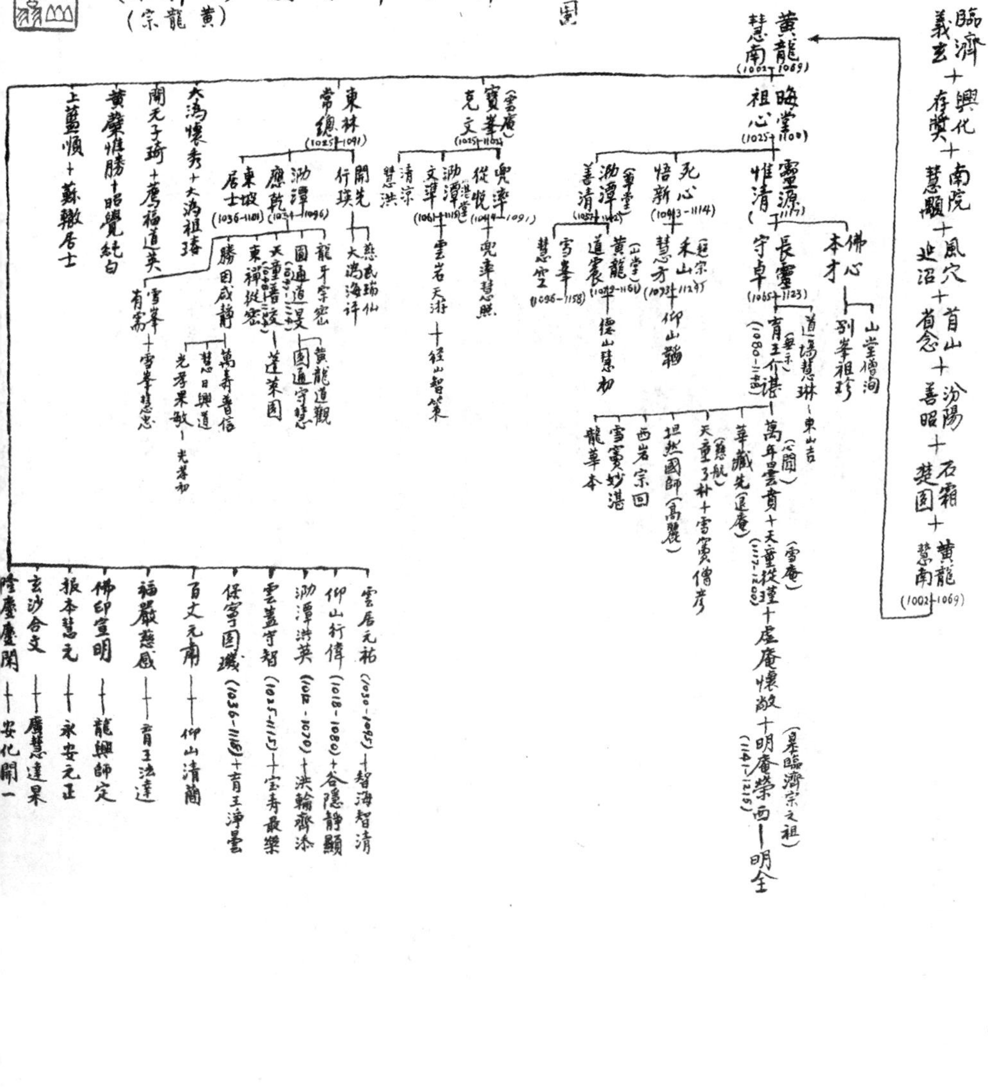

臨濟義玄＋興化＋南院＋存獎＋慧顒＋風穴＋延沼＋首山＋省念＋善昭＋汾陽＋石霜＋楚圓＋黃龍慧南（1002-1069）

黃龍慧南（1002-1069）

晦堂祖心（1025-1100）

東林常總（1025-1091）

寶峰克文（雲庵）（1025-1102）

靈源惟清（1117）
長靈守卓（1065-1123）
佛心本才
山堂道洞
別峰祖珍
楊岐慧琳～東山吉
（心聞）
萬年曇貴＋天童正覺＋虛庵懷敞＋明庵榮西—明全

死心悟新（1043-1114）
妙喜宗杲（徑山）
起宗
禾山
仰山鞠

悟新慧才（1024）仰山鞠

兜率從悅（1044-1091）
兜率慧照

湛堂文準（1061-1115）
清涼慧洪（石門）
泐潭善清
泐潭懷澄＋黃龍（草堂）＋雲蓋妙湛＋龍華本

居士韓駒（1036-1101）
東坡蘇軾＋東禪從密

開先行瑛
廬山智策＋雲岩天游＋徑山智策

大潙懷秀＋大潙祖珣
南元子琦＋慮福道英
黃龍惟勝＋晦覺純己
上藍順＋蘇轍居士

雲居元祐（1050-1085）＋智海智清
仰山行偉（1018-1080）＋合隱靜顯
泐潭洪英（1012-1070）＋洪通守恂
雲蓋守智（1025-1115）＋宇壽最樂
保寧圓璣（1036-1118）＋宇淨淨雲
百丈元肅＋仰山清簡
福嚴慈感＋育王法達
佛印宣明＋龍興師定
振本慧元＋永安元正
玄沙合支＋厲慧達果
雪竇慶閑＋安化開一

禪宗師承圖　（臨濟宗）（楊岐宗）

錫山漢俗

由此以上……

義玄 十 存獎 十 慧顒 十 延沼 十 省念 十 善昭 十 楚圓 十 方會（992―1049）

義玄 十 存獎 十 慧顒 十 延沼 十 省念 十 汾陽 十 石霜 十 楊岐

楊岐方會（992―1049）
白雲守端（1025―1072）
保寧仁勇
雲蓋智本
五祖法演（―1104）
昭覺克勤（1063―1135）

虎丘紹隆（見易圖）（1077―1136）
　應菴曇華 十 淨慈曇密（1116―1184）
　　密菴咸傑 十 破菴祖先 十 無準師範
　　　龍翔南雅（祖堂）
　　　鼓山安永（東庵）十 淨慈慧明
　　　西禪鼎需

大慧宗杲（1089―1163）
　懶菴鼎需
　東林道顏（佛心）
　拙菴德光
　　徑山如琰 十 徑山師範
　　天童了瑮
　　雲巖元善 十 密庵咸傑
　　空叟宗印
　　　火瀾居簡
　　　天佑思順

育王淨曇
育王淨慧師
　育王大觀
　　龍翔大訢（別山）
　　東巖正祖（日本）
　　天界宗泐
　　　靈隱竹泉
天童善濟（1178―1186）
　天童智顒
　桂山如珏
　　虎丘善濟

端裕（1085―1150）
護國景元（1094―1146）
竹菴士珪
靈隱慧遠
徑山宗杲

雲隱（1153―1186）
　潛菴道濟（1148―1207）
　疎山如本
　敬山覺阿（日本）
　桂山如珏

太平慧懃（1059―）
　佛眼守淨 十 綱菴了贊
　女珠心道 十 楚雲慧方

龍門清遠（1067―1120）
　竹菴士珪
　龍翔士珪
　烏巨道行
　　佛惠清
　　鐵牛礼
　　無著元璹

開福道寧（?―1113）
　月庵善果
　大洪祖證 十 萬杉師觀 十 興門慧開 十 法燈覺心（日本）

大隨元靜（1065―1135）
　在頭自回 十 雲居德會
　保安可封

天目禮 十 懶牛和 十 竹林寶 十 竹林安 十 海西堂（谷庵）十 中和璋 十 海雲印簡（1202―1257）十 可庵朗 十 劉秉忠（1216―1274）

正員

祖禪整備（日本）
中峰空谷有

定嚴濟戒

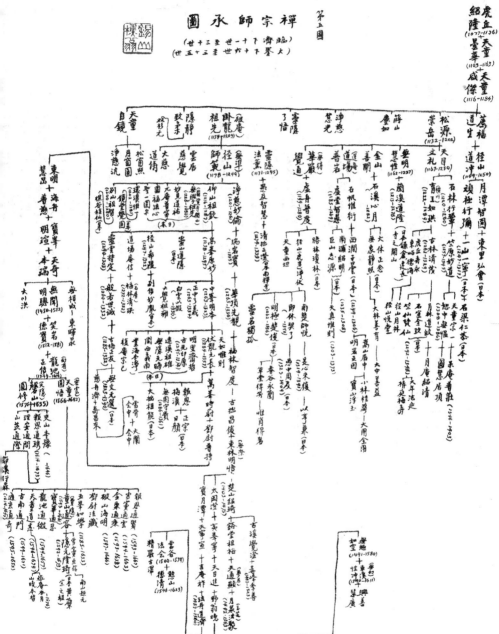

禪宗師承圖

（臨濟下十一世至三十世）
（大鑒下十六世至三十五世）

禪宗師承圖〔曹洞宗〕

（大鑒下第五世至第三三世）

錫蘭

洞山良价
(802-869)

洞山道全
龍牙居遁
曹山本寂
(840-901)

金峯從志
疎山匡仁
曹山慧霞
曹山慧霞正慧

九峯普滿
雲居道膺
(853-902)

同安丕
同安常察
同安觀志
大陽警玄
(943-1027)

青林師虔
石門獻藴
石門慧徹
石門紹遠

芙蓉道楷
(1043-1118)

鹿門自覺
(-1147)

丹霞子淳
(1064-1117)

真歇清了
(1090-1151)

天童正覺
(1091-1157)

華嚴慧蘭
慈雲覺
青州希辯
(1031-1149)

青州大明僧寶
(1114-1173)

長蘆宗賾

天童宗珏
雪竇智鑑
(1105-1192)

天童如淨
(1163-1228)

雪巖妙覺

廣福道勤

曹君默覺
東谷妙光

雪竇智鑑＋天童如淨

永平道元（日本曹洞宗初祖）

鎣山紹瑾（日本）

玉山體
雲居慧淵＋萬松行秀

雪巖慧滿

少室文泰
寶應福遇＋少室道成

少室文才

萬容子嚴

宗鏡
(1500-1567)

宗書

常忠
(1514-1588)

常潤
(-1585)

大覺方念
(-1594)

雲門圓澄

少室正道
湛然圓澄
雲門湛然＋夢泽明懷

博山元來
(1575-1630)

東苑元鏡
(1577-1630)

覺浪道盛

壽昌慧經
(1548-1618)

無異元來

鼓山元賢
(1578-1657)

永覺元賢

石濤宗

禪宗師承圖
（雲門宗）

雲門文偃（864~949）

師寬
師戒
福昌重善
白雲樂淨
子祥舍匡
洞山良雅
宇初
潭州道乾
衡岳赦
德山文殊
洞山
緣密
應真＋曉聰（1030）
香林澄遠（~987）
智門光祚
雙峰竟欽（910~977）
南台
道通
雙峰
慧真
慧真
雙泉
仁郁＋德山慧遠

五祖師戒
洞山自寶
興化紹銑
佛日智嵩（1007~1072）
宇初
潭州道乾

渤潭懷澄
靈隱雲知
青王懷璉
佛日或卿
徑山維琳（~1118）
天宮慧徵
洞山曉舜
雲居曉舜＋蔣山法泉
大潙懷秀＋歸宗慧通

南華
寶緣
子榮＋圓通居訥
進慶
雪寶重顯（980~1052）
天衣義懷（993~1064）
百支智映
長蘆福

圓通法秀
圓照宗本
興國智圓

佛印智才
天鉢重元＋靈巖智明
長蘆應夫＋波潮宗賾＋洪潮璟
長蘆福
慧林宗本
慧林宗本

佛國惟白＋慧林慧海
保寧子英＋廣福惟尚
圓先智珦＋進福思詠
佛印了元（1032~1098）

禾山楚材＋曹山本寂
開先善道
佛印了元（1032）

智海本逸
黃檗志因

天中德隆

善權淨悟
慶善淨悟

高麗僧義天

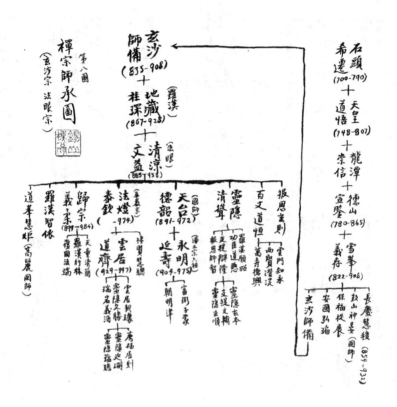

第八圖　禪宗師承圖

（玄沙宗　法眼宗）

玄沙
師備
（835-908）
＋
（羅漢）
地藏
桂琛
（867-928）
＋
（玄眼）
清涼
文益
（885-958）

石頭
希遷
（700-790）
＋
天皇
道悟
（748-807）
＋
龍潭
崇信
＋
德山
宣鑒
（780-865）
＋
雪峯
義存
（822-908）

長慶慧稜（854-932）
鼓山神晏（國師）
保福從展
安國弘瑫
玄沙師備

道峯慧炬（高麗國師）
羅漢智依
歸宗　義柔（879-984）　羅漢行林　護國法瑞
法燈　泰欽（-974）　雲居　道齊（929-997）　雲居契環　廬福居則　瑞巖義海　靈隱地珊　靈隱瑫鵬
天台　德韶（891-972）　永明　延壽（904-975）　富鄧守豪　朝明津
清聳　羅漢願昭　功臣道慇　支提辯隆　報恩師智　靈隱玄順
靈隱
百丈道恆　萬壽俊興
報恩玄則　西賢澄湜　雲門知永
天童清簡

History of Zen in China

英汉对照

中国禅宗史

（美）顾毓琇 著　陈人哲 谈谷铮 译

外语教学与研究出版社
FOREIGN LANGUAGE TEACHING AND RESEARCH PRESS
北京 BEIJING

图书在版编目（CIP）数据

中国禅宗史 ：英汉对照 ／（美）顾毓琇著；陈人哲，谈谷铮译 . -- 北京 ：外语教学与研究出版社，2016.11（2023.11 重印）

ISBN 978-7-5135-8479-1

I.①中… II.①顾… ②陈… ③谈… III.①禅宗－佛教史－中国－英、汉 IV.①B946.5

中国版本图书馆 CIP 数据核字（2017）第 020835 号

出 版 人　王　芳
系列策划　吴　浩
责任编辑　段会香
装帧设计　视觉共振设计工作室
出版发行　外语教学与研究出版社
社　　址　北京市西三环北路 19 号（100089）
网　　址　https://www.fltrp.com
印　　刷　三河市北燕印装有限公司
开　　本　650×980　1/16
印　　张　17.5
版　　次　2017 年 2 月第 1 版　2023 年 11 月第 7 次印刷
书　　号　ISBN 978-7-5135-8479-1
定　　价　45.00 元

如有图书采购需求，图书内容或印刷装订等问题，侵权、盗版书籍等线索，请拨打以下电话或关注官方服务号：
客服电话：400 898 7008
官方服务号：微信搜索并关注公众号"外研社官方服务号"
外研社购书网址：https://fltrp.tmall.com

物料号：284790001

"博雅双语名家名作"出版说明

　　1840 年鸦片战争以降，在深重的民族危机面前，中华民族精英"放眼看世界"，向世界寻求古老中国走向现代、走向世界的灵丹妙药，涌现出一大批中国主题的经典著述。我们今天阅读这些中文著述的时候，仍然深为字里行间所蕴藏的缜密的考据、深刻的学理、世界的视野和济世的情怀所感动，但往往会忽略：这些著述最初是用英文写就，我们耳熟能详的中文文本是原初英文文本的译本，这些英文作品在海外学术界和文化界同样享有崇高的声誉。

　　比如，林语堂的 *My Country and My People*（《吾国与吾民》）以幽默风趣的笔调和睿智流畅的语言，将中国人的道德精神、生活情趣和中国社会文化的方方面面娓娓道来，在美国引起巨大反响——林语堂也以其中国主题系列作品赢得世界文坛的尊重，并获得诺贝尔文学奖的提名。再比如，梁思成在抗战的烽火中写就的英文版《图像中国建筑史》文稿（*A Pictorial History of Chinese Architecture*），经其挚友费慰梅女士（Wilma C. Fairbank）等人多年的奔走和努力，于 1984 年由麻省理工学院出版社（MIT Press）出版，并获得美国出版联合会颁发的"专业暨学术书籍金奖"。又比如，1939 年，费孝通在伦敦政治经济学院的博士论文以 *Peasant Life in China—A Field Study of Country Life in the Yangtze Valley* 为名在英国劳特利奇书局（Routledge）出版，后以《江村经济》作为中译本书名——《江村经济》使得靠桑蚕为生的"开弦弓村"获得了世界性的声誉，成为国际社会学界研究中国农村的首选之地。

　　此外，一些中国主题的经典人文社科作品经海外汉学家和中国学者的如椽译笔，在英语世界也深受读者喜爱。比如，艾恺（Guy S. Alitto）将他 1980 年用中文访问梁漱溟的《这个世界会好吗——梁漱溟晚年口述》一书译成英文（*Has Man a Future? —Dialogues with the Last Confucian*），备受海内外读者关注；

此类作品还有徐中约英译的梁启超著作《清代学术概论》(*Intellectual Trends in the Ch'ing Period*)、狄百瑞（W. T. de Bary）英译的黄宗羲著作《明夷待访录》(*Waiting for the Dawn: A Plan for the Prince*)，等等。

有鉴于此，外语教学与研究出版社推出"博雅双语名家名作"系列。

博雅，乃是该系列的出版立意。博雅教育（Liberal Education）早在古希腊时代就得以提倡，旨在培养具有广博知识和优雅气质的人，提高人文素质，培养健康人格，中国儒家六艺"礼、乐、射、御、书、数"亦有此功用。

双语，乃是该系列的出版形式。英汉双语对照的形式，既同时满足了英语学习者和汉语学习者通过阅读中国主题博雅读物提高英语和汉语能力的需求，又以中英双语思维、构架和写作的形式予后世学人以启迪——维特根斯坦有云："语言的边界，乃是世界的边界"，诚哉斯言。

名家，乃是该系列的作者群体。涵盖文学、史学、哲学、政治学、经济学、考古学、人类学、建筑学等领域，皆海内外名家一时之选。

名作，乃是该系列的入选标准。系列中的各部作品都是经过时间的积淀、市场的检验和读者的鉴别而呈现的经典，正如卡尔维诺对"经典"的定义：经典并非你正在读的书，而是你正在重读的书。

胡适在《新思潮的意义》(1919 年 12 月 1 日，《新青年》第 7 卷第 1 号)一文中提出了"研究问题、输入学理、整理国故、再造文明"的范式。秉着"记载人类文明、沟通世界文化"的出版理念，我们推出"博雅双语名家名作"系列，既希望能够在中国人创作的和以中国为主题的博雅英文文献领域"整理国故"，亦希望在和平发展、改革开放的新时代为"再造文明"、为"向世界说明中国"略尽绵薄之力。

外语教学与研究出版社

人文社科出版分社

Respectedly dedicated to:

Wuchi Tashih Shihtou Hsichien
(Musai Sekitō Zenji, 700-790)

and

Abbot Hsu Yun
(Kiun, 1840-1959)

谨献给
无际大师石头希迁
佛慈弘法大师虚云

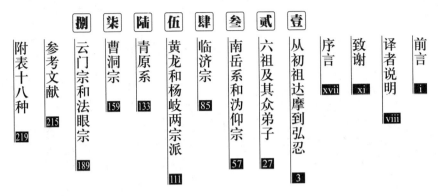

前言

《禅史》本是我父亲顾毓琇（一樵）先生用英文所著，于 1979 年在美国出版。2000 年中国社会科学院组织专家学者编辑完成了他的全集，共 16 卷，由辽宁教育出版社出版，其中第 10 卷收入了《禅史》（英文）。2001 年，我征得父亲同意后，将英文原著交专家翻译成中文，后历时多年，中文版于 2009 年由上海古籍出版社出版。可惜我父亲已于 2002 年 9 月 9 日逝世，他没能亲自校阅和看到中文版《禅史》。今蒙外语教学与研究出版社吴浩博士策划出版《禅史》的英汉对照本，虽只收录英文原著的上篇《中国禅宗史》，未包括下篇《日本禅宗史》，但它的问世，同样可以告慰他的在天之灵，也是对他很好的纪念。

现在介绍一些关于作者的情况，供读者参考。

※　※　※

我父亲于 1902 年诞生在江苏无锡虹桥湾故居（今学前街 3 号，由中央批准已成为"顾毓琇纪念馆"），以后在北京、上海、南京、重庆以及美国等地度过了丰富多彩传奇般的百龄岁月。他在 2002 年逝世之前，曾以"学者、教授、诗人、清风、明月、劲松"来概括自己的一生。

1915 年他未满 13 岁时北上进入清华学堂（后为清华大学），1923 年公费留学美国，在麻省理工学院专攻电机工程，1928 年不满 26 岁时获得科学博士学位，是该校电机系获此学位的第一个中国人。在求学期间，即先后发明了"四次方程通解法"和"顾氏变数"，以后又以许多科研成果和学术论文，奠定了他在国际电工界的权威地位。20 世纪 50 年代初起，他又开始研究自动控制，特别是非线性系统控制，成为国际上公认的控制理论的先驱。1972 年荣获 IEEE（电气电子工程师学会）兰姆金奖，2000 年他 98 岁时又荣获千禧金奖和电路及系统学会的杰出成就金奖。此外还曾获得中国电机学会金质奖章等多种奖项。

1929 年他学成回国，从此开始了漫长的教学生涯，担任过浙江大学、中央大学、清华大学等校教授、电机系主任、工学院院长。抗日战争时期他以无党派人士的身份出任国民政府教育部政务次长达六年半，后又担任中央大学校长。抗战胜利后，曾任上海市教育局局长、国立政治大学校长。但他从未放弃专业，一直兼任大学教授，亲自为学生讲课。他在上海交通大学任教时，江泽民主席曾是他的学生，他们之间的师生情谊已经成为历史佳话。

他自述"一贯服膺'关怀天下，服务民众，业精于勤，业博于文，好古敏求，淡泊自持，得天下英才而育之'"的古训。1950年移居美国后他先是回到母校麻省理工学院任教，以后又应聘到宾夕法尼亚大学担任终身教授。

从20世纪70年代起，他曾多次回国讲学，担任了两岸五所交通大学、清华大学、北京大学、南京大学、东南大学、浙江大学、东北工业大学、北京航空航天大学、西北电子科技大学、四川大学、江南大学等十多所著名学府的名誉教授，并为中美文化教育的交流做了许多工作。

20世纪30年代初，他与好友创办了中国电机工程学会，曾担任会长，又曾担任中国工程师学会副会长多年。从1946年开始，当选国际理论及应用力学组织个人理事，连选连任达半个世纪。还曾被聘为美国国家科学院理论及应用力学委员会委员，当选台湾"中央研究院"院士。

※ ※ ※

他主张文理并重、理工并重，自己兼好文艺。早年在清华读书时，就开始写作并发表了不少小说、诗歌、话剧，参加了具有深远影响的"文学研究会"，此后在文艺方面的创作从未中断。抗日战争期间，他创办了国立音乐院（今中央音乐学院前身），并兼任院长。他曾解开中国古乐谱的许多谜团，将古乐译成五线谱，他又是第一个翻译贝多芬《第九交响乐》即《欢乐颂》的中国人。他所作的话剧都富有爱国激情，多次公演；抗战胜利后在上海冲破多种阻力，创办了上海实验戏剧学校（今上海戏剧学院前身）。他特别喜爱诗词，所作诗词歌赋近八千首，曾获得"国际桂冠诗人"称号，晚年仍常有新作，乐此不疲。由于他在多方面的贡献，宾夕法尼亚大学授予他名誉文学硕士和法学博士学位。

※　※　※

父亲一生遵循江东顾氏先贤炎武先生关于"天下兴亡，匹夫有责"的遗训，热爱祖国，热爱人民。早年积极参加五四运动，又曾多次到灾区赈灾。1931年担任中央大学工学院院长时，曾率领师生欢送十九路军抗日。抗战军兴，曾率领清华大学工学院师生研制防毒面具，亲自送往前线。抗战期间他从事战时教育事业，不遗余力。抗战胜利后，他向往民主、和平、建设，曾发表《中国经济的改造》、《中国的文艺复兴》等文章。1947年他的同学、好友闻一多惨遭国民党特务暗杀，他义无反顾地公开发表了《怀故友闻一多先生》，称闻一多"真是中华民族的忠实斗士！"1949年后他侨居海外，但一直关注祖国和家乡。从1973年起他先后八次回到祖国，受到周恩来、邓小平、江泽民等多位领导人的会见，使他感到亲切，同时也不断建言献策。例如，他建议"文化开发、经济开放、政治开明"，很早就建议科教兴国，藏富于民，实行股份制等等，并为祖国的和平统一和改善中美关系做了许多实际的工作。

※　※　※

父亲喜欢广交朋友，可谓朋友遍天下。他对朋友不分籍贯职业、富贵贫寒、地位高低、年龄大小，都一视同仁，坦诚、热情相交。他看人相当透彻，是非分明，抗日战争时痛恨汉奸，生前反对"台独"，他常对朋友说，要多看人家的长处，而不必计较人家的不足。他从不在背后说别人的坏话，而朋友之间出现纷争来向他诉说时，总是劝人要宽宏大量。他记性很好，晚年还能记得很多朋友的情况。他助人为乐，帮助别人从来不求回报。他又喜欢请客，我母亲年轻时会做一手好菜，因此许多朋友尤其是在美国的中国留学生常常成为座上客，但父亲自己吃得很简单。他一生实际上是工薪阶层，晚年更是靠养老金生活，自己非常节俭，但稍有积蓄，就拿出来办奖学金或捐给慈善事业（他在国内外许多大学都设有奖学金）。

※　※　※

人们称我父亲是博古通今、学贯中西的文理大师。作为他的儿子，在长期的观察中，我感到他确实博学多才。除了不可否认的天资聪颖、从小得到良好的教育之外，他的成就更在于勤奋努力。他坚持"今日事今日了"，非常珍惜时间。他说所谓"天下无难事，只怕有心人"，应该是"只怕用心人"；人都有心，贵在"用心"，用心就是开动脑筋，认真思考。他讲我们老家早年有"清楚真实"四个字的祖传匾额，遇事能弄清楚，求真实，就会有成果。他晚年除了读书、看报、写作之外，几乎没有任何嗜好，又喜欢与人特别是青年人交谈，因此平时不太有空闲。他有时想起什么就提笔写出来（基本不打草稿），从不间断。我母亲劝他"歇一歇"时，他说"老天爷不叫我去，就是叫我还要做点事情"。他不做什么锻炼，也不吃什么补品，认为多动脑筋和心气平和、乐观开朗，就是养生之道。

※　※　※

我父母养育了八个子女，我幼时父亲很忙，都由母亲抚养教导。但父母的言行举止和人格魅力，起着潜移默化的作用。父亲对子女要求严格，但主要看重待人接物、为人处世，对我们的兴趣爱好从不横加干涉。他自己是电机工程博士，当然希望有子女能继承这个专业。我读中学时比较喜欢数理化，想长大后当个工程师，为此他感到高兴；而我的大哥慰连却对工科不感兴趣，父亲也绝不勉强（以后我大哥学了农业，曾任洛阳农业大学校长、博士生导师，不幸于1990年逝世）。受父亲的影响，我们兄弟（妹）从小养成了读书看报、关心时事的习惯。上海解放前我和大哥慰连、大妹慰文看了许多进步书刊和小说，当我们还是中学生时，出于爱国心和正义感，都满腔热情地参加了学生运动，以后又先后秘密参加了中国共产党地下组织，我们家还一度成为地下党的活动场所。当时我们的有些行为比较幼稚，难免不引起父母的注意，但他们相信自己的子女不会去做坏事，并没有严加阻止，以至临近解放时我们三个大孩子不肯随他们离开上海，从此父母同我们隔离了24年之久，形成了父亲所说的"一个家庭，两个世界"！

解放前父母隐隐约约地知道我们这三个子女对国民党不满而思想"左倾"，但不知道也没有想到，才十几岁的孩子竟会是共产党员！直到1973年他们应邀回到祖国，周恩来总理接见他们和我们兄妹时，总理风趣地对我母亲说"感谢你为我们生了三个共产党员"，父母这时才知道我们兄妹三人早已是共产党员。当时"十年动乱"尚未结束，总理还说我们是"经过无产阶级文化大革命考验和锻炼的共产党员"，此后父母从陪同人员处知道我们曾备受冲击，更因为父亲的关系而"罪加一等"，对我们加深了谅解和亲情。

自从1973年父母第一次返回祖国开始，特别是"文革"结束以后，我们书信来往不断。此后父母八次回国，我都全程陪同，由此也对老人家有了更深的了解，常恨忠孝不能两全！

1989年起我几次因公访美，顺便去探望父母，但每次在家不过两三天。直到1993年后我从工作岗位上退居二线，才有机会每年都赴美探亲。父母逐渐年迈体弱，我大哥、大妹先后去世，在美国的弟妹又不在父母身边，我想多陪伴侍奉他们，但由于当时我还没有离休，从1993年起又担任了全国政协第八、第九届委员共十年，父亲认为我在国内还有许多事情要做，应当"多为国家效力"，要我不必为了他们而在美国久留，所以每次我只在家两三个月。我每次到家时父母都非常高兴，在美国的弟妹和小辈也都前往团聚，共享天伦之乐，但我每次离开时父母又不免伤感。起初我赴美时，人生地不熟，父亲还亲自到机场迎送，朋友们说，这使人想起了朱自清先生所写的《背影》……那时他已是90多岁的老人！

※　※　※

据我的前辈们说，祖母生我父亲时曾梦见一位罗汉立在面前，父亲生下时脐带绕在脖子上，用我们无锡话叫作"盘在颈根上"，像是佛珠，因此取乳名为"盘盘"。我的祖父晦农公早年接受了当时的新思想，相信读书救国、科学救国，不幸在35岁时英年早逝，留下七个子女，当时我的大伯父才15岁，我父亲排行老二，只有14岁，最小的叔父是遗腹子。遭此巨变，家道中落，我祖母王诵芬太夫人深明大义，秉承夫志，节衣缩食，坚持让子女求学。为了祈求保佑家人平安吉利，我的曾祖母、祖母都信奉佛教，父亲并不迷信，但中国传统文化包括佛教在内的许多精华，想来肯定对他会有影响。他一生刚正不阿、清廉自守、清心寡欲、诚信待人、乐善好施、慈悲为怀，追求忠孝仁爱、超凡脱俗，似乎都有儒、释、道的烙印。他非常喜欢旅行，遍游名山古寺，寻访高僧大德，以至晚年研究禅史，我想，他更看重的是对哲理的探索。

在写《禅史》之前，他还曾用中文写有《禅宗师承记》（1976年出版）和《日本禅僧师承记》（1977年出版），也已收入《顾毓琇全集》第9卷。

父亲自号"梁溪居士"，博览群书，除佛教著作之外，对其他宗教学说也有兴趣。1946年他在一篇讲话中说："请教全世界从古到今的哲学家和宗教家、科学家和教育家，做我们的老师，来创造世界的和平和幸福。"他曾提出："世界文明须重建，中华文化应发扬。"

※　※　※

父亲在美国著名学府宾夕法尼亚大学任教并在费城定居50年之久，直到2001年9月11日美国纽约发生恐怖事件那天，我小妹慰民和妹夫接父母到俄克拉何马（父母离开费城与纽约出事无关，在同一天只是巧合）。

2002年8月底父亲病重，我赶到医院时他神志仍异常清楚，以微弱的声音询问国内的情况，仍在关心即将召开的中共十六大、中美关系和台海形势，多次说对中国的事情包括和平统一要抱有乐观态度。

9月上旬俄克拉何马天气一直晴朗，到9月9日早晨突然下了阵雨，而父亲也平静地停止了呼吸。我不知道在宗教里对这个现象作何解释，不由自主地引起许多遐想，只能强忍悲痛安慰母亲说："你看老天爷也晓得爹爹去了，现在安息了，我们也不必过于难过！"

说来又是凑巧，2002年9月9日正是我满70岁的生日。人们说，年已古稀的人为父亲送终，是他老人家一生积德修来的福气。9月9日是一个值得纪念的日子，1945年9月9日，父亲曾扬眉吐气地在南京紫金山参加了日本投降的受降典礼。2000年9月9日，我和三弟慰华、儿子宜凡曾陪父亲从费城到纽约再次会见江泽民主席。

父亲离开我们已经14年多了，他的音容笑貌仍历历在目。写此文时，心潮起伏，难以平静。谨以此寄托我和家人的哀思！

我母亲与父亲相依相伴七十多年，同甘共苦，伉俪情深。父亲生前常说没有母亲他不会活得这么长久。父亲的许多著作都是由母亲题写书名，父亲都写明是献给她的。我想这部书也应该献给我的慈母——王婉靖夫人！

最后要衷心感谢外语教学与研究出版社使《禅史》上篇《中国禅宗史》（英汉对照版）问世，《禅史》中文版早已脱销，这次英汉对照版的出版可填补空缺。

顾慰庆

2016 年 11 月

译者说明

《禅史》译自顾毓琇先生关于中日禅宗发展简史的英文原著。众所周知，顾先生作为一代宗师，博学多能，桃李遍天下，其治学不仅专于电机科技，而且更广泛涉及文学、艺术、音乐、戏剧及宗教文化等，在各方面多有深入研究和专门著作问世。作为一位著名学者，他是兼治工程科技和人文科学的光辉典范，值得我们崇敬和学习。顾先生曾著有《禅宗师承记》（中国部分）及《日本禅僧师承记》两专著，内容甚为详尽。不过两书是以古汉语写成，现今广大读者不易看懂。本书则取材于该两书中的精华部分，故内容十分简明扼要，叙述清楚易懂，更适合于一般读者。书末还附有顾先生多年来从中、日各地精心收集到的禅宗传承世系表等有关资料，很有参考价值。现受戚文先生之托，将该英文原著译成现代汉语，提供给国内广大读者。此外，该英文原著中有较多部分直接引用了西方学者在这方面的译述和著作，足以表明西方人士对东方佛教文化的研究、理解和重视。在当今全球经济一体化、倡导各种文化多样化的趋势之下，该书对沟通东西方文化，促进相互理解，也能起到一定的作用，更希望能因此引起国内大众对这方面的重视和关注。

佛教禅宗始祖菩提达摩在南北朝时自印度来到中国，传授其佛教思想和哲理。初曾受阻，后来不断兴盛。代代相传，绵延不绝。在唐中期以后禅宗就成为一支重要的佛教宗派。通过历代禅师卓越的智慧和努力，禅宗不断发扬壮大。在其发展过程中，又部分结合和吸收了中国固有文化的儒家和道家思想，终于成为颇具中国特色且独放异彩的禅宗思想，深得人心。禅宗宣扬众生佛性平等，佛性即在每个人心中，任何人都能明心见性；去除迷惘，则人可以顿悟佛性；并且还主张不一定要出家为僧，即使在家（称为居士），也能修行成佛。所以，禅宗不仅受到普通百姓的信奉，还深得众多士大夫阶层人士的欢迎和崇敬。例如，唐代著名诗人王维、白居易，宋代大文人苏轼和苏辙都是禅宗居士。禅宗的广泛传播，对中国的社会和文化产生了重大影响。而且各禅宗教派，不仅在中国兴旺繁衍，还远播日本、朝鲜等国，继续在那繁衍昌盛，直至今日。禅宗也是历代向日本等国传播中国文化的主要桥梁，对沟通中、日、朝、韩等国文化都起了重要作用。在20世纪初期，又由日本学者将禅宗思想传向欧美，引起了西方学者的注意和兴趣，这充分显示了禅宗思想的智慧魅力和社会价值。

禅宗虽属佛教，但禅宗思想则在一定程度上超越了宗教领域的界限。它蔑视祖师权威，突破戒律束缚，反对仅凭借文字经典和苦行修炼，而提倡明心即是佛性、以自我为主，实现自我价值和自我解放，具有一定的先进意义，值得我们去研究和探讨。《禅史》共十六章，由陈人哲译第一至第五章，谈谷铮译第六至第八章，郑鹏译第九至第十六章。译者深感才疏学浅，难以当此重任，恐多谬误不当之处，希望广大读者不吝赐正，以备再版时予以更正，在此谨表衷心感谢！

ACKNOWLEDGMENTS

The author is grateful to Pantheon Books, 201 East 50th Street, New York, N.Y., 10022, for kind permission to use excerpts from *A History of Zen Buddhism*, by Heinrich Dumoulin, S. J., translated by Paul Peachey, and *Original Teachings of Ch'an Buddhism: Selected from the Transmission of the Lamp*, translated by Chang Chung-yuan, and *The Way of Zen*, by Alan W. Watts.

The First Zen Institute of America, Inc., 113 East 30th Street, New York, N.Y., 10016, has been generous in granting permission to quote passages from *The Development of Chinese Zen*, by Heinrich Dumoulin, S. J., translated with additional notes and appendices by Ruth Fuller Sasaki. The Princeton University Press has kindly given permission to reprint certain passages from *Zen and Japanese Culture* by Daisetz T. Suzuki. The author wishes to express his indebtedness and gratitude.

Harcourt Brace Jovanovich, Inc., 757 Third Avenue, New York, N.Y., 10017, has kindly written to the author. They foresee no difficulty with the author's request to reprint certain excerpts from *Zen Dust* by Isshu Miura and Ruth Fuller Sasaki. The author is grateful for such permission.

The author is also grateful to Grove Press, Inc., 196 W. Houston St., New York, N.Y., 10014, for permission to quote from *Essays in Zen Buddhism*, by D. T. Suzuki; to Shambhala Publications, Inc., 1123 Spruce Street, Boulder, Colorado 80302, for permission to quote the fourteenth case from *The Blue Cliff Record*, translated by Thomas and J. C. Cleary; and to Samuel Weiser, Inc. 625 Broadway, New York, N.Y., 10012, for permission to quote Mr. Christmas Humphreys' Foreword to *Living by Zen* by D. T. Suzuki.

As *Zen and Zen Classics* by R. H. Blyth has been most helpful to the author, besides the works of Dumoulin, Suzuki, and Ruth Fuller Sasaki, the author has requested permission from The Hokuseido Press, No. 12, 3-chome, Nishikicho, Kanda, Chiyodaku, Tokyo, for quotations from Volumes 2 and 3. The author was informed by The Hokuseido Press that

Dr. Frederick Franck had made selections from Blyth's five volumes and these selections are published as a Vintage Book.

The author wishes to thank the Random House for permission to use excerpts from the Selections edited by Frederick Franck, and also to thank the Perennial Library for permission to quote from *The Practice of Zen*, by Garma C. C. Chang.

致谢

作者在此谨向下列各有关文献作者和机构深表谢意：

感谢潘塞恩图书出版公司慷慨允许摘录它所出版的《佛教禅宗史》，杜慕林著，保罗·披切译（由德文译成英文）；以及《佛教禅宗之源》，选自《传灯录》，张钟元译；还有《禅道》，艾伦·瓦茨著。

美国第一禅堂慷慨允许摘录引用它所出版的《中国禅宗的发展》，杜慕林著，由罗丝·富勒·佐佐木自德文译成英文，并加附注和附录。又普林斯顿大学出版社慷慨允许重印铃木大拙著《禅宗与日本文化》中的某些段落。作者在此深表感谢。

承蒙哈考特·布雷斯·乔瓦诺维奇出版公司来信对作者的请求表示同意：自其出版的《禅尘》一书（三浦一舟和罗丝·富勒·佐佐木著）中摘录引用某些内容。作者对此表示感谢。

作者还要感谢丛树出版社允许摘录引用铃木大拙著《佛教禅宗论文集》。感谢北正堂出版社允许摘录引用由托马斯和J. C. 克利里所译的《碧岩集》。感谢萨姆尔·威塞尔出版公司同意引用铃木大拙所著《依禅生活》中由克里斯马斯·汉弗莱先生所作的前言。

除了杜慕林、铃木大拙和罗丝·富勒·佐佐木等译述著作之外，由布莱思所著《禅与禅宗经典》对作者帮助最人，作者要求从该书第2和第3卷中摘录某些段落，已获北星堂的同意；该出版社并告诉作者已有弗雷德里克·弗兰克博士对布莱思的五卷本作了精选，精选本由古典书局出版。

本书作者感谢兰登书屋允许引用弗雷德里克·弗兰克所编选集中的一些选段，并感谢佩里尼尔图书馆允许引用张澄基的《禅宗的修行》。

The author must also acknowledge his indebtedness to:

Outlines of Mahayana Buddhism, by D. T. Suzuki, Schocken Books Inc., 1963

The Practice of Zen, by Garma C. C. Chang, Perennial Library, 1970

The World of Zen, by Nancy Wilson Ross, Vintage Book, 1960

The Platform Scripture, translated by Wing-tsit Chan, St. John's University Press, Jamaica, N.Y., 1963

The Golden Age of Zen, by John C. H. Wu, Hwa Kang Bookstore, Taipei, 1975

Lao Tzu: Tao Teh Ching, translated by John C. H. Wu, St. John's University Press, Jamaica, N.Y., 1961

The Three Pillars of Zen, by Philip Kapleau, Beacon Press, 1967

Zen Is Eternal Life, by Jiyu Kennett, Dharma Publishing, Emeryville, California, 1976

Zen-shū Shi, by Reverend Keidō Chisan, Tokyo, 2nd edition, 1974

Sōtō-shū Zensho, published by Sōtō-shū Office, Tokyo, 1976

Shen-hui Ho-shan I-chi, compiled and edited by Hu Shih, "Academia Sinica", Taipei, 1970

Chung-kuo Ch'an-tsung Shih, by Reverend Yin Shun, Taipei, 1975

Meibatsu Chūkoku Bukkyō Kenkyū, by Reverend Sheng-yen, Tokyo, 1975

Daishō Shinshū Daizōkyō, published 1924-1934

Kinse Zenrin Sōhō Den, Vol. I, by Reverend Doku'en Jōju, 1890, 1973; Vols. II and III, by Shōhata Buntei, 1938, 1973.

The author is most grateful to Sōtō-shū Daihonzan Sōji-ji for supplying the color photo of Musai Sekitō Zenji, and to Gold Mountain Temple, San Francisco, for supplying the photo of Abbot Hsu Yun.

The author is glad to add the following acknowledgments:

(1) In a letter dated September 18, 1978, Harper & Row Publishers, Inc., 10 East 53rd St., New York, gave permission to quote from pages 75-76 in *The Practice of Zen* by Garma C. C. Chang (Perennial Library Edition).

作者还应该向下列众多文献作者和出版单位表示深切感谢：

《大乘佛教概论》，铃木大拙著，邵肯出版社，1963

《禅宗的修行》，张澄基著，佩里尼尔图书馆，1970

《禅的世界》，南希·威尔逊·罗斯著，古典书局，1960

《六祖坛经》，陈荣捷译，圣约翰大学出版社，纽约州牙买加，1963

《禅学的黄金时代》，吴经熊著，华冈书店，台北，1975

《老子：道德经》，吴经熊译，圣约翰大学出版社，纽约州牙买加，1961

《禅门三柱》，菲利普·卡普乐著，灯塔出版社，1967

《禅是永恒的生命》，法云慈友著，正法出版社，加利福尼亚埃默里维尔，1976

《禅宗史》，莹堂智璨著，东京，第二版，1974

《曹洞宗全书》，曹洞宗办事处，东京，1976

《沈慧和尚志》，胡适汇编，"中央研究院"，台北，1970

《中国禅宗史》，印顺法师著，台北，1975

《明末中国佛教研究》，圣严法师著，东京，1975

《大正新修大藏经》，1924—1934

《近世禅林僧宝传》，卷一，独园承珠法师著，1890，1973；卷二、卷三，小畠文鼎著，1938，1973

作者非常感谢曹洞宗大本山总持寺提供的无际石头希迁的彩照，并感谢旧金山金山寺提供了虚云大师的照片。（因清晰度不足，原书所提及照片均未收录。）

作者还很乐意对下列作者和机构表示衷心感谢：

（1）哈柏和罗出版公司1978年9月18日来信同意作者引用张澄基所著《禅宗的修行》（佩里尼尔图书馆出版）的第75—76页。

(2) In a letter dated December 19, 1978, Random House, Inc. Permissions Editor Nina Garfinkel gave the author the following answer: "Since you have let us know that you have already obtained permission from the Hokuseido Press in Tokyo for use of selections from R. H. Blyth's works, and since they actually control publication rights in his texts, we can assure that we have no objection to your including excerpts from our book, in your forthcoming volume." (Random House, Inc. is the Publisher of *Selections from R. H. Blyth*, edited by Frederick Franck.)

（2）兰登书屋的版权编辑尼娜·加芬克尔在 1978 年 12 月 19 日给作者的回信中说："因为你已告诉我们你已经获东京北星堂的同意以引用布莱思著作中的片段，而因为实际上是他们控制该著作的版权，所以我们向你保证，对于你在你要出版的书中引用我们书中的片段，我们没有反对意见。"（兰登书屋是弗兰克所编《布莱思选集》[即前述《禅与禅宗经典》] 一书的出版商。）

INTRODUCTION

In 1976, the author published (in Chinese) *History of Chinese Zen Masters* with eight charts on the dharma lineages. In 1977, the author published (in Chinese) *History of Japanese Zen Masters* with twenty-eight lineage charts. In the present volume, most of the basic materials are taken from the two previous volumes. However, in rendering certain passages from Chinese into English, it is deemed desirable to utilize many excellent translations that are already available to the English-reading public. Although it is possible to give all personal names in English either according to the Chinese pronunciation or to the Japanese pronunciation, in the main text the Japanese pronunciation is preferred for the reason that many English-reading readers are already familiar with the Japanese pronunciation from recent books on Zen.

This volume is divided into two parts: each part has eight chapters. Part I is concerned with "History of Zen in China." Chapter 1 tells the brief story from Daruma the First Patriarch to Gunin the Fifth Patriarch. Chapter 2 is concerned with Enō the Sixth Patriarch and his disciples. From the First Patriarch to the Sixth Patriarch, Zen School had a single line of transmission. After Enō, it must be pointed out that Zen lineage did not limit itself to a single line of transmission. As was well known, Enō had at least *five* prominent dharma-heirs, which included Shen-hui (Jinne), with an Imperial-designated title of the Seventh Patriarch.

The two famous branches—Nangaku branch and Seigen branch—are the headings of Chapters 3 and 6, respectively. Both branches flourished from their second-generation masters to the present day. Nangaku's dharma-heir was Baso (Matsu), and Seigen's dharma-heir was Sekitō (Shih-tou), whose body was recently enshrined at Sōji-ji, Tsurumi, near Yokohama, Japan.

In Chapter 3, the Igyō School, founded by Isan and Kyōzan, was included. Chapter 4 is concerned with the Rinzai School (in China). Both the Igyō School and the Rinzai School belonged to the "Five Houses," but only the Rinzai School and the Sōtō School have flourished both in China and in Japan until the present day. As the Rinzai School was divided into the Ōryū and Yōgi Sects, Chapter 5 is concerned with both Sects. It can be pointed out that although the Ōryū Sect Masters succeeded in the transmission of the lamp to Eisai, founder of the Rinzai School in Japan,

序言

　　本书作者前著中文版《禅宗师承记》出版于 1976 年，附有八张禅宗世系图。后又于 1977 年出版了作者所著中文版《日本禅僧师承记》，附有二十八张世系图。本书大部分内容译自以上两书（汉译英），不过在将两书中某些段落转译成英语时，作者认为最好还是充分引用一些已有文献中（对于英语读者来说是很易找得的）许多现成的优秀译文。对于所有人名的英译，虽可根据汉语发音，也可根据日语发音，但考虑到许多英语读者已很熟悉最近出版的众多禅宗书籍中的日语发音，所以本书主要也采用了按照日语发音的英语译名。

　　本书可分为两部分，各八章。第一部分为"中国禅宗史"，其中第一章叙述从始祖达摩到五祖弘忍的简史，第二章是关于六祖慧能和他的众多弟子。禅宗自始祖到六祖是单系传承。在慧能以后禅宗就不再是单系传承了。我们知道，慧能至少有五位卓越的法嗣，其中包括神会，获有朝廷钦赐尊号，为七祖。

　　禅宗的两大著名支系——南岳系和青原系——分别是第三和第六章的章名。此两系自其第二代大师开始一直兴盛繁衍，直至今天。南岳怀让的法嗣是马祖道一，青原行思的法嗣是石头希迁，石头希迁的真身近被祀奉于日本横滨附近鹤见的总持寺中。

　　第三章中包括沩仰宗，是由沩山灵祐和仰山慧寂所创建；第四章则是关于中国的临济宗。沩仰宗和临济宗都属于原先"五宗"，但在五宗中只有临济和曹洞两宗既在中国也在日本兴旺繁衍直至今天。临济宗后又分为黄龙和杨岐两派，第五章就叙述这两个宗派。可以指出，虽然首先是由历代黄龙宗禅师成功地将禅宗之灯传给了日本临济宗的创建人荣西，但将禅宗火炬

the dharma descendants of the Yōgi Sect were responsible for carrying the torches further on. Note that Master Kidō, the teacher of Nampo Jōmyō, belonged to the Yōgi Sect. Ingen Ryūki, who went to Japan in 1654 and became the founder of the Ōbaku School, also belonged to the Yōgi lineage. There were four famous Chinese painters who were monks by the end of the Ming Dynasty. Pa-Ta and Shih-tao (1641-1708) were Zen monks, and Shih-tao's dharma-teacher was Lü-an Pen-yueh (Ryo'an Hongetsu, d. 1676). Ryo'an Hongetsu was a contemporary of Ingen; both Ryo'an and Ingen were second-generation dharma-heirs of Mitsu'un Engo (1566-1642).

As mentioned before, Chapter 6 is concerned with the Seigen branch, and Seigen's dharma-heir was Sekitō (700-790). Just as Baso's line led to Rinzai, Sekitō's line led to Tōzan and Sōzan, founders of the Sōtō School. Chapter 7 is concerned with the Sōtō School (in China). Master Nyojō of Tendō became the dharma teacher of Dōgen, who was the founder of the Sōtō School in Japan. Since Dōgen studied under Eisai's disciple, Myōzen, Dōgen could also be considered as belonging to the Rinzai School in Japan.

The Ummon School and the Hōgen School were included in Chapter 8, the last chapter in Part I.

Part II is concerned with "History of Zen in Japan." Chapter 9 starts with Eisai, the founder of the Rinzai School in Japan, after his return from his second trip to China. Chapter 10 is concerned with the Era of the Five Mountains. As the Kenchō-ji was founded by the Chinese monk Rankei Dōryū and the Engaku-ji was founded by the Chinese monk Mugaku Sogen, the close relationship between the Chinese Zen School and the Japanese temples was evident. Enji Ben'en, Shōichi Kokushi, founder of the Tōfuku-ji, and Mukan Fumon, founder of the Nanzen-ji, were "return monks" from China. There were so many Japanese monks who went to seek and learn Zen in China, that the Chinese influence kept on from Sung to Yuan times. Of the founders of the forty-six sects in Japanese Zen, sixteen were Chinese Masters; fifteen were Japanese

Masters who visited Sung-China; and fifteen were Japanese Masters who visited Yuan-China.

Chapter 11 is concerned with the Era of Daiō, Daitō, and Kanzan. Nampo Jōmyō (1235-1308), Daiō Kokushi, went to China in 1259, and became the most important disciple of Kidō Chigu (1185-1269).

继续传承发扬的则是众多杨岐宗的后代法嗣。例如南浦绍明的师父虚堂禅师就属于杨岐宗；而在 1654 年去日本的隐元隆琦，后成为黄檗宗的创建人，也属于杨岐宗。明末清初有四位很有名的国画大师都是僧人，其中八大山人朱耷（1626—1705）和石涛（1641—1708）就是禅僧。石涛师从旅庵本月（？—1676），旅庵则与隐元隆琦（1592—1673）是同时代人，旅庵和隐元都是密云圆悟（1566—1642）的第二代法嗣。

如上所述，第六章是关于青原系及其法嗣石头希迁（700—790）。就像南岳系由马祖道一传向临济义玄那样，青原系则由石头希迁传向洞山良价和曹山本寂，两人就是曹洞宗的创建人。第七章是关于在中国的曹洞宗。天童寺如净大师的法嗣是道元希玄，而道元则是日本曹洞宗的创建人。又因道元也曾师从明全学禅，而明全又是日本临济宗荣西的弟子，所以也可以认为道元属于日本临济宗。

云门宗和法眼宗都包括在第八章内，即本书上篇的最后一章。

本书第二部分为"日本禅宗史"。第九章从荣西开始，在他第二次从中国返回日本后，成为日本临济宗的创始人。第十章是有关于五山派时代。建长寺是由中国僧人兰溪道隆所创建，而圆觉寺是由中国僧人无学祖元所创建，可见中国的禅宗与日本寺庙之间的密切关系是明显的。东福寺的创建人圣一国师圆尔和南禅寺的创建人无关普门都是从中国归来的僧人。有众多的日本僧人曾到中国寻求并学习禅法，所以从宋朝乃至元朝期间，日本禅宗一直保持有中国的影响。在日本禅宗四十六宗派的创建人中，有十六位是中国的大师，有十五位日本大师曾经访问过宋朝时的中国，还有十五位日本大师曾经访问过元朝时的中国。

第十一章是有关大应、大灯与关山的时代。南浦绍明（1235—1308），即大应国师，于 1259 年去过中国，成为虚堂智愚（1185—1269）

His disciple, Shūhō Myōchō (1282-1336), Daitō Kokushi, was the founder of Daitoku-ji. Shūhō's disciple, Kanzan Egen (1277-1360), was the founder of Myōshin-ji. Both the Daitoku-ji and the Myōshin-ji have flourished until the present day. The author accompanied by his wife, Wei Zing, made a special trip to Kyoto in July 1978, to visit the Myōshin-ji.

Chapter 12 starts with Hakuin (1685-1768) and traces the Inzan (1751-1814) and Takujū (1760-1833) lines to the present day. The Institute for Zen Studies at Hanazone University, Kyoto, has kindly supplied the author with a big chart tracing the lineages from Shōgen Sūgaku (1132-1202), Kidō's dharma grandfather, to the present. So it is gratifying for the author to report the lineages of Reverend Kajiura Itsugai (1896-), the recently retired Chief Abbot, and Reverend Yamada Mumon (1900-), the present Chief Abbot of Myōshin-ji. (In Chart 14, *History of Japanese Zen Masters* by the author these two lineages can be easily completed.)

Chapter 13 is concerned with the Ōbaku School in Japan founded by Ingen Ryūki.

Chapter 14 is concerned with the Sōtō School in Japan. Dōgen Kigen (1200-1253), founder of the Sōtō School, may well be "the strongest and most original thinker that Japan has so far produced," according to Father Dumoulin, author of *A History of Zen Buddhism* (English translation by Paul Peachey, Pantheon Books, 1963).

Chapter 15 starts with Keizan Shōkin (1268-1325), the Fourth Patriarch of the Japanese Sōtō School, and traces the Gasan Shōseki (1274-1365) and the Myōhō Sotetsu (1277-1350) lines to the present day. The author and his wife made a special trip in July 1978 to the Sōtō School's Daihonzan Sōji-ji at Tsurumi to pay homage at the shrine of Musai Sekito Zenji (700-790). The author was fortunate to receive the help of Sōtō-shū Main Office in Tokyo, to obtain important lineages from the newly published *Sōtō-shū Zenshō*. The author was further gratified to receive official documents from Sōji-ji concerning the lineages of

Reverend Iwamoto Shōshun, the recently retired Chief Abbot, and Reverend Ichikawa Kin'ei, the present Chief Abbot of Sōji-ji. Mention must be made of the monumental work of Reverend Keidō Chisan (1879-1967) entitled *History of Zen School* in Japanese, first published in 1919, and its second edition recently published in 1974. This *History* includes both the History of Zen in China and the History of Zen in Japan.

最重要的弟子。他的弟子宗峰妙超（1282—1336），即大灯国师，是大德寺的创建人。宗峰的弟子关山慧玄（1277—1360）是妙心寺的创建人。大德寺与妙心寺迄今香火犹盛。本书作者由其妻婉靖伴同，于1978年7月，专程到京都访问过妙心寺。

第十二章是从白隐慧鹤（1685—1768）开始，沿隐山惟琰（1751—1814）与卓洲胡仙（1760—1833）的世系直到现今。京都花园大学禅宗研究院慷慨地向作者赠送了一份从松源崇岳（1132—1202）即虚堂的法祖直到现今的大幅世系表。这样就使得作者可以记述妙心寺最近退休的住持梶浦逸外（1896—）法师与现今的住持山田无文（1900—）的世系，令人欣慰。（在作者所著的《日本禅僧师承记》第十四图中即可很容易地完善这两个世系。）

第十三章是有关由隐元隆琦所创建的日本黄檗宗。

第十四章是有关在日本的曹洞宗。按照《佛教禅宗史》（该书由保罗·披切译为英文，潘塞恩图书出版公司，1963）的作者杜慕林的说法，日本曹洞宗创建人道元希玄（1200—1253）可能是"迄今日本所造就的最强、最有创见的思想家"。

第十五章是从日本曹洞宗的四世祖莹山绍瑾（1268—1325）开始，追寻峨山绍硕（1274—1365）与明峰素哲（1277—1350）的世系直到现在。本书作者偕妻于1978年7月专程赴曹洞宗的鹤见大本山总持寺向无际大师石头希迁（700—790）真身致敬。作者有幸得到了东京曹洞宗总部的帮助，从最新版《曹洞宗全书》中获得了重要的曹洞宗世系图。作者更高兴的是从总持寺收到了有关最近退休的住持岩本胜俊法师与现任住持乙川瑾映法师世系的正式文本。还要提到的是莹堂智璨（1879—1967）所著的《禅宗史》日文本是一部不朽著作，该书初版于1919年，最近于1974年再版发行。这部《禅宗史》兼收并蓄了禅宗在中国与在日本的历史。

As a child, the author visited the Tien-nin Temple (Tennei-ji) at Changchow (near Wusih) in the company of his grandmother. During the Anti-Japanese War (1937-1945), the author had the opportunity of meeting with Abbot Tai Hsu (Taiki) at Tsin-yun Shan (Shin'un Zan). Then in June 1941, the author visited the Nan-hua Temple (Nanka-ji) at Shao-kuan, paid homage at the shrine of the Sixth Patriarch, and met with Abbot Hsu Yun (Kiun, 1840-1959), the foremost Zen Master in China. On January 7, 1943, the author had the good fortune of meeting with Abbot Hsu Yun again at Tzu-yun Temple (Jiun-ji) near Chungking. In the autumn of 1975, the author wrote a long poem commemorating Musai Sekitō Zenji, as his body was enshrined at Sōji-ji at Tsurumi, near Yokohama, Japan. In July 1978, the author, accompanied by his wife, visited the shrine of Master Shih-tou Hsi-chien (Sekitō) in Japan. So this humble volume is respectfully dedicated to Master Shih-tou (700-790) and Abbot Hsu Yun (1840-1959), on the fifteenth day of the seventh month in the year of the *horse* (1978), the ninety-fifth birthday of the author's beloved mother. (A sad note must be added to record the passing of the author's older brother, Dr. Yo-chi Ku, M.D., on August 5, 1978, corresponding to the second day of the seventh month, at the age of seventy-eight.)

作者在孩提时，曾随祖母参拜过常州（临无锡）的天宁寺。在中国抗战期间，作者有机会在缙云山会晤太虚大师。随后于1941年6月，作者赴韶关南华寺参拜六祖慧能大师的真身，并会晤了中国当代最杰出的禅宗大师虚云老和尚（1840—1959）。1943年1月7日，作者有幸在重庆附近的慈云寺再次会晤虚老。1975年秋季，作者写了一首长诗以纪念无际石头希迁大师真身奉安于日本横滨附近鹤见的总持寺。1978年7月，作者由妻子伴同参拜了在日本的石头希迁大师真身。因此将本书在1978年（即马年）农历七月十五日作者慈母95岁生辰之际，敬献给石头大师与虚云大师。

还须添附一项悲痛悼念：作者长兄顾毓琦医学博士于1978年8月5日（农历七月二日）逝世，享年78岁。

CHAPTER 1   FROM DARUMA TO GUNIN

Bodhidharma or Daruma was the First Patriarch of Ch'an (Zen) Buddhism, developed in China some fifteen hundred years ago. According to historian Tao-hsuan (Dōsen, 596-667) in his *Further Biographies of Eminent Monks* (645 A.D.), Daruma reached the southern coast of China from India in 470 A.D., that was, near the end of the Sung (Sō) Dynasty (420-479). This Sung Dynasty succeeded the Eastern Tsin (Tō Shin) Dynasty, which ended in 420, the sixteenth year of the Yi-Hsi (Giki) era. A historical account can also be found in Tao-yuan's (Dōgen's) *Ching-te Chuan-teng Lu* (*Keitoku Dentō Roku*), compiled in 1004 A.D. We shall refer to this reference as simply the *Lamp Records* from now on. Another reference is *Lieh-dai Fa-pao Chi* (*Rekidai Hōbō Ki*), which will be referred to as simply the *Dharma Records*. Both the *Lamp Records* and the *Dharma Records* were reproduced in Volume 51 of the *Buddhist Encyclopedia* (*Daishō Daizōkyō*). For example, Daruma's record as given in the *Dharma Records* appears on pages 180-181 in Vol. 51, while Daruma's record as given in the *Lamp Records* appears on pages 217-220 in Vol. 51 of *Daishō Daizōkyō*.

In 520 A.D., the first year of the Pu-Tung (Futsu) era, Daruma arrived at Chingling (present Nanking). The ruling King, Wu-ti (r. 502-550), of the Kingdom of Liang (or Liang Dynasty), asked Daruma what he had brought from India. Daruma answered: "Not a word." Liang Wu-ti asked: "I have built many temples, copied numerous Buddhist sutras, and put up many Buddhist images, for the salvation of my people, do I have achieved any merit or virtue?" Daruma answered straightforwardly: "No merit or virtue at all!" The King could not understand and was apparently offended. So Daruma left the Kingdom of Liang and traveled north to enter the Kingdom of Wei.

Wei Wen-ti, the King of later Wei, ascended the throne in 471 A.D., and moved his Capital to Lo-yang (Honan Province) in 494 A. D. He built the Shao-lin Temple (Shōrin-ji) at Sung Shan (Mount Sū) in 496 A.D., and died three years after. Wei Wu-ti succeeded to the throne, and died in 515 A.D. Wei Ming-ti succeeded to the throne in 517 A.D. and built the Yung-ning Temple (Einei-ji), which was destroyed by fire in 534 A.D. Daruma did visit the Yung-ning Temple before its destruction. In the *Lo-yang Chieh-lan Chi* (*Rakuyō Garan Ki*), authored by Yang Hsuan-chih (*Yō Genshi*) in 547, it was mentioned that when Yang was visiting the Yung-

壹 从初祖达摩到弘忍

　　佛教禅宗大约于 1500 年前在中国创建并发展，菩提达摩（简称达摩）是中国禅宗的初祖。根据道宣（596—667）撰写的《续高僧传》（公元 645 年）记载，达摩于公元 470 年从印度来到中国南部海岸，当时已接近南朝宋代（420—479）末年。公元 420 年（晋恭帝元熙二年），东晋灭亡，南朝宋政权建立。还有道原在公元 1004 年撰写的《景德传灯录》（简称《传灯录》）中对此事也有记载。另有一参考著作是《历代法宝记》。《传灯录》和《历代法宝记》两书都已收入《大正藏》第 51 卷中，例如《历代法宝记》中所载达摩生平可见该书第 51 卷第 180—181 页，而《传灯录》中所载达摩生平则可见该书第 51 卷第 217—220 页。

　　公元 520 年，即南朝梁普通元年，达摩来到建康（即今南京），当时统治南朝的国君梁武帝（在位 502—550）问达摩从印度带来了什么。达摩回答："没带一个字。"梁武帝问："我建造了许多寺庙，抄写了许多佛经，立了许多佛像，以超度和拯救我的百姓，我有何功德？"达摩直接回答说："根本没有什么功德。"武帝不能理解，明显觉得被冒犯了。于是达摩离开建康，再往北行，来到了北方的北魏。

　　北魏孝文帝即位于公元 471 年，494 年把国都迁到河南洛阳，496 年就在嵩山建造了少林寺，三年后逝世。魏宣武帝继位，于 515 年逝世。魏孝明帝即位于 517 年，建造了永宁寺，此寺于 534 年被烧毁。在未毁之前，达摩确实曾访问过此寺。据杨衒之在 547 年所著的《洛阳伽蓝记》中称，作者在访永宁寺时，正好遇到了

＊　公元 419 年 1 月（义熙十四年），晋安帝驾崩，晋恭帝即位后改元元熙元年。

ning Temple, he came upon Bodhidharma (Daruma), the monk from the western land (India), sitting in quiet admiration before the beauty of the shrines and the pagodas. The old monk (Daruma) said that he was one hundred and fifty years old, and had come from far away, traveling over many lands. This account authenticated the appearance of Daruma at the temple between 517 and 534.

There were three possible dates concerning Daruma's passing: (1) 528 A.D., (2) 532 A.D., and (3) 536 A.D. It is more probable that Daruma passed away in 532, as his disciple and dharma-heir Hui-ke (Eka, 487-593) moved around for some years after the Master's passing by the Yellow River, before he went to Nieh-tu, the Capital of the eastern half of the Wei Kingdom (534-537). Dumoulin in his *A History of Zen Buddhism* mentioned that Daruma "died (before 534) at a ripe age." (See English translation by Paul Peachey, Pantheon Books, 1963.)

In Tao-hsuan's biography of Daruma, and also in the text of *Two Entrances and Four Acts* with a Preface by Tan-lin (Donrin), Daruma mentioned the Two Entrances as: (1) the Entrance by Reason (*li*), and (2) the Entrance by Conduct (*hsing*). According to Tan-lin's Preface:

> In the Entrance by Reason, the unity of all living beings in the one true nature is grasped, a nature which cannot fully disclose itself because it is hidden by the dust of external things and by confusing ideas. When one, abandoning the false and embracing the true, in simplicity of thought abides in *pi-kuan*, one finds that there is neither selfhood nor otherness, that the masses and the worthies are of one essence.

Tan-lin was one of Daruma's students, although he was not considered as a Zen Master. The term, *pi-kuan*, literally "wall-gazing," was praised by Tao-hsuan as Daruma's greatest achievement in his teaching of Mahayana Buddhism. A companion term, *chueh-kuan* (Kakukan), meaning "vision of enlightenment," is also to be found in Zen literature. To quote Dumoulin-Peachey in *A History of Zen Buddhism*, page 71:

The calming of the spirit through sudden enlightenment and the understanding of the true Buddha nature is designated in the text (of *Two Entrances and Four Acts*) as the "Entrance by Reason," while the goal which is attained is called *tao*.

Note that the Entrance by Conduct consists of the Four Acts. To quote again:

> 来自西方（印度）的僧人达摩，静坐在那里赞赏该寺和宝塔之美。老僧达摩自称已有 150 岁高龄，来自很遥远的地方，游历了许多国家。这一记载可以确证达摩现身于永宁寺的时间是在公元 517—534 年之间。
>
> 关于达摩去世之年，推测有三种可能：（1）528 年，（2）532 年，（3）536 年。比较可靠的是达摩卒于 532 年。因为他的弟子即法嗣慧可（487—593）在其师父去世后，曾在黄河周边地方云游了几年，然后在 534—537 年间到了东魏的都城邺都。根据杜慕林在其《佛教禅宗史》中称：达摩"以高寿终（在 534 年之前）"（参见保罗·披切的英译本，潘塞恩图书出版公司，1963）。
>
> 在道宣著的《续高僧传·达摩》中，以及在昙琳作序的《二入四行》中，达摩讲到两种入门为：（1）由"理"入门，（2）由"行"入门。昙琳在序中说：

> 理入者，谓藉教悟宗，深信含生同一真性，但为客尘妄想所覆，不能显了。若也舍妄归真，凝住壁观，无自无他，凡圣等一。

昙琳是达摩众多弟子之一，虽然他还没有被认为是禅师。这里"壁观"二字，从字面上讲，就是面对着墙壁，道宣称颂这是达摩在对大乘佛教讲授中最大的成就。另一相伴随的用语是"觉观"，意思是启发领悟的观点，也同样出现在禅宗文献中。下文引自杜慕林《佛教禅宗史》第 71 页：

> 通过顿悟而领会了佛教真义，使心灵平静，这在《二入四行》中就称为"由理入门"，这时达到的目标就称为道。

这里可以指出，"由行入门"包含了四种行动，再引该书中一段译文如下：

In the Entrance by the Four Acts, the general Mahayanist attitudes, based on various passages in the *Vimalakirti* and the *Nirvana Sutras* and issuing from the doctrines of the Perfect Virtues (*paramita*), *karma*, and the emptiness of all things, are set forth.

The Chinese text can be found in Abbot Yin-shun's *History of Zen School in China* (in Chinese), 1971, 1975, pages 8-13.

Hui-ke (Eka) was born in 487 A.D., the eleventh year of the Tai-Ho era under the reign of Wei Wen-ti, and passed away in 593 A.D., the thirteenth year of the Kai-Huang era under the reign of Sui Wen-ti (first Emperor of Sui Dynasty). Eka was a native of Wu-lao (Burō) in present Honan Province. His father was waiting anxiously for a child. One night he became aware that the bedroom was filled with a strange light, and his wife conceived a child. So the new born child was named Kuang (Kō), meaning "light." Later when he was forty years old, Eka dreamed of a divine giant advising him to go south and then changed his name to Shen-Kuang (Jinkō), meaning "divine light."

According to the *Dharma Records*, Hui-ke visited Daruma at the age of forty. He stood before the Master while the heavy snow reached his waist. He cut off one arm in order to show his devotion to seek the Dharma. The Master was impressed and accepted him as one of his disciples. After six years, he received the sacred transmission as Daruma's dharma-heir. As the story was told, Hui-ke received his Master's marrow: Tao-fu (Dōfuku) received his skin, Taoyu (Dōikū) received his bones, and Nun Tsung-chih (Ni Sōji) received his flesh. So Hui-ke became the Second Patriarch in the Zen School. Daruma gave Eka the *Lankavatara Sutra* in 4 *chuan*, according to Dōsen's *Further Biographies of Eminent Monks*, with the words: "I have observed that in this land of China there is only this *sutra*. If you depend upon this *sutra*, you will be able to save the world." Eka was advised by Daruma to be a hermit; accordingly he spent about forty years in Nee-Shan (Gei-san). After he found his dharma-heir Seng-tsan (Sōsan), he entered Shi-kung Shan (Shikū-san) and pretended to be a lunatic. It was a dangerous undertaking to spread the Dharma of Ch'an (Zen), and Eka was executed. However, Emperor Wen-ti of Sui (Zui) Dynasty regretted that an old monk of one hundred and seven years of age was thus brutally treated. So Eka was revered as a Bodhisattva, and Buddhism was revived.

Eka's doctrine can be given as follows. (See D. T. Suzuki: *Essays in Zen Buddhism*, First Series, pages 194-195).

在由四行入门中提出了：根据《维摩诘经》和《涅槃经》中多段经文中大乘佛教信众的态度，完美道德原则的论点，烦恼以及所有事物的空虚实质（一切皆空）。

中文原文可见印顺《中国禅宗史》1971、1975 年版，第 8—13 页。

慧可出生于公元 487 年，即魏孝文帝太和十一年；于 593 年去世，即隋朝开国皇帝隋文帝开皇十三年。出生地为武牢，属今河南省。其父亲当时正迫切盼望生子。有一天晚上，他忽觉卧室内充满了异光，妻子就怀孕了，于是就把新生儿取名为"光"。后来，慧可在 40 岁时，梦见一巨神鼓励其南游，所以又改名"神光"。

根据《历代法宝记》中记载，慧可在 40 岁时拜见达摩，恭立在师前，正下着大雪，积雪达到腰间。为表达其拜师的诚意，慧可自断一臂。达摩深为感动，就接纳他作为众弟子之一。六年后慧可继承达摩衣钵，成为他的法嗣。故事中传称，有四个弟子得传达摩大师之法：道副得其皮，道育得其骨，尼总持得其肉，而慧可得其精髓。于是，慧可就成为禅宗的第二代祖师。根据道宣所著《续高僧传》记载，达摩授给慧可四卷《楞伽经》，并说："我观汉地，唯有此经。仁者依行，自得度世。"达摩还嘱咐他可以隐居山林。慧可遵从师嘱，隐居在尼山约四十年。当他找到了他的法嗣弟子僧璨后，又隐入司空山，假装疯痴。宣扬达摩禅宗是一项危险的任务，慧可被处决。然而，隋文帝后悔如此残酷地对待这位 107 岁高龄的老僧，便尊崇他为菩萨，佛教得以再度兴盛。

慧可宣讲的教旨如下（参见铃木大拙：《佛教禅宗论文集》系列 I，第 194—195 页）：

The deepest truth lies in the principle of identity. It is due to one's ignorance that the mani-jewel is taken for a piece of brick, but lo! when one is suddenly awakened to self-enlightenment it is realized that one is in possession of the real jewel. The ignorant and the enlightened are of one essence, they are not really to be separated. We should know that all things are such as they are. ... When we know that between this body and the Buddha there is nothing to separate one from the other, what is the use of seeking after Nirvana (as something external to ourselves)?

In 535 A.D., when Seng-tsan (Sōsan) was over forty years old, he paid his respects to Hui-ke and said: "I am diseased; I beg you to cleanse me of my sin." Hui-ke said: "Bring me your sin and I will cleanse you of it." Seng-tsan thought for a long while, but could not find the sin. Hui-ke then said: "I have cleansed you of your sin. From now on, obey Buddha, Dharma, and Sengha." Seng-tsan said: "Since I met you, I know Sengha, but what are Buddha and Dharma?" Hui-ke said: "Mind is the Buddha; Mind is the Dharma; Dharma and Buddha are one, and so is Sengha." Seng-tsan said: "Now I realize that the nature of SIN is neither inside, nor outside, nor in between. Just as the Mind, Buddha and Dharma are one." Hui-ke then ordained him and gave him the name "SENG-TSAN," meaning Monk the Brilliant. Hui-ke warned him that there would be great disaster later. Seng-tsan became a hermit at Nee-Kung Shan (Geikū-san) for more than ten years. He passed away in 606 A.D., while standing, holding a tree branch in his hand.

In 592 A.D., the twelfth year of the Kai-Huang era under the reign of Sui Wen-ti, a young monk of fourteen years of age by the name Tao-hsin (Dōshin, 580-651) came to salute Seng-tsan, the Third Patriarch, and served under him for nine years before he received the ordainment and the transmission.

Seng-tsan left an important document to posterity, known as *Hsin-hsin-ming* (*Inscribed on the Believing Mind*). Dr. D. T. Suzuki made an English translation, which appeared in his *Essays in Zen Buddhism*, Series

I, pages 196-201. R. H. Blyth in his *Zen and Zen Classics*, Volume 1 (The Hokuseido Press, 1960, 1974, Tokyo) also gave an English translation. We shall compare the two versions as follows:

(Suzuki) The Perfect Way knows no difficulties

Except that it refuses to make preference:

　　最深层次的真理是等同一致的原理。由于人的愚昧无知，把真玉宝石当作了砖瓦。但是，你瞧！当你顿然自我启发而醒悟时，就会发觉你完全拥有真正的宝石。无知和得到启悟原是一个实体，并非分开的。我们应该知道，万事万物都保有其本来面目……当我们懂得了在自身与佛性间本来一致，无可分割，如果再要到自身以外去寻求涅槃，那又有何用呢?

　　公元 535 年，僧璨已有 40 多岁，他拜见慧可，并说:"弟子有病，请求师父为弟子忏悔罪孽。"慧可说:"把你的罪孽找来，我为你忏悔罪孽。"僧璨沉思了很久，却未能找到。于是慧可说:"我为你忏罪已毕，从今以后，你就应依从佛、法、僧三宝。"僧璨说:"我既已拜见师父，懂得了僧的意义，但什么是佛和法？"慧可回答:"心即是佛，心即是法，法和佛是统一体，僧也同样。"僧璨说:"今天我懂得了罪性不在内，不在外，也不在中间。正与'心'这个概念相同，所以说佛法合一。"于是慧可就接纳他为弟子，并给他取名为"僧璨"，意思就是有大智慧的和尚。慧可告诫他说今后可能会有大灾难。僧璨在尼空山隐居了十多年。他于公元 606 年去世，去世时身体站立，手中执一树枝。

　　公元 592 年，即隋文帝开皇十二年，有一年仅 14 岁的小和尚，名道信（580—651）来拜见禅宗第三祖僧璨。他服侍师父九年之后受了戒，得传其衣法。

　　僧璨留给后世一篇重要著述《信心铭》。铃木博士把它译成英文，见《佛教禅宗论文集》，系列 I，第 196—201 页。另外 R. H. 布莱思在《禅与禅宗经典》第 1 卷中也把它译成英文（东京北正堂出版社，1960，1974）。对照两种译文的大意如下:

　　完美之路并没有任何困难，

　　不过不要去作任何挑拣，

Only when freed from hate and love,

It reveals itself fully and without disguise.

A tenth of an inch's difference,

And heaven and earth are set apart:

If you want to see it manifest,

Take no thought for or against it.

(Blyth) There is nothing difficult about the Great Way,

But, avoid choosing!

Only when you neither love nor hate,

Does it appear in all clarity.

A hair's breadth of deviation from it,

And a deep gulf is set between heaven and earth.

If you want to get hold of what it looks like,

Do not be anti- or pro- anything.

There are altogether 146 lines. Let us just compare the last twelve lines:

(Suzuki) What is is the same with what is not,

What is not is the same with what is:

Where this state of things fails to obtain,

Be sure not to tarry.

One in all,

All in one—

If only this is realized,

No more worry about your not being perfect!

The believing mind is not divided,

And undivided is the believing mind—

This is where words fail,

For it is not of the past, future, or present.

(Blyth) What is, is not;

What is not, is.

只有在既无爱又无恨时，
它就完全显出了本色，没有伪饰……

只有毫厘之差，
结果却是天壤之别；
如要见到真相显示，
就不要去考虑是或否。（铃木）

伟大之路并无什么困难，
但是，不要去挑拣；
只要既不恨，也不爱，
它就会清清楚楚显示出来……

只要偏离了一发之差，
就在天地间划下一条鸿沟；
要想看到真相如何，
就不要去反对或赞成什么。（布莱思）

（原偈：至道无难，惟嫌拣择。但莫憎爱，洞然明白。毫厘
有差，天地悬隔。欲得现前，莫存顺逆。）

译文一共有 146 行。以下是最后 12 行（布译为 13 行）的对照。

存在与不存在相同，
不存在与存在也一致；
当这样的事态不能达到时，
一定不要在那里停滞。

一在全内，
全也在一内——
只要这点能够实现，
就不用担心你不会完美！

虔诚不会被分心，
不分心就是虔诚——
这不是言辞所能表达，
因为它既非过去和将来，也非现在。（铃木）

存在的并不存在，
不存在的则存在。

Until you have grasped this fact,

Your position is simply untenable.

One thing is all things;

All things are one thing.

If this is so for you,

There is no need to worry about perfect knowledge.

The believing mind is not dual;

What is dual is not the believing mind.

Beyond all language,

For it, there is no past, no present, no future.

These 146 lines were the sources of many dialogues in future generations.

Tao-hsin (Dōshin, 580-651) became the Fourth Patriarch. Contemporary with Dōshin was the Japanese monk Dōshō (Tao-chao), who was a disciple of Hui-man (Eman), Seng-tsan's dharma brother. In 617 A.D., Tao-hsin (Dōshin) arrived at Chi-chou (present Kiangsi Province) with his disciples, while the city was under siege by the bandits. A miracle happened such that the bandits retreated at the sight of Dōshin's group, and the city was saved from destruction. In 624 A.D., Dōshin moved to Pu-tou Shan (literally, "Broken-Head Mountain"). The mountain was later known as Shuang-feng Shan ("Double-Peak Mountain").

While visiting Huang-mei (Ōbai) in present Hupeh Province, Dōshin met a child of extraordinary features. He asked the child's parents to let the child be a monk under his care. This child was later known as Hung-jen (Gunin). In 643 A.D., Emperor Tai-tsung of the Tang Dynasty wished to summon Master Dōshin to visit the Capital. For three times the Master refused the invitation. In the fourth time, the Emperor sent word that if the Master could not come, the emissary should bring his head instead. The Master was extremely calm and ready to give up his head. The Emperor did order the emissary not to harm the Master, and revered him even more after this incident. Dōshin lived to seventy-two years old. Besides Hung-jen (Gunin), the Fifth Patriarch, Dōshin had another disciple, Fa-yung (Hōyū, 594-657), founder of the Niu-tou Shan (Gozu-san) School.

> 如果还未能掌握这一事实，
> 那么你的立足处就根本站不住。
>
> 一件事就是全部事，
> 全部事也就是一件事。
> 如果你确实能如此，
> 那就不用担心不能完全认知。
>
> 信心不是怀疑心，
> 怀疑心也不是信心。
> 所有言语都不能表达，
> 因为这里没有过去，没有现在，
> 也没有未来。（布莱思）

（原偈：有即是无，无即是有。若不如是，必不须守。一即一切，一切即一。但能如是，何虑不毕。信心不二，不二信心。言语道断，非去来今。）

这146行是禅宗以后许多代的对话的源泉。

道信（580—651）是禅宗第四祖。与道信同时代的日本和尚道昭，是僧璨师兄慧满的弟子。公元617年，道信带领他的众弟子来到吉洲（在今江西省），此时该城正被一群盗匪所包围。奇迹出现了，盗匪看到了道信众师徒后，即行退却，于是该城免遭劫难。公元624年道信搬迁到破头山，此山以后被称为双峰山。

在道信游黄梅（在今湖北省）时，遇到一儿童，气质非凡。于是道信求得其双亲同意，让该儿在他的教诲培养下成为一名僧人，此儿即是后来的弘忍。公元643年唐太宗想要召道信大师进京，大师前后三次回绝了皇帝的召请。第四次太宗传旨说，大师如再不来，那么使者就要取其头来见。大师极为平静，准备弃头不惜。不过实际上太宗却是命令使者不要去伤害大师，之后对大师更为尊敬。道信年72岁圆寂。除弘忍（禅宗第五祖）之外，道信另有一弟子法融（594—657），是牛头禅的创建人。

According to the *Lamp Records* (see *Daishō Daizōkyō*, Vol. 51, pages 226-228; English translation in Professor Chang Chung-yuan's *Original Teachings of Ch'an Buddhism*, pages 17-26), Niu-tou Fa-yung was a native of Yenling in Jun-chou (now Chinkiang, Kiangsu Province). When he was nineteen years old, he was thoroughly acquainted with all the Chinese classics. Subsequently he read the *Mahaprajna-paramita Sutra*, and gained a deep understanding of the real void. One day, he realized that the *prajna* doctrine of Buddhism was the ferryboat that takes one to the other shore. He shaved his head and went into Mount Mao. Later he stayed in a rock cave in a cliff north of the Yu-hsi Monastery in the Niu-tou Mountain. As the legends went, a hundred birds brought flower offerings to Fa-yung.

In the middle of the Chen-Kuan era (627-649) of the Tang Dynasty, the Fourth Patriarch, Tao-hsin, observed the Niu-tou Mountain from a distance and conjectured that some outstanding Buddhist must be living there. Therefore Tao-hsin went to the mountain and searched for him. On his arrival he saw Fa-yung sitting, quiet and self-possessed, paying no attention to his visitor.

The Patriarch asked him: "What are you doing here?"

"I am contemplating Mind."

"Who is he that contemplates and what is the Mind that is contemplated?"

Fa-yung did not answer, but immediately stood up and made a deep bow. ...

The Fourth Patriarch expounded thus:

"All systems of Buddhist teaching center in Mind, where immeasurable treasures originate. All its supernatural faculties and their transformations revealed in discipline, meditation, and wisdom are sufficiently contained in one's mind and they never depart therefrom. All the hindrances to the attainment of *bodhi* which arise from passions that generate *karma* are originally non-existent. Every cause and effect is but a dream. There is no Triple World which one leaves, and no *bodhi* to search for. The inner reality and outer appearance of man and a thousand things are identical. The Great Tao is formless and boundless. It is free from thought and anxiety. You have now understood this Buddhist teaching. There is nothing lacking in you, and you yourself are no different from Buddha. There is no way of achieving Buddhahood other than letting your mind be free to be itself. You should not

根据《传灯录》所载（参见《大正藏》第51卷，第226—228页，及张钟元教授英译本《佛教禅宗之源》第17—26页），牛头法融是润州（今江苏省镇江）延陵人。19岁即已熟读了全部中国儒家经史。然后读了佛教大部《般若经》，获得了对"真空"的深刻理解。有一天，他领悟了佛教"般若"的道理是到达彼岸的出世渡船，于是剃了发，入隐茅山，然后又居入牛头山幽栖寺寺北一个峭壁的山洞内，传说有百鸟来献鲜花给法融。

唐朝贞观（627—649）中期，四祖道信从远处遥望牛头山，猜想一定有高僧住在那里，于是就进山寻访。到达后看到法融静坐在那里，镇定自若，根本不顾来访的客人。

四祖问他："你在此做什么？"

"我在沉思我心。"

"是谁在沉思，沉思的心又是什么？"

法融不回答，立刻站了起来，深深行了一礼。

四祖这样解释：

全部佛教教义的核心就是心。心是无量珍宝的源泉。一切由戒规、禅定和智慧所显示的神通和变化都充分包含在人心内，也永不离人心。一切妨碍达到菩提而由痴心造成的烦恼业障原本空寂，都不存在。一切因果，也都如梦如幻。人都逃不出三界，也没有菩提可求。人和万千事物、内心和外部全都平等。大道无形，也无边界。无所思也无所虑。现在你已悟解了佛法教义，你就不再缺少什么，你自己就无异于佛。除了让你的心自身完全解脱之外，别无其他成佛之道。不必要沉思，也不必要

contemplate nor should you purify your mind. Let there be no craving and hatred, and have no anxiety or fear. Be boundless and absolutely free from all conditions. Be free to go in any direction you like. Do not act to do good, nor to pursue evil. Whether you walk or stay, sit or lie down, and whatever you see happen to you, all are the wonderful activity of the Great Enlightened One. It is all joy, free from anxiety—it is called Buddha."

Hung-jen (Gunin, 602-675) was only seven years old, when Dōshin adopted him as his protege. For thirty years he never left the Fourth Patriarch. He was eight feet (Chinese measure) tall, and had extraordinary features. He was the founder of Tung-Chan Temple (Tōzen-ji) at Huang-mei, Hupeh Province. The time had finally come for a full proclamation of Ch'an (Zen). So the Fifth Patriarch was the first to preach openly and give lessons to his five hundred pupils.

Hung-jen (Gunin) had many promising disciples, among them were Shen-hsiu (Jinshū, d. 706), Hui-neng (Enō, 638-713), and Chih-sien (Chisen, 609-702). Shen-hsiu (Jinshū) was very brilliant, and he was Chief Priest at the Tung-Chan Temple. Later he became the founder of the Northern School. Hui-neng (Enō) was a kitchen aide and came from the Canton region. A well-known anecdote told the unusual story that both Shen-hsiu and Hui-neng submitted gāthās to the Fifth Patriarch, who would decide the dharma-heir based upon the understanding of basic ideas revealed in these gāthās. Shen-hsiu's gāthā was written on the wall of the Meditation Hall. The English translations are:

> (Suzuki) This body is the Bodhi-tree,
> The soul is like a mirror bright;
> Take heed to keep it always clean,
> And let not dust collect on it.

> (A. W. Watts) The body is the Bodhi Tree;
> The mind like a bright mirror standing.
> Take care to wipe it all the time,

And allow no dust to cling.

Hui-neng submitted his gāthā and asked somebody who could write to write it on the wall. The English translations follow:

澄净此心。无所贪求，无所嗔恨，无所焦虑，无所恐惧。不受任何条件的约束和限制，自由自在地走向任何要去之处。既不为善，也不作恶。或行或止，或坐或卧，不论见到或遇到什么事物，都是伟大启示的奇妙作用，尽是欢乐，全无忧虑，这就称为佛。

弘忍（602—675）年仅七岁时就被道信收纳为弟子，前后三十年之久，从未离开其师父即禅宗第四祖。他身高八尺，气质不凡。他是湖北省黄梅东山寺的创建人（弘忍在东禅寺传衣钵后创建东山寺）。此时，朝廷对佛教禅宗完全开禁的日子终于到来，作为禅宗的第五祖，他也就成为能公开传播禅宗教义的第一人，向他的五百个弟子们传授佛法。

弘忍大师有许多优秀弟子，如神秀（？—706）、慧能（638—713）和智诜（609—702）等，而以神秀为上座，是东禅寺的首座法师，以后成为禅宗北支的始祖。慧能是一个食堂的役工，来自广东地区。有一众所周知的传说，讲述了这样一个不寻常的故事：弘忍要求神秀和慧能各交一首诗偈（佛教诗歌）给他，由他根据诗偈中所显示各人对佛法基本教义的领悟深度来判定谁可以继承他，作为他的法嗣。神秀的偈写在寺内禅堂廊壁上，铃木和艾伦·瓦茨的译文如下：

身是菩提树，
心像明亮的镜子；
注意保持永远洁净，
不让尘埃积在上面。（铃木译）

身是菩提树，
心像明亮的镜台。
注意时时刻刻勤拂拭，
不让沾尘埃。（艾伦·瓦茨译）

（原偈：身是菩提树，心如明镜台，时时勤拂拭，勿使惹尘埃。）

慧能也作了一偈，请会写字的人替他写在墙壁上，偈的译文为：

(Suzuki) The Bodhi is not like the tree,

The mirror bright is nowhere shining;

As there is nothing from the first,

Where can the dust itself collect?

(A. W. Watts) There never was a Bodhi Tree,

Nor bright mirror standing.

Fundamentally, not one thing exits,

So where is the dust to cling?

Thereby the Fifth Patriarch secretly chose Hui-neng (Enō) to be the Sixth Patriarch. Hui-neng was advised by Hung-jen to leave Huang-mei, and go south. The story will be told in Chapter 2. Hui-neng (Enō) was noted for his *Platform Scriptures*—an English translation was recently made by Professor Wing-tsit Chan and published by St. John's University, Jamaica, N.Y. Professor Chan's translations of the two gāthās will be given in Chapter 2 .

Shen-hsiu (Jinshū) had two able disciples: Pu-chi (Fujaku, 651-739) and Yi-fu (Gifuku, 658-736). Pu-chi's disciple, Tao-hsuan (Dōsen, 702-760), went to Japan. Dōsen's disciple, Hsing-piao (Gyōhyō, 722-797), was the teacher of Saichō (767-822), who visited China and went back to Japan to become the founder of the Tendai School in Japan. While in China, Saichō studied under Yu-lao Hsiao-jan (Gyokurō Kyūnen), who was Ma-tsu Tao-i's (Baso Dōitsu's) disciple. While Tao-hsuan (Dōsen) brought to Japan the Zen teachings of the Northern School, Saichō was able to bring back the Zen teachings of the Sixth Patriarch. Saichō also visited many masters of the Tien-tai (Tendai) School in China. The Tien-tai School (in China) considered Nagarjuna as its First Patriarch. The Ninth Patriarch was Ching-chi Chan-jan (Keikei Tannen, 711-782). Keikei's disciple was Tao-sui (Dōsui), and Saichō became Dōsui's disciple. After Saichō went back to Japan, he became the founder of the Tendai School in Japan. However, out of respect for his Chinese teacher, the official honorary founder of the Japanese Tendai School was Dōsui.

Going back to the Niu-tou Shan School, the lineage was given below:

(1) Fa-yung (Hōyū, 594-657);

(2) Chih-yen (Chigen, 600-677);

(3) Hui-fang (E'hō, 629-695);

(4) Fa-chih (Hōji, 635-702);

(5) Chih-wei (Chi'i, 646-722);

(6) Hui-chung (Echū, 683-769).

菩提不像树，

明镜也不存在。

根本什么都没有，

哪里会积尘埃？（铃木译）

既无菩提树，

也无明镜台。

根本不存在，

哪里会沾尘埃？（艾伦·瓦茨译）

（原偈：菩提本无树，明镜亦非台，本来无一物，何处惹尘埃。）

于是五祖就暗自选中慧能继承他，成为禅宗第六祖。且又劝告他离开黄梅，远去南方。详细故事留待第二章再讲。慧能以其传世之作《六祖坛经》而著名，近已由陈荣捷教授把它译成英文，中英文对照本由美国纽约州牙买加圣约翰大学出版。陈教授对此两偈的译文也将在第二章中再转译成中文。

神秀有两个优秀弟子：普寂（651—739）和义福（658—736）。普寂的弟子道璇（702—760）去了日本。道璇的弟子行表（722—797）是最澄（767—822）的师父。最澄在中国时，拜马祖道一的弟子玉姥憍然为师，学习佛法。道璇把禅宗北支的教义带去日本，而最澄则把禅宗南支六祖的教义带到日本。最澄又曾拜访了中国天台宗的许多大师。中国天台宗认龙树为第一代始祖，九祖则是湛然（711—782）。湛然的弟子是道邃，道邃的弟子即是最澄。最澄回日本后成为日本天台宗的创建人。但出于对他中国师父的尊敬，就公认道邃为日本天台宗的荣誉始祖。

再回到牛头山这一宗，其传承世系如下：

（1）法融（594—657）　　（2）智岩（600—677）

（3）慧方（629—695）　　（4）法持（635—702）

（5）智威（646—722）　　（6）慧忠（683—769）

Hui-chung's dharma brother was Hsuan-su (Genso), whose disciple was Ching-shan Tao-chin (Keizan Dōkin, 714-792).

Besides Shen-hsiu and Hui-neng, the Fifth Patriarch (Gunin) had another disciple: Chih-sien (Chisen, 609-702), whose dharma-heirs were successively:

(1) Chu-chi (Shojaku, 665-732)

(2) Wu-hsiang (Musō, 684-762)

(3) Wu-ji (Muju, 714-774)

The Sixth Patriarch and his disciples will be the subject of Chapter 2.

To conclude this Chapter, the posthumously bestowed honorary titles of the first Six Patriarchs in the Chinese Zen School will be given:

Bodhidharma (Daruma), Yuan-chueh Ta-shih (Engaku Daishi)
> bestowed by Dai-tsung (r. 763-779) of Tang Dynasty

Hui-ke (Eka, 487-593), Ta-tsu Ta-shih (Daiso Daishi)
> bestowed by Te-tsung (r. 780-804) of Tang Dynasty

Seng-tsan (Sōsan, d. 606), Chien-chih Ta-shih (Kanchi Daishi)
> bestowed by Hsuan-tsung (r. 713-755) of Tang Dynasty

Tao-hsin (Dōshin, 580-651), Ta-i Chan-shih (Dai-i Zenshi)
> bestowed by Dai-tsung (r. 763-779) of Tang Dynasty

Hung-jen (Gunin, 602-675), Ta-man Chan-shih (Daiman Zenshi)
> bestowed by Dai-tsung (r. 763-779) of Tang Dynasty

Hui-neng (Enō, 638-713), Ta-chien Chan-shih (Daikan Zenshi)
> bestowed by Hsien-tsung (r. 806-820) of Tang Dynasty

Note that Emperor Hsuan-tsung (Gensō), who reigned 713-755, was the first Tang Emperor who bestowed a posthumous honorary title to a Zen Patriarch, who was the Third Patriarch Seng-tsan. Emperor Dai-tsung (Daisō), who reigned 763-779, bestowed posthumous honorary titles on Bodhidharma (Daruma), the First Patriarch, Tao-hsin (Dōshin), the Fourth Patriarch, and Hung-jen (Gunin), the Fifth Patriarch. According to Dr. Hu Shih, in his *Biography of Shen-hui*, page 72, it was in the first year of the Chien-yuan (Kengen) era, i.e., 758 A.D., under the reign of

Shu-tsung (Shukusō, r. 756-762) that General Kuo Tzu-i recommended to the Emperor Shu-tsung to bestow an honorary title to the First Patriarch, probably at the request of Shen-hui, the able disciple of Enō, the Sixth Patriarch. However, it was not until the reign of Dai-tsung (Daisō, r. 763-779) that Bodhidharma received the title of Yuan-chueh (Engaku) Ta-shih, meaning "Perfect Enlightenment." The Second Patriarch, Hui-ke (Eka, 487-593), received the posthumous honorary title, Ta-tsu (Daiso) Ta-shih, meaning "Great Founder." The Third Patriarch's posthumous

慧忠的师兄弟是玄素，玄素的弟子则是径山道京（714—792）。

五祖弘忍的弟子除神秀和慧能外，还有一位是智诜（609—702）。智诜的法嗣相继为：

（1）处寂（665—732）

（2）无相（684—762）

（3）无住（714—774）

六祖和他的众弟子将是第二章的主题内容。

在本章结束之前，把当初朝廷对中国禅宗最早的六位祖师的敕谥列举如下：

菩提达摩，由唐代宗（在位763—779，按另作762—779）敕谥圆觉大师

慧可（487—593），由唐德宗（在位780—804，按另作780—805）敕谥大祖大师

僧璨（？—606），由唐玄宗（在位713—755，按另作712—756）敕谥鉴智大师

道信（580—651），由唐代宗（在位763—779）敕谥大医禅师

弘忍（602—675），由唐代宗（在位763—779）敕谥大满禅师

慧能（638—713），由唐宪宗（在位806—820）敕谥大鉴禅师

这里应指出，唐玄宗统治年代是713—755年，所以是先向禅宗三祖僧璨赐谥尊号的第一位皇帝，然后方才是唐代宗向始祖菩提达摩、四祖道信和五祖弘忍赐谥尊号。根据胡适博士《神会传》第72页中记载，在唐肃宗（在位756—762）乾元初年，即公元758年，由郭子仪将军向肃宗举荐：要对禅宗始祖赐谥尊号。这很可能是由于神会的请求，而神会则是慧能的一个很有

honorary title, Chien-chih (Kanchi) Ta-shih, bestowed by Hsuan-tsung, meant "Mirror Wisdom." From Tao-hsin (Dōshin) to Hui-neng (Enō), the honorary titles were designated Chan-shih (Zenshi) instead of Ta-shih (Daishi). The Fourth Patriarch's title Ta-i Chan-shih (Daii Zenshi) meant "Great Healing," while the Fifth Patriarch's title Ta-man Chan-shih (Daiman Zenshi) meant "Great Fulfillment." The Sixth Patriarch posthumous honorary title, bestowed by Emperor Hsien-tsung (Kensō, r. 806-820), Ta-chien (Daikan) Chan-shih, meant "Great Mirror."

According to the *Biography of Shen-hui* by Kuei-feng Tsung-mi (Keihō Shūmitsu, 780-841), Shen-hui (Jinne, 670-762) received the posthumous honorary title of Cheng-tsung Ta-shih (Shinsō Daishi) in 770 A.D., the fifth year of the Ta-lieh (Daireki) era under the reign of Dai-tsung (Daisō, r. 763-779). Then in 796 A.D., the twelfth year of the Chen-yuan (Teigen) era, under the reign of Te-tsung (Tokusō), Shen-hui was bestowed the title of the Seventh Patriarch by the Emperor. Note that by declaring Shen-hui (Jinne) as the Seventh Patriarch, the Sixth Patriarch in the Chinese Zen School was definitely his dharma-teacher, Hui-neng (Enō). As it was mentioned before, Hui-neng (Enō) did not get his posthumous honorary title until Emperor Hsien-tsung (Kensō, r. 806-820) came to the throne.

The list of Buddhas and Patriarchs in India was taken from the *Lamp Records* (*Daishō Daizōkyō*, Vol. 51, pages 202-220. See Appendix to Chapter 1). The Japanese pronunciations were based on Rōshi Jiyu Kennett's *Zen Is Eternal Life*, page 284, and also supplied by Reverend John Daishin Buksbazen, Vice President for Education, Zen Center of Los Angeles.

才能的弟子。不过事实上一直等到唐代宗统治年间，菩提达摩才正式得到了赐谥尊号为圆觉大师。圆觉的含义是圆满的觉醒或领悟。二祖慧可的赐谥尊号大祖大师，意思是伟大的缔造者。三祖由唐玄宗赐谥尊号鉴智大师，意思是明镜般的智慧。自道信开始至慧能的谥号由大师改为禅师。四祖的谥号为大医禅师，意思是人世间的大医师。五祖的谥号为大满禅师，意思是大圆满。六祖由唐宪宗赐谥为大鉴禅师，意思是智慧如一面大明镜。

根据圭峰宗密（780—841）撰《禅门师资承袭图》中记载，神会（670—762）是在公元770年即唐代宗大历五年获谥真宗大师尊号，然后在公元796年即贞元十二年，再由唐德宗赐尊号为禅宗第七祖。但应注意到，既然公布认定神会是禅宗七祖，那么他的师父慧能当然就应是禅宗六祖了。不过事实上如前所述，要等唐宪宗即位（在位806—820）后才正式向慧能赐谥这一尊号。

禅宗始祖达摩来自印度，达摩之前的各代佛和祖师参见本章附录，摘自《传灯录》（《大正藏》第51卷，第202—220页）。日文注音参考法云慈友著《禅是永恒的生命》第284页，洛杉矶禅学中心主管教育的副校长约翰·布科斯巴泽恩法师也提供了帮助。

Appendix to Chapter 1
第一章附录

Buddhas and Patriarchs
七佛天竺祖师

1) Bibashi Butsu   毗婆尸佛

2) Shiki Butsu   试诘佛（尸弃佛）

3) Bishafu Butsu   毗舍浮佛

4) Kuruson Butsu   拘留孙佛

5) Kunagonmuni Butsu   拘那含牟尼佛

6) Kashō Butsu   迦叶佛

Shakyamuni Butsu
释迦牟尼佛

1) Makakashō   摩诃迦叶

2) Ananda   阿难陀

3) Shōnawashu   商那和修

4) Ubakikuta   优婆毱多

5) Daitaka   提多迦

6) Mishaka   弥遮迦

7) Bashumitsu   婆须蜜

8) Butsudanandai   佛陀难提

9) Fudamitta   伏驮蜜多

10) Barishiba   婆栗湿缚（胁尊者）

11) Funayasha   富那夜奢

12) Anabotei	阿难菩底（马鸣大士）
13) Kabimora	迦毗摩罗
14) Nagyaharajuna	那迦阏剌树那（龙树大士）
15) Kanadaiba	迦那提婆
16) Ragorata	罗侯罗多
17) Sōgyanandai	僧迦难提
18) Kayashata	伽耶舍多
19) Kumorata	鸠摩罗多
20) Shayata	阇夜多
21) Bashubanzu	婆修盘头
22) Man'ura	摩拏罗
23) Kakurokuna	鹤勒那
24) Shishibodai	师子菩提（师子尊者）
25) Bashashita	婆舍斯多
26) Funyomitta	不如蜜多
27) Hannyatara	般若多罗
28) Bodaidaruma	菩提达摩

CHAPTER 2 THE SIXTH PATRIARCH AND HIS DISCIPLES

Hui-neng (Enō, 638-713) was the Sixth Patriarch of the Zen School. His family name was Lu. His ancestors resided in Fan-yang, southwest of present Peking. In the middle of Wu-te era (618-626), his father was demoted from office and banished to Hsin-chou, the present Hsin-hsing District in southwestern Kwangtung Province. He lost his father when Hui-neng was three years old. The family was poor, and he peddled firewood in the city. One day when he was twenty years old, he heard a traveler who recited the *Diamond Sutra*. He was told that the Fifth Patriarch Master Hung-jen (Gunin) of Huang-mei (Hupeh Province) was expounding the *Diamond Sutra*. Hui-neng was greatly impressed and asked his mother's permission to seek the dharma (law) some five hundred miles to the north. Arriving at Shao-chou on his northward trip, he met Liu Chih-lioh, whose aunt was a nun, by the name Wu-chin-tsang (Mujinzō). The nun read *Nirvana Sutra* to Hui-neng and explained its meaning. Hui-neng did not know the words, but was interested in the meaning. The nun said: "You do not recognize the words. How can you understand the meaning?" Hui-neng said: "The essence of Buddhism does not depend on words." The nun was surprised, but she spread the word that Hui-neng is a man of Tao and he should be treated with respect. The country people repaired the old Paolin (Hōrin) Temple and requested Hui-neng to reside there. One day Hui-neng realized that he should not stop in midway, and started his journey north again the next day. At Lo-Chang he met Chih-yuan (Chi'on), a Ch'an (Zen) Master. Master Chih-yuan told him that Bodhidharma of India transmitted his mind-seal to Huang-mei (meaning Hung-jen) and he should go to Master Hung-jen at Tung-ch'an Temple (Tōzen-ji). Hui-neng arrived at Huang-mei around 660 A.D. and left Huang-mei in 661 A.D.

According to *Lieh-dai Fa-pao Chi* (*Rekidai Hōbō Ki*, reprinted in *Daishō Daizōkyō*, Vol. 51, page 182), Hui-neng arrived at Huang-mei (Ōbai) when he was twenty-two years old. When he first paid his respects to Master Hung-jen (Gunin), Hung-jen asked him: "Where do you come from?" Hui-neng answered: "I came from Hsin-chou, and I wish to be Buddha." Hung-jen said: "Hsin-chou is a place for barbarians." Hui-neng said: "Although I am a barbarian, but can my Buddha-nature be different from the Master's?" Hung-jen was greatly impressed, but assigned Hui-neng to work in the mill for the next eight months.

贰 六祖及其众弟子

　　禅宗第六祖慧能（638—713）未出家时俗姓卢，祖居范阳（在今北京西南。译者注：范阳为河北省涿县）。唐武德（618—626）中期，父亲被贬官，流放到新州（今广东省新兴县东）。慧能3岁时，父亲去世，家里很穷，长大后就在城里卖柴度日。在他20岁时，有一天，听到一旅客在读《金刚经》，旅客告诉他，五祖弘忍正在黄梅（在今湖北省）讲解《金刚经》。慧能听后深有感悟，求其母亲准许他北行千里去拜师。在北行途中到达韶州时，遇见一人名刘志略。刘的姑母是一尼姑，法名叫无尽藏。尼姑读《涅槃经》给他听，并向他解释经中意义。慧能不识字，却听得懂经中意义，感受很深。尼姑问："你不识字，怎么能听得懂经中的意义呢？"慧能说："佛法妙理不在文字上。"尼姑大为惊异，告诉乡里人说，此人很不寻常，是一得道之人，应该对他尊敬和供养。于是众人就把当地的宝林古寺修缮好，请慧能住进去，为大家讲佛法。一天，他想到自己原来的目的是要去求大法，怎么能到此为止、半途而废呢？第二天就告别离去，继续北行。到达乐昌县时，遇到了智远禅师，智远告诉他说，来自西方印度的菩提达摩曾在黄梅传授衣钵心印，现已传到了第五代弘忍大师，应该到东禅寺去拜师求教。慧能大约是在660年到达了黄梅，然后在661年离开了那里。

　　根据《大正藏》第51卷第182页《历代法宝记》中的记载，慧能到达黄梅时，年方22岁。第一次拜谒弘忍禅师时，师问："你从何处来？"答："来自新州，愿作佛。"弘忍说："新州是南蛮之地。"慧能答："虽是南蛮人，同样也有佛性，与师父的佛性能有什么差别呢？"这给弘忍禅师留下了很深刻的印象，于是就接受了他，不过只是安排他去磨坊踏碓（舂米的石具），让他干了八个月的活。

Then we come to the account of Hung-jen's transmission of the Lamp as given in Hui-neng's *Platform Sutra* (See Professor Wing-tsit Chan's translation, *The Platform Scripture*, St. John's University Press, Jamaica, N.Y., 1963, pages 31-43).

One day the Fifth Patriarch suddenly called his disciples to come to him. When the disciples had already assembled, the Fifth Patriarch said: "Let me say this to you: Life and death are serious matters. You disciples are engaged all day in making offerings, going after fields of blessings only, and you make no effort to achieve freedom from the bitter sea of life and death. If you are deluded in your own nature, how can blessings save you? Go to your rooms, all of you, and think for yourselves. Those who possess wisdom use the wisdom (*prajna*) inherent in their nature. Each of you must write a verse and present it to me. After I see the verses, I will give the robe and the Law (Dharma) to the one who understands the basic idea and will appoint him to be the Sixth Patriarch. Hurry, hurry!"

Head Monk Shen-hsiu (Jinshū, d. 706) thought, "These people would not present verses to show their minds because I am an instructor. If I do not present a verse to show my mind, how can the Fifth Patriarch see whether my understanding is shallow or deep? I shall present the verse of my heart (mind) to the Fifth Patriarch to show him my ideas. ... If I do not present a verse to manifest my mind, I shall never acquire the Law." He thought for a long time but found it an extremely difficult matter. He then waited until midnight, and without allowing anyone to see him, went to the wall of the southern corridor and wrote a verse to manifest what was in his mind, thus wishing to seek the Law. ...

At midnight Head Monk Shen-hsiu, holding a candle, wrote a verse on the wall of the southern corridor, without anyone knowing about it, which said:

"The body is the tree of perfect wisdom (*bodhi*).
The mind is the stand of a bright mirror.

At all times diligently wipe it.

Do not allow it to become dusty."

... Suddenly the Fifth Patriarch saw the verse. After reading it, he

慧能传给后世的《坛经》中关于弘忍向慧能传授衣钵的故事如下（参见陈荣捷教授的《坛经》译本第31—43页，美国纽约牙买加圣约翰大学出版社，1963）：

有一天，五祖突然召集弟子们都来到他面前。众弟子到齐后，五祖就说："我要对大家讲，生与死是十分严肃的大事，你们终日做功课，企求福德。不过你们事实上并没有努力去寻求如何脱离生死苦海，获得自由自在。如已迷失了自己本有的佛性，那么福德又怎能拯救你们呢？你们大家都要用自己本心所固有的佛性智慧，回自己室内去深入思考，每人写一首诗偈交给我。等我看后就会决定究竟谁确能领悟佛性的根本，我就会将衣钵和禅宗佛法传授给他，成为禅宗第六祖。大家都快快回去吧！"

神秀是首座教授师（于706年去世），心想："大家都不想呈上诗偈以表示所领悟的佛性，因为我已是教授师了。但如果我也不呈上诗偈来表示我心中所领悟的佛性，那么师父又怎能知道我对佛性领悟程度的深浅呢？所以我还是应该向师父呈上诗偈来表示我心中的领悟……如果我不呈诗偈来显示我的领悟，那我就永远得不到佛法的传授了。"他想了很久，觉得这件事毕竟太难了。就这样一直等到半夜，想趁此时不让任何人看到，悄悄走到禅堂南面房廊处，在墙壁上写下一首诗偈，来显示其心中的领悟，盼望能得到佛法的传授……

就在半夜无人看见时，首座神秀手持蜡烛，在南廊墙壁上写诗偈如下：

身体是一颗完美的智慧之树（菩提树），

心就像明亮的镜台。

时时刻刻都要勤加拂拭，

不让它沾染尘埃。

（此偈原文为：身是菩提树，心如明镜。时时勤拂拭，莫使有尘埃。）

……五祖突然见到此偈，读后就对一位宫廷画师（原被请来准备

said to the court artist, "I will give you thirty thousand cash and will be much obliged to you for your coming from afar. But we will not paint the transfigurations. The *Diamond Scripture* says, 'All characters are unreal and imaginary.' It is better to keep this verse and let deluded people read it. If people practice according to it, they will not fall into the Three Evil Stages. People who practice according to the Law will enjoy great benefits."

Thereupon the Fifth Patriarch called Head Monk Shen-hsiu into the hall and asked, "Was this verse written by you? If you wrote it, you should receive the Law."

Head Monk Shen-hsiu said, "Please pardon me. In fact, I did write it. Yet I dare not seek the position of the patriarch. I hope your Holiness will be compassionate and see if your disciple possess a small amount of wisdom and understand the basic idea."

The Fifth Patriarch said, "The verse you wrote shows some but not complete understanding. You have arrived at the front door but you have not yet entered it. Ordinary people, by practicing in accordance with your verse, will not fail. But it is futile to seek the supreme perfect wisdom while holding to such a view. One must enter the door and see his own nature. Go away and come back after thinking a day or two. Write another verse and present it to me. If then you have entered the door and have seen your own nature, I will give you the robe and the Law."

As the boy led me (Hui-neng) to the southern corridor, I immediately paid reverence to the verse. As I did not know how to read, I asked someone to read it to me. After I heard it, I immediately understood the basic idea. I also composed a verse and asked a person who could read to write it on the wall of the western corridor to manifest what was in my own mind. It is useless to study the Law if one does not understand his own mind. Once a person understands his own mind and sees his own nature, he will immediately understand the basic idea. My verse says:

"Fundamentally perfect wisdom has no tree.

Nor has the bright mirror any stand.

Buddha-nature is forever clear and pure.

在壁上画佛经故事的）说："我给钱三万，劳驾你远道而来，深表感谢。不过，现在我们又不想画了。《金刚经》上这样说：'所有事物的相状，都是虚妄不实的假象。'不如就把此偈保留在这里，好让众多迷悟之人能经常读到它。如果确能按照它去修行，那就不会堕入三恶道中（地狱、饿鬼和畜生），这样按照佛法去修行的人就会得到很大的福。"

随后，五祖就叫首座神秀来到禅堂，问："此偈是你写的吗？如果是你写的，你应能得到佛法的传授。"

首座神秀答："请宽恕我，这确实是我写的。但弟子不敢妄求禅法的继承，只望师父慈悲，审察一下弟子是否略有粗浅智慧，能稍微悟解根本的佛性大意。"

五祖说："你写的这首诗偈表示你虽有所悟解，但还不能说已经完全透彻，只可以说已到了大门口，却还未能入门。一般人遵照你这首诗偈去修行，当然不会没有收获。但仅仅持这样的看法，要想求得最高最透彻的智慧，那还是无效的，必须要进入真理大门的里面去认识自己本有的佛性。现在回去继续思考一两天，再作一首诗偈给我。如果你确已跨进了真理大门，认识了自己本有的佛性，那我就可以把衣钵和佛法传授给你了。"

有一童子，带引慧能来到南面房廊下，即向壁上那首诗偈参拜致礼。慧能不识字，请人读给他听，听后马上理解了诗中的基本大意。于是慧能也作了一首诗偈，再请一识字的人把它写在西面房廊的墙壁上，表白自己所认识的本心。任何人如果不明白自己本心，那么学佛法也是无用的。如果能明白了自心并认识了本性，那就会立即领悟佛法的根本。慧能的诗偈是：

完美透彻的智慧根本没有什么树，

明亮的镜子也根本没有什么台。

佛性永远是洁净的，

Where is there any dust?"

(Another verse was recorded in the *Platform Scriptures*, but it is not important.)

The Fifth Patriarch suddenly realized that I (Hui-neng) alone had the good knowledge and understanding of the basic idea but he was afraid lest the rest learn it. He therefore told them, "He does not understand perfectly after all."

The Fifth Patriarch waited till midnight, called me (Hui-neng) to come to the hall, and expounded the *Diamond Scripture*. As soon as I heard this, I understood. That night the Law (Dharma) was imparted to me without anyone knowing it, and thus the method of sudden enlightenment and the robe were transmitted to me.

The Fifth Patriarch said to Hui-neng: "You are now the Sixth Patriarch. This robe is the testimony of transmission from generation to generation. As to the Law (Dharma), it is to be transmitted from mind to mind. Let people achieve enlightenment through their own effort."

According to *Lieh-dai Fa-pao Chi* (*Rekidai Hōbō Ki*), it took three days and three nights for the secret transmission of the Law. The Master advised Hui-neng to leave Huang-mei, cross the Yangtze river, and go south. After three days, the Fifth Patriarch told the disciples that the Buddha-Law had gone to Ling-nan. When the disciples asked who is at Ling-nan, Fa-ju (Hōnyo) replied: "It is Hui-neng." As the story was told, one military officer, by the name of Hui-ming, on hearing this, chased Hui-neng to Ta-yu-ling. Hui-neng was scared, and was ready to give up the robe. Hui-ming said: "I do not come for the robe. Please tell me what the Fifth Patriarch has instructed you upon your departure." Hui-neng then gave Hui-ming some instructions concerning the Law of the mind and the direct seeking into one's nature.

Returning to the *Lamp Records*, the Fifth Patriarch ordered Hui-neng to be a hermit in the Ssu-hui and Huai-chi Districts in south China. So

Hui-neng moved about quietly and preached in these districts for the next sixteen years. (Hui-neng left Huang-mei in 661 A.D. and reached Canton in 676 A.D.)

哪里会有什么尘埃？

（此偈原文为："菩提本无树，明镜亦非台。佛性常清净，何处惹尘埃？"《坛经》中记载另一诗偈，这里从略。）

五祖见了此诗后，顿时觉得只有慧能方才是真正能领悟佛性大意的人，但又怕众人不服气，会给慧能带来麻烦。所以不想明讲，只对众人说："这首诗偈最终也没有完全领悟。"

当天半夜，五祖把慧能叫到禅堂内，向他讲解《金刚经》，慧能听后，马上能领悟经中要旨。就在当天深夜，五祖向慧能传授了佛法。在寺内并无任何人知晓之下，慧能就获得了传授给他的顿悟佛法和传承衣钵。

五祖对慧能说："你当上了禅宗第六代祖师，这件袈裟是嗣承祖师的信物，代代相传。至于顿悟的佛法，就只能以心传心，要通过自己的努力去达到领悟境界。"

根据《历代法宝记》记载，这一在秘密中进行的佛法传授经历了三天三夜之后，五祖建议慧能从速离开黄梅，过长江南行。也就在三天之后，五祖方才向众弟子宣布：佛法继承人现已去了岭南。众弟子问："是谁去了岭南？"法如回答说："那是慧能。"故事还说：有一僧人名慧明，过去做过将军，听后马上就去追赶慧能，直到大庾岭才追上了。慧能受到惊吓，准备把衣钵让他拿去。慧明说："我来不是要这衣钵，请你教给我在你离开之时师父传授给你的佛法指示。"于是慧能就向他讲授了一些心法，指示应该怎样去寻求人的本性。

再回到《传灯录》中所载，五祖当时曾命慧能隐居于南方四会和怀集两地之间。所以在以后 16 年间，慧能就平静地云游于此两地区，传播佛法（慧能在 661 年离开黄梅，经历 16 年，即在 676 年到了广州）。

In the first year of the Yi-feng era (676), Hui-neng met Yin-tsung (Inshū), an expert on the Nirvana scripture, in the Fa-hsing Temple (Hōsei-ji) at Canton. One day when Yin-tsung was lecturing, a banner was streaming in the wind. A dispute arose between two monks, one insisting that the wind was moving and the other, the banner was moving. Hui-neng said to them: "Neither the wind nor the banner moves; what moves is your mind." Yin-tsung, overwhelmed by Hui-neng's profound insight, wanted to become his disciple. On the fifteenth day of the first month (677 A.D.), Yin-tsung shaved Hui-neng's head; and on the eighth day of the second month Law Master Chih-kuang (Chikō) ordained Hui-neng.

Exactly one year later, he was invited to go back to the Pao-lin Temple. The prefect of Shao-chou, Wei Chu, invited him to preach in the Ta-fan Temple (Daibon-ji). In this lecture he emphatically declared that all people possess the Buddha-nature and that one's nature is originally pure. If one puts his self-nature into practice, he will be equal to Buddha. Instead of taking refuge in the Buddha outside, one should take refuge in the nature within him, for all Buddhas, all Dharmas, and all scriptures are immanent in it.

The Sixth Patriarch resided at Shao-chou for forty years. He entered nirvana in 713 at the age of seventy-six. Posthumously he was honored by the title Ta-chien Chan-shih (Daikan Zenji), the Zen Master of "Great Mirror."

Father Heinrich Dumoulin, S. J., studied the famous *kōan* collection *Mumonkan*, which reflected the history of Zen Buddhism in China during a span of nearly five centuries. He then wrote a summary of the history of Chinese Zen Buddhism in German and published it in *Monumenta Series* (Vol. 6, 1941, pages 40-72). Later Mrs. Ruth Fuller Sasaki translated it into English and published it with her annotations and indices as *The Development of Chinese Zen After the Sixth Patriarch in the Light of Mumonkan*, New York, 1953. At Mrs. Ruth Fuller Sasaki's suggestion, Dumoulin wrote *A History of Zen Buddhism* in German in 1959. This was translated into English by Paul Peachey and published in New York by Pantheon Books in 1963. The first four chapters dealt with: (1) The Mystical Element in Early Buddhism and Hinayana; (2) Mysticism Within Mahayana; (3) The Mahayana Sutras and Zen; and (4) the Anticipation of Zen in Chinese Buddhism. It is highly recommended that the reader read

唐高宗仪凤元年（676），慧能在广州法性寺遇见一位专门讲解《涅槃经》的印宗法师。有一天，印宗在讲经时，寺中旗幡正在风中飘扬，有两名僧人发生了争辩。一人坚持说风在动，另一人则说幡在动。慧能就跟他们说："既不是风在动，也不是幡在动，真正在动的只是你们自己的心。"印宗听到了这一深刻见识后，就决定要向慧能学习佛法。677 年的正月十五日，印宗法师为慧能剃了发，在二月八日慧能又在法系祖师智光那里受了戒。

整整一年后，慧能被邀请返回韶州的宝林古寺。韶州刺史韦琚就邀请他到大梵寺去讲经说法。在他的讲解中，特别着重指出，众生都有佛性，人的本性原来都是很纯洁清净的。只要按自己的本性去修行，他就将等同于佛。所以不需向外界去求佛，而应该向自己的本性来求佛。所有佛性、所有佛法和所有经文都是内在固有的。

六祖慧能在韶州居住了近四十年，于 713 年圆寂，终年 76 岁，朝廷敕谥尊号为大鉴禅师。

S. J. 海因立希·杜慕林研究了公案集《无门关》，该集反映了约五百年间的中国禅宗史。然后他就用德文写了中国佛教禅宗史的纲要，出版于《纪念集》系列中（1941 年版，第 6 卷，第 40—72 页）。后来再由罗丝·富勒·佐佐木夫人把它译成英文，1953 年在纽约出版：《中国禅宗在第六祖以后的发展——在〈无门关〉启示下》，附有她的注解和索引。在罗丝·富勒·佐佐木夫人的建议下，杜慕林在 1959 年又用德文写了《佛教禅宗史》，并由保罗·披切译成英文，1963 年由纽约潘塞恩图书出版公司出版。在该书开头四章中论述的内容是：（1）早期佛教和小乘佛教的神秘要素；（2）大乘佛教内部的神秘性；（3）大乘佛经与禅宗；（4）中国禅宗的冀望。读本书之前，推荐读者最好先去读一下

Dumoulin-Peachey's *A History of Zen Buddhism*, especially the first four chapters, before he goes into the present book.

Dumoulin-Peachey's Chapter 5 is entitled: Zen Patriarchs of the Early Period. The material covered is comparable to Chapter 1 of this book. Their Chapter 6 is entitled: The High Period of Chinese Zen. The material covered is comparable to this chapter, starting from the Sixth Patriarch. To quote from Dumoulin-Peachey: *A History of Zen Buddhism*, page 94:

> The philosophy of Mahayana Buddhism must be regarded as the first source of the metaphysical conception of Hui-neng. One can detect in the expression and development of his thought much of the legacy of China. When, for example, Hui-neng employs the conceptual scheme of substance and function in order to elucidate the relationship of contemplation (*samadhi*) and wisdom (*prajna*), he actually pours Buddhist content into Chinese molds. Likewise, he speaks of the Dharma-world in much the same way that the Taoists speak of the universe. Nonetheless his cosmology stays within the Buddhist framework. The combination of the concepts of self-nature (*svabhava*), Buddha-nature, and Buddha-knowledge is anticipated in the great Mahayana sutras. Therefore it is difficult to point to anything completely new in Hui-neng's teaching. And yet, even though the various elements of his proclamation existed beforehand, we can recognize his originality, the originality not of a thinker but of a mystic. Just as Meister Eckhart drew his teachings from scholastic philosophy, the Fathers of the Church, and Neo-Platonism, and formulated them anew in his mysticism, so Hui-neng assimilated in his personal experience the Mahayanist metaphysics, enriched by Taoist influence, and proclaimed this message with the fervor of an evangelist.
>
> Hui-neng and his sect have not the remotest interest in a philosophical elaboration of the contents of enlightenment. For them, everything depends on the liberating experience. The realization of

enlightenment brings final liberation. This liberation is experienced immediately, as "a person feels both warm and cold when he drinks water." Words are of no avail.

From Alan W. Watts: *The Way of Zen*, page 88, we can summarize the essence of Ch'an or Zen School of Buddhism by the following criteria: (1) Outside teachings, apart from tradition; (2) Not founded on words

杜慕林著、保罗·披切译的《佛教禅宗史》，尤其是开头的四章。

该书第五章为"禅宗初期祖师"，内容与本书第一章相似。第六章为"中国禅宗兴盛期"，内容与本章相仿，即从六祖开始讲起。下文引自该书第94页：

大乘佛教哲学肯定可以看作是慧能玄学思维的第一源泉。在其思想的表达和发展中，人们还可找到很多中国本身文化遗产内容。例如，当他用物与物性的概念来解释沉思与智慧之间的关系时，他实质上就把佛教内容注入中国模式之中。同样，当他谈及佛法世界时，也就非常像中国道家谈论宇宙一样。不过他的宇宙观当然还是在佛教框架之内。有关自性、佛性和佛性认识等概念的结合，都可预期在大乘佛经中找到。所以也很难在慧能的说教中找到有什么完全崭新的内容。不过，即使说他所宣示说教的许多内容都是本来早已有的，我们却仍应承认他的原创性，但不是思想家而是玄秘主义的原创性。就好像玄秘大师埃克哈特的说教源自学院哲学、教会神父和新柏拉图主义，把它们重新系统化地表达在他的玄秘主义中，慧能同样也是在他个人认识和经验上吸收了大乘佛教的玄学体系，再丰富和充实了道家学说的影响，以传教士的热心激情来传教播道。

慧能和他的宗派对于领悟启示的内容在哲学上的详尽阐述却并无多大关心。在他们看来，一切都取决于自我解脱的经历。实现启示领悟就会带来最终的解脱。这种顿悟的经历，就好像人在饮水时立刻就知道是暖是冷一样，任何言词都没用。

根据艾伦·瓦茨《禅道》第88页，可以对佛教禅宗的要旨总结为以下几点：（1）对外说教，背离过去传统；（2）不以语言文字

and letters; (3) Pointing directly to the human mind; (4) Seeing into one's nature and attaining Buddhahood.

Among Hui-neng's dharma-heirs, at least FIVE were prominent: (1) Ho-tse Shen-hui (Kataku Jinne, 670-762); (2) Nan-yang Hui-chung (Nan'yō Echū, d. 775); (3) Yung-chia Hsuan-chueh (Yōka Genkaku, 665-713); (4) Nan-yueh Huai-jang (Nangaku Ejō, 677-744); and (5) Ching-yuan Hsing-ssu (Seigen Gyōshi, d. 740).

Shen-hui (Jinne) was born in 670 A.D. According to Dr. Hu Shih, author of *Biography of Shen-hui*, Shen-hui passed away in 762 A.D. at the age of ninety-two. Shen-hui fought the critical battle between the so-called Northern and Southern Schools and won, and thus established Hui-neng (Enō) as the Sixth Patriarch (Rokuso).

There was one reference that the Emperor Te-tsung (Tokusō) in the twelfth year of the Chen-yuan (Teigen) era betsowed upon Shen-hui the title of the Seventh Patriarch. This corresponded to 796 A.D. See Hu Shih: *Biography of Shen-hui*, pages 70-71. However, this honor was not so important in Zen Buddhist history. The Ho-tse (Kataku) branch had a fourth-generation dharma heir, Kuei-feng Tsung-mi (Keihō Shūmitsu, 780-841), who was revered as the Fifth Patriarch of the Hua-yen (Kegon) School in China. The lineage can be given below:

(1) Ho-tse Shen-hui (Kataku Jinne, 670-762)

(2) Tzu-chou Chih-ju (Jishū Chijo, 749-834)

(3) I-chou Nan-yin (Ekishū Nan'in)

(4) Sui-chou Tao-yuan (Suishū Dōen)

(5) Kuei-feng Tsung-mi (Keihō Shūmitsu)

The lineage of Hua-yen School can be given as follows:

(1) Fa-shun (Hōjun, 557-640)

(2) Yun-hua Chih-yen (Unka Chigen, 602-668)

(3) Hsien-shou Fa-tsang (Kenshu Hōzō, 643-712)

(4) Ching-liang Cheng-kuan (Seiryō Chōkan, 738-839)

(5) Kuei-feng Tsung-mi (Keihō Shūmitsu, 780-841)

(6) Chang-shui Tzu-hsuan (Chōsui Shisen, 965-1038)

There was another connection between Shen-hui and Ching-liang Cheng-kuan. Shen-hui had another disciple Wu-tai Wu-min (Godai Mumyō, 722-793), who was also Cheng-kuan's teacher. Note that I-chou Nan-yin had another disciple Tung-king Shen-chao (Tōkyō Jinshō, 776-838).

A recent Chinese Zen Master, Hsu Yun (Kiun, 1840-1959), gave a sermon at the Jade Buddha Monastery (Gyoku-Butsu-ji) in Shanghai:

为基础;（3）直指人的内心;（4）窥见人的本性而获得了佛性。

在继承慧能的许多法嗣中至少有五人比较卓越：

（1）荷泽神会（670—762）（2）南阳慧忠（？—775）

（3）永嘉玄觉（665—713）（4）南岳怀让（677—744）

（5）青原行思（？—740）

根据胡适博士所著《神会传》，神会生于670年，于762年圆寂，高寿92岁。他参与了禅宗南北两个宗派之间激烈的论争并获得了胜利，这就最终确定了慧能作为禅宗六祖的地位。

根据记载，唐德宗贞元十二年（796）向神会赐谥，尊号为禅宗第七祖，见胡适《神会传》第70—71页。不过这一荣誉称号在佛教禅宗史上也不算非常重要。荷泽神会分支（称为荷泽宗）的第四代法嗣圭峰宗密（780—841）被尊为中国华严宗的第五祖。其传承世系如下：

（1）荷泽神会（670—762）（2）磁州智如（749—834）

（3）益州南印　　　　　　（4）遂州道圆

（5）圭峰宗密

华严宗的传承世系如下：

（1）法顺（557—640）　　（2）云华智俨（602—668）

（3）贤首法藏（643—712）（4）清凉澄观（738—839）

（5）圭峰宗密（780—841）（6）长水子璇（965—1038）

在神会与清凉澄观之间还有另一个传承关系，即神会的另一弟子五台无名（722—793）也是澄观的师父。这里还可以提一下，益州南印还有一个弟子是东京神照（776—838）。

近代中国禅宗大师虚云大师（1840—1959）在上海玉佛寺讲道时曾说：

Once the Seventh Patriarch, Shen-hui, asked the Sixth Patriarch, Hui-neng (Enō), "Through what practice should one work that one may not fall into a category?" The Sixth Patriarch replied, "What have you been doing?" Shen-hui (Jinne) answered, "I do not even practice the Holy Truth!" "In that case, to what category do you belong?" said the Master. Shen-hui: "Even the Holy Truth does not exist, so how can there be any category?" Hearing this answer, the Sixth Patriarch was impressed by Shen-hui's understanding. (See *The Practice of Zen*, by Garma C. C. Chang, pages 75-76).

From the above passage, we learned that Abbot Hsu Yun (Kiun, 1840-1959), who lived to one hundred and twenty years, not only recognized Shen-hui (Jinne) as the Seventh Patriarch, but also quoted the conversation between Hui-neng and Shen-hui as a good lesson for the students of Zen.

Nan-yang Hui-chung (Nan'yō Echū, d. 775) lived very long and was revered by many masters. He was National Teacher (Kokushi), because both Emperors Shu-tsung (r. 756-762) and Dai-tsung (r. 763-779) were his disciples. He passed away in the tenth year of the Ta-lieh (Daireki) era under the reign of Emperor Dai-tsung.

Yung-chia Hsuan-chueh (Yōka Genkaku, 665-713) studied in the Tien-tai School under its Seventh Patriarch Tien-kung Hui-wei (Tenkū E'i) with Tsu-chi Hsuan-lang (Sakei Genrō, 673-754), who later became the Eighth Patriarch in the Tien-tai (Tendai) School. Tsu-chi (Sakei) encouraged Yung-chia (Yōka) to pay homage to Hui-neng of Tsao-hsi (Sōkei) at Shao-chou (now Kwangtung Province). He was known as Chen-chueh Ta-shih (Shinkaku Daishi). He left posterity with his "Cheng-tao-ke" ("Shōdōka"). The following lines were taken from R. H. Blyth: *Zen and Zen Classics*, Vol. 1, page 107:

The really wise man, always at ease, unmoved.

He does not get rid of illusion, nor does he seek for the truth.

Ignorance is intrinsically the Buddha nature.

Our illusory unreal body is the cosmic body.

...

From the time I recognized the road to Tsao Chi,

I realized I had nothing to do with birth and death.

Walking is Zen, sitting is Zen;

Talking or silent, moving, unmoving,

　　有一次七祖神会问六祖慧能："应怎样去修行方能不堕入尊卑上下的等级？"六祖问："你是怎样做的呢？"神会答："我并没有去学习践行圣人的真理！"六祖问："那么你是属于哪一等级呢？"神会答："即使圣人真理也未存在，哪里还有什么等级呢？"六祖听了这些应答，对神会的悟解深度留下了非常深的印象。（见张澄基：《禅宗的修行》，第75—76页）

　　由上面这段，我们可知活到近120岁高龄的虚云大师（1840—1959）不仅承认神会为禅宗第七祖，而且还引用此段慧能与神会之间的对话，对禅学学子们进行一次有意义的讲课。

　　南阳慧忠（？—775）很长寿，为很多大师所尊敬。他是国师，唐肃宗（在位756—762）和唐代宗（在位763—779）都是他的弟子。他在唐代宗大历十年圆寂。

　　永嘉玄觉（665—713）与左溪玄朗（673—754）一起师事天台宗七祖天宫慧威。左溪后为天台宗第八祖，他鼓励永嘉去拜见韶州（今广东省）曹溪的慧能大师，向他致敬。永嘉被称为真觉大师，他留给后世一首《证道歌》，以下几行引自R. H. 布莱思《禅与禅宗经典》第1卷第107页：

　　　　真正有智慧的人，一直平静，不动心。
　　　　既不排除幻想，也不苦苦去求真。
　　　　无知在本质上就是佛性。
　　　　我们虚幻之体就是这世界之身。
　　　　……
　　　　自从那时我认知了来曹溪之路，
　　　　我也认知了已无关于生和死。
　　　　行即禅，坐即禅；
　　　　或谈吐或无语，或动或静止，

The essence is at ease.

...

All principles are no principles;

They have no relation to spiritual perception.

...

It never leaves this place, and is always perfect.

When you look for it, you find you can't see it.

You can't get at it; you can't be rid of it.

When you do neither, there it is!

When you are silent, it speaks; when you speak, it is silent.

This "It" must be referred to the Tao, or the Way.

The account of the meeting of Yung-chia with Hui-neng was given in the *Platform Scriptures*. (See also R. H. Blyth: *Zen and Zen Classics*, Vol. 1, page 105). While Hui-neng became enlightened on reading the *Diamond Sutra* and Yung-chia became enlightened on reading the *Vimalakirti Nirdesa Sutra*, both insisted that their realization came from within, not from the sutras.

R. H. Blyth gave the following translation:

Yung-chia walked round the Sixth Patriarch three times (without bowing) and merely shook his Buddhist staff with iron rings. The (Sixth) Patriarch said, "A Sramana embodies the 3,000 rules of deportment and the 80,000 minute moral rules. From whence does your honour come, may I ask, with your overweening self-assurance?" Yung-chia replied, "Birth-and-death is a problem of great moment; all changes ceaselessly." Hui-neng asked, "Why not embody the unborn and grasp the timeless?" Yung-chia replied, "To be unborn and deathless is to embody it; to be timeless is to grasp it." "That is so. That is so," assented the Patriarch. At this, Yung-chia acted according to the prescribed ceremonial, and prostrated himself, and then soon after bade farewell to the Patriarch.

Nan-yueh Huai-jang (Nangaku Ejō, 677-744) was the founder of the

Nangaku Branch. According to the *Lamp Records* (*Daishō Daizōkyō*, Vol. 51, pages 240-241), the following conversation took place between Enō and Nangaku Ejō:

精髓所在是安稳松弛。

……

一切原则均非原则；

无关于心灵直觉。

……

它永不离此地，而永远完美无缺。

你到处去找它，但就是见不到它。

你不能得到它，但又不能脱离它。

你什么都不做时，啊！它就在那里！

你不作声时它在讲，你在讲时它默默无语。

这里的"它"当然就应是"道"或"路"。

在《坛经》中讲述了永嘉拜见慧能时的故事（亦见 R. H. 布莱思：《禅与禅宗经典》第 1 卷，第 105 页）。慧能是读了《金刚经》而得到了启悟，永嘉则是读了《维摩诘经》而得到了启悟。但两人都坚持认为他们的启悟是来自内心，而并不是来自读经。

R. H. 布莱思在其书中的译文如下：

永嘉围着六祖绕行了三周，不向六祖施礼，而只是振动手中有铁环的锡杖。六祖问："僧人有三千种威仪，八万条详细的戒行。请问尊座来自何地？为什么这样自信和傲慢？"永嘉答："生死事至关重大，万物又迅速变化，永不止息。"慧能问："为什么不去体会和掌握'无生'和'无时'？"永嘉答："不生不灭就是本体，'无时'即在掌握。"五祖表示赞同说："确是这样，确是这样！"于是永嘉就遵照规定的礼仪，向六祖礼拜，然后马上辞别而去。

南岳怀让（677—744）是禅宗南岳支系的创建人。根据《传灯录》所载（见《大正藏》第 51 卷，第 240—241 页），在慧能与南岳怀让之间有一段对话如下：

Enō asked: "Where do you come from?"

Ejō replied: "I come from Sung Shan (Mount Sū)."

Enō said: "What sort of thing comes from there this way?"

Ejō said: "If a person says I am a thing, he is not right."

The above English translation appeared in *The Development of Chinese Zen* by Heinrich Dumoulin, S. J., English translation by Ruth Fuller Sasaki, The First Zen Institute of America, Inc., New York, 1953.

In 713 A.D. the second year of the Sien-tien (Senten) era under the reign of Emperor Sui-tsung (Eisō), Huai-jang (Ejō) moved to Heng Shan (Nangaku) and resided at Po-jo Temple (Hanjaku-ji). Note that 713 was the year Enō (Rokuso) entered nirvana. It was recorded that Ejō served under Master Enō for fifteen years. Ejō's dharma-heir was Ma-tsu Tao-i (Baso Dōitsu, 709-788). Baso was sitting in meditation at Chuan-fa Yuan (Denhō-in) all day long. Master Ejō approached him and asked: "What is your aim for *zazen* (sitting in meditation)?" Baso said: "I want to be a Buddha." Ejō took a tile and tried to polish it. Baso asked: "Master, what is this for?" Ejō said: "I want to make it a mirror." Baso said: "How can you make a mirror by polishing a tile?" Ejō then said: "One cannot get a mirror by polishing a tile. How can one become a Buddha by *zazen*?" Ma-tsu (Baso) had many disciples, among them:

Po-chang Huai-hai (Hyakujō Ekai, 720-814)

Ta-chu Hui-hai (Daishu Ekai)

Yu-lao Hsiao-jan (Gyokurō Kyūnen)

Yen-kuan Chi-an (Enkan Saian, 750?-842)

Kuei-tsung Chih-chang (Kisū Chijō)

Wu-hsieh Ling-mo (Gosetsu Reimoku, 747-818)

Nan-chuan Pu-yuan (Nansen Fugan, 748-834)

Hsi-tang Chih-tsang (Saidō Chizō, 735-814)

Ta-mei Fa-chang (Daibai Hōjō, 752-839)

Chang-ching Huai-hui (Shōkei Eki, 756-815)

Go-hu Ta-yi (Gako Daigi, 746-818)

Hsing-shan Wei-kuan (Kōzen Ikan, 755-817)

Fen-chou Wu-nieh (Bunsō Mugyō, 760-821)

> 慧能问："你来自何地？"
>
> 怀让答："来自嵩山。"
>
> 慧能说："什么物，与么来？"
>
> 怀让说："说似一物即不中。"

这些内容出自 S. J. 海因立希·杜慕林著的《中国禅宗的发展》，由罗丝·富勒·佐佐木从德文译成英文，纽约州的美国第一禅堂于 1953 年出版。

公元 713 年，即唐玄宗先天二年（睿宗传位于玄宗后改元先天），怀让迁居衡山，住在般若寺。应注意到，慧能的圆寂也是在 713 年，据记载怀让侍从于慧能左右已有十五年之久。怀让的法嗣是马祖道一（709—788），马祖原在传法院终日坐禅沉思。怀让禅师见到了，问他："你坐禅在求什么？"马祖答："为求成佛。"怀让就拿了一块砖，试图去磨光它。马祖问："大师在做什么？"师答："我要把它磨作镜子。"马祖问："怎么能把砖磨成镜子呢？"怀让说："磨砖不能成镜，那么坐禅又怎样能成佛呢？"马祖恍然大悟，他后来有很多弟子，其中如：

百丈怀海（720—814）

大珠慧海

玉姥翛然

盐官齐安（750？—842）

归宗智常

五泄灵默（747—818）

南泉普愿（748—834）

西堂智藏（735—814）

大梅法常（752—839）

章敬怀晖（756—815）

鹅湖大义（746—818）

兴善惟宽（755—817）

汾州无业（760—821）

Pang Yun (Hō Kōji, d. 811)

Teng Yin-feng (Tō Impō)

Po-chang Huai-hai (Hyakujō Ekai, 720-814) had several disciples: (1) Kuei-shan Ling-yu (Isan Reiyū, 771-853); (2) Huang-po Hsi-yun (Ōbaku Kiun, d. 850); (3) Chang-ching Ta-an (Chōkei Daian, 793-883); and (4) Ta-tzu Huan-chung (Daiji Kanchū, 780-862). Kuei-shan and his disciple Yang-shan Hui-chi (Kyōzan Ejaku, 807-883) were the founders of the Igyō School. Huang-po Hsi-yun (Ōbaku Kiun) was the teacher of Lin-chi I-hsuan (Rinzai Gigen, d. 866), who was the founder of the Rinzai School.

Yu-lao Hsiao-jan (Gyokurō Kyūnen) was the teacher of the Japanese monk Saichō (767-822), who went back to Japan to be the founder of the Tendai School in Japan. Yen-kuan Chi-an (Enkan Saian, 750?-842) was the teacher of I-kung (Gikū) and Tao-chu (Dōjo), both of whom were invited to go to Japan.

Kuei-tsung Chih-chang (Kisū-Chijō) had one disciple Kao-an Ta-yu (Kōan Daigu). Nan-chuan Pu-yuan (Nansen Fugan, 748-834) had several dharma heirs: Chao-chou Tsung-shen (Jōshū Jūshin, 778-897), Chang-sha Ching-tsen (Chōsha Keijin, 788-868), and Lu Keng (Riku Kō, 764-834). Ta-mei Fa-chang (Daibai Hōjō, 752-839) had a disciple Hang-chou Tien-lung (Kōshū Tenryū), whose disciple was Chu-chi (Gutei).

Besides Lin-chi I-hsuan (Rinzai Gigen), Ōbaku had other disciples: Mu-chou Tao-tsung (Bokujū Dōshō, 780?-877?), Pei Hsiu, the Prime Minister (Haikyū Shōkoku), O-shih Ling-kuan (Useki Reikan), and Chien-ching Tsu-nan (Senkei Sonan). Besides Yang-shan Hui-chi (Kyōzan Ejaku), Isan had other disciples: Hsiang-yen Chih-hsien (Kyōgen Chikan) and Ling-yun Chih-chin (Reiun Shigon). Chang-ching Ta-an (Chōkei Daian) had two disciples: Ling-shu Ju-min (Reiju Nyobin, d. 918) and Ta-sui Fa-chen (Daizui Hōshin).

The Nangaku Branch and the Igyō School are presented in Chapter 3. The Lin-chi or Rinzai School is presented in Chapter 4.

While the Nangaku Branch was the subject of R. H. Blyth's *Zen and*

Zen Classics, Vol. 3, the Seigen Branch was the subject of Vol. 2. In his Preface to Vol. 2, R. H. Blyth wrote:

This volume purports to be the History of Zen from Enō to Ummon, that is, of the Seigen Branch of the double-forked tree of Zen, but what the reader actually gets is something better, a selection of the anecdotes concerning the line of patriarchs. It was from such stories that

庞蕴（？—811）

邓隐峰

百丈怀海（720—814）有几位弟子如下：（1）沩山灵祐（771—853），（2）黄檗希运（？—850），（3）长庆大安（793—883），（4）大慈寰中（780—862）。沩山和他的弟子仰山慧寂（807—883）是沩仰宗的创建人。黄檗希运是临济义玄（？—866）的师父，而临济则是临济宗的创建人。

玉姥翛然是日本僧人最澄（767—822）的师父，最澄即是日本天台宗的创建人。盐官齐安（750？—842）是义空和道助两人的师父，两人都被邀请去了日本。

归宗智常只有一个弟子高安大愚。南泉普愿（748—834）则有好几个法嗣：赵州从谂（778—897）、长沙景岑（788—868）和大夫陆亘（764—834）。大梅法常（752—839）有一弟子是杭州天龙，天龙有一弟子是俱胝。

黄檗的弟子除临济义玄之外，其他还有：睦州道纵（780？—877？）、相国裴休、乌石灵观以及千顷楚南。沩山弟子除仰山慧寂之外，其他还有香严智闲和灵云志勤。长庆大安有两弟子：灵树如敏（？—918）和大隋法真。

南岳支系和沩仰宗将在第三章、临济宗则将在第四章中叙述。

南岳支系是 R. H. 布莱思《禅与禅宗经典》第 3 卷的主题，而青原支系则是该书第 2 卷的主题。布莱思在第 2 卷序言中写道：

本卷的要旨是叙述从慧能到云门的禅宗历史，也就是禅宗世系分支中的青原支系。不过读者在这里可读到一些更有趣的内容，即有关各代祖师的轶事精选。如《碧岩集》、《无门关》

the *Hekigan-roku, Mumonkan,* and *Shōyōroku* were composed. These three works, as in the case of a selection of the best poems of the best poets, give us a somewhat partial and excessively lofty view of Chinese Zen geniuses.

Ching-yuan Hsing-ssu (Seigen Gyōshi, d. 740) was the founder of the Seigen Branch. Seigen occupied perhaps the first place among the disciples of the Sixth Patriarch (Rokuso). To him Enō entrusted the Buddha-robe and bowl, without appointing him his successor. Nor was Seigen permitted to hand down the precious symbols of the dharma tradition. The robe and the bowl were to be placed in the Monastery at Tsao-hsi (Sōkei).

Seigen's dharma-heir was Shih-tou Hsi-chien (Sekitō Kisen, 700-790). Sekitō was the author of *Tsan-tung-chi* (*Sandōkai*) and *Tsao-an Ke* (*Sōanka*). In *Sandōkai*, Sekitō spoke of Buddha as the "Great Hermit"; the meaning and foundation of all things he called the "spiritual source" (reigen). The dialectical resolution of the dualistic pairs of opposites *ji* (things) and *ri* (reason), and *myō* (light) and *an* (darkness) into a higher unity, developed by Sekitō in the *Sandōkai*, can be regarded as the foundation of, or first step toward, the later doctrine of the "Five Ranks" (go'i) in the Sōtō School.

Sekitō's disciples were:

(1) Yueh-shan Wei-yen (Yakusan Igen, 751-834)

(2) Tien-huang Tao-wu (Tennō Dōgo, 748-807)

(3) Tan-hsia Tien-jan (Tanka Tennen, 739-824)

Yakusan's disciples were: (1) Yun-yen Tan-sheng (Ungan Donjō, 782-841); (2) Tao-wu Yuan-chih (Dōgo Enchi, 769-835); and (3) Chuan-tzu Te-cheng (Sensu Tokusei). Ungan was the teacher of Tung-shan Liang-chieh (Tōzan Ryōkai, 807-869), founder of the Tsao-tung (Sōtō) School. Dōgo Enchi's disciple was Shih-shuang Ching-chu (Sekisō Keisho, 807-888). Sensu Tokusei's disciple was Chia-shan Shan-hui (Kassan Zenne, 805-881).

Tanka Tennen's disciple was Tsui-wei Wu-hsueh (Suiba Mugaku), whose disciple was Tou-tzu Ta-tung (Tōsu Daidō, 819-914).

Tennō Dōgo was the teacher of Lung-tan Chung-hsin (Ryūtan Sūshin), whose disciple was Te-shan Hsuan-chien (Tokusan Senkan, 782-865). Tokusan's disciples were: (1) Hsueh-feng I-tsun (Seppō Gison, 822-908), (2) Yen-tou Chuan-huo (Gantō Zenkatsu, 828-887), and (3) Kan-tan Tzu-kuo (Kantan Shikoku). Seppō's disciples were: (a) Hsuan-sha Shih-pei

和《从容录》都是根据这些轶事编写的。这三篇作品就好像是最佳诗人的最佳诗篇选集，会给我们提供有关中国禅宗大师们一部分非常崇高的见解和观点。

青原行思（？—740）是禅宗青原系的创建人，或许也是六祖慧能的首座弟子。六祖虽然向他传授了衣钵，但并未明确指定他是继承人，虽将珍贵的禅宗传统信物交给了他，不过仍留在曹溪寺内，镇守山门。

青原的法嗣是石头希迁（700—790），著有《参同契》和《草庵歌》。在《参同契》中石头称佛是大隐者，称所有事物的意义和基础为精神本原（"灵源"）。石头在《参同契》中阐述了对立双方"事"和"理"、"明"和"暗"的辩证关系，在分解后可以提升到更高层次的统一整体，这可以认为是走向石头宗随后"五级"原理的根本基础或第一步。

石头的弟子有：

（1）药山惟俨（751—834）（2）天皇道悟（748—807）

（3）丹霞天然（739—824）

药山的弟子有：（1）云岩昙晟（782—841），（2）道吾圆智（769—835），（3）船子德诚。而云岩昙晟的弟子洞山良价（807—869）则是曹洞宗的创建人。道吾圆智的弟子是石霜庆诸（807—888），船子德诚的弟子则是夹山善会（805—881）。

丹霞天然的弟子是翠微无学，翠微的弟子是投子大同（819—914）。

天皇道悟是龙潭崇信的师父，龙潭的弟子是德山宣鉴（782—865）。德山的弟子有：（1）雪峰义存（822—908），（2）岩头全奯（828—887），（3）感潭资国。雪峰的弟子则有

(Gensha Shibi, 835-908); (b) Yun-men Wen-yen (Ummon Bun'en, 864-949), founder of the Ummon School; (c) Pao-fu Tsung-chan (Hofuku Jūten, d. 928); (d) Chang-ching Hui-leng (Chōkei Eryō, 854-932); (e) Tsui-yen Ling-tsan (Suigan Reisan); and (f) Ku-shan Shen-yen (Kozan Jin'an, 863-939).

Gensha Shibi was the teacher of Lo-han Kuei-chen (Rakan Keijin, 867-928), whose disciple was Fa-yen Wen-i (Hōgen Bun'eki, 885-958), founder of the Fa-yen or Hōgen School. Fa-yen (Hōgen) had a disciple Tien-tai Te-shao (Tendai Tokushō, 891-972), whose disciple was Yung-ming Yen-shou (Yōmyō Enju, 904-975).

Ummon's disciples were: Hsiang-lin Cheng-yuan (Kyōrin Chōon, d. 987), Tung-shan Shou-chu (Tōzan Shusho, 910-990), Pa-ling Hao-chien (Haryō Kōkan), and Te-shan Yuan-mi (Tokusan Emmitsu). Kyōrin was the teacher of Chih-men Kuang-tsu (Chimon Kōso, d. 1031), whose disciple was Hsueh-tou Chung-hsien (Setchō Jūken, 980-1052). Setchō Jūken was the author of one hundred verses upon which the *Blue Cliff Records* (*Pi-yen-lu* or *Hekigan-roku*) were based. Setchō's dharma-heir, Tien-i I-huai (Tenne Gikai, 993-1064), had two disciples: Hui-lin Tsung-pen (Erin Sōhon, 1020-1099), and Yuan-tung Fa-hsiu (Enzū Hōshū, 1027-1090).

Tōzan Ryōkai's disciples were: (1) Tsao-shan Pen-chi (Sōzan Honjaku, 840-901), (2) Yun-chu Tao-ying (Ungo Dōyō, d. 902), (3) Chiu-feng Pu-man (Kyūhō Fuman), (4) Lung-ya Chu-tun (Ryūga Koton, 835-923), (5) Su-shan Kuang-jen (Sozan Kōnin, 837-909), and others.

Tōzan and Sōzan were the founders of the Sōtō School. Sōzan's disciple was Tsao-shan Hui-hsia (Sōzan Eka), whose disciple was Hua-yen Cheng-hui (Kegon Shō'e). Ungo Dōyō's disciples were: Tung-an Tao-pei (Dōan Dōhai, 889-955), and Yun-chu Huai-yueh (Ungo Egaku). Kyūhō Fuman's disciple was Tung-an Wei (Dōan I), whose disciples were: Tung-an Kuan-chih (Dōan Kanshi) and Chen-chou Shih-ching (Chinshū Sekkyō). Dōan Kanshi's disciples were: Liang-shan Yuan-kuan (Ryōsan Enkan) and Chen-chou Ling-tung (Chinshū Reitsū). Ryōsan's disciple was Ta-yang Ching-yuan (Daiyō Keigen, 943-1027). Daiyō was not able to find a dharma-heir when he was very old. He entrusted Fushan Fa-yuan (Fusan Hō'en, 991-1067) to find a worthy heir. Thus Tou-tzu I-ching (Tōsu Gisei, 1032-1083) became the dharma-heir of Daiyō Keigen and continued on the line. Tōzu was known as Miao-shu Ta-shih (Myōzoku Daishi), meaning Master of "Miraculous Continuity." Tōzu's disciple was Fu-yung Tao-kai (Fuyō Dōkai, 1043-1118). Fuyō's dharma

（a）玄沙师备（835—908）;（b）云门文偃（864—949），是云门宗的创建人;（c）保福从展（？—928）;（d）长庆慧稜（854—932）;（e）翠岩令参;（f）鼓山神晏（863—939）。

玄沙师备是罗汉桂琛（867—928）的师父，桂琛的弟子法眼文益（885—958）是法眼宗的创建人。法眼有一弟子天台德韶（891—972），天台的弟子是永明延寿（904—975）。

云门的弟子有：香林澄远（？—987）、洞山守初（910—990）、巴陵颢鉴和德山圆密。香林是智门光祚（？—1031）的师父，智门的弟子是雪窦重显（980—1052）。雪窦写了一百首禅诗,《碧岩集》就是在这些诗的基础上写成的。雪窦的法嗣天衣义怀（993—1064）有两弟子：慧林宗本（1020—1099）和圆通法秀（1027—1090）。

洞山良价的弟子有:（1）曹山本寂（840—901），（2）云居道膺（？—902），（3）九峰普满，（4）龙牙居遁（835—923），（5）疏山匡仁（837—909），等等。

洞山良价和曹山本寂是曹洞宗的创建人。曹山本寂的弟子是曹山慧霞，慧霞的弟子是华严正慧。云居道膺的弟子是同安道丕（889—955）和云居怀岳。九峰普满的弟子是同安威，同安威的弟子有同安观志和陈州石镜。同安观志的弟子是梁山缘观和陈州灵通。梁山的弟子是大阳警玄（943—1027）。大阳很老时还未能找到合适的后继法嗣，拜托福山法圆（991—1067）代他找一个合适者。于是投子义青（1032—1083）成为继承大阳警玄衣钵的法嗣。投子的尊号是妙续大师，意思是妙心相续不绝。投子的弟子是芙蓉道楷（1043—1118）。芙蓉的法嗣有

heirs were: Tan-hsia Tzu-chun (Tanka Shijun, 1064-1119), Lo-men Tzu-chueh (Rokumon Jikaku, d. 1117), and Ku-mu Fa-cheng (Komoku Hōjō). Tanka's heirs flourished in the south. His fourth-generation disciple was Tien-tung Ju-ching (Tendō Nyojō, 1162-1228), whose disciple Dōgen Kigen became the founder of the Sōtō School in Japan. Rokumon's heirs flourished in the north, and his line was continued to Hsin-yueh Hsing-shu (Shinetsu Kōchū, 1642-1696), who went to Japan.

The above lineage of the Sōtō School in China was based on *Ching-te Chuan-teng Lu* (*Keitoku Dentō Roku*). See Y. H. Ku, *History of Chinese Zen Masters.*

Liu Ke (Ryūka), a layman, who was a great admirer of Sekitō, said:

> Westward from the river (Kiangsi), Daijaku (i.e., Baso Doitsu) is the Master; southward from the lake (Hunan), Sekito is the Master. People flock thither in crowds. He who has not seen both these great masters consider himself an ignoramus.

This quotation in English translation was taken from *The Development of Chinese Zen*, by Heinrich Dumoulin, S. J., English translation by Ruth Fuller Sasaki, published by The First Zen Institute of America, Inc., New York, 1953, page 6. The Chinese text appeared on page 46.

The Nangaku and Seigen Branches were to flourish side by side. Although there were developed FIVE Schools later on, the Rinzai and the Sōtō Schools would continue on not only in China, but also in Japan.

In the Sōtō School in China, Rokumon's heirs led to the Chiao-shan (Shōzan) line which has flourished to the present day. (See Charts X and X A).

In a parallel way, the Rinzai School in China could be traced from Engo Kokugon (1063-1135) to Mujun Shihan (1178-1249) and then branched out into two long lines. (See Chart VI). The first line started from Seggan Sokin (1216-1287) and continued for fifteen generations to Ingen Ryūki (1592-1673) who went to Japan to be the founder of the Ōbaku School. The second line started from Jōji Myōrin (1201-1261) and continued for fourteen generations to Kōan Ensei, who started the

Ku-shan (Kozan) line. The Kozan line (See Chart VI A) has flourished to the present day. According to *Star-Lamp Records* edited by Abbot Hsu Yun (Kiun, 1840-1959), the Kozan line continued to Abbot Hsu Yun, and his dharma-grandson, Abbot Ling-yuan (Reigen, 1902-), who was the founder of Daikaku-ji at Keelung, Taiwan.

丹霞子淳（1064—1119）、鹿门自觉（？ —1117）和枯默法成。丹霞的众多法嗣在中国南方传道兴旺，其第四代弟子是天童如净（1162—1228）。天童的弟子道元希玄成为日本曹洞宗的始祖。至于鹿门自觉的众后嗣则兴盛于中国北方，他的世系继续不断传到心越兴俦（1642—1696），心越也去了日本。

上述曹洞宗在中国的传承世系来自《景德传灯录》，见拙著《禅宗师承记》。

有一刘某，十分崇拜石头希迁，曾说：在江之西有马祖道一是大师，在湖之南有石头希迁是大师。百姓众人群集去到那里朝拜大师，谁没有去拜见这两位大师就会自认愚昧无知。

上文引自 S. J. 海因立希·杜慕林《中国禅宗的发展》（由罗丝·富勒·佐佐木译成英文，纽约州美国第一禅堂出版）1953 年版第 6 页;《禅宗师承记》第 46 页。

中国禅宗的南岳和青原两大支系同时发展，一起繁盛兴旺。后又发展成为五个宗系，其中临济和曹洞两宗，则不仅在中国，而且在日本也都继续不断繁衍兴盛。

曹洞宗在中国，由鹿门自觉的众多法嗣一直传到焦山系，继续兴盛，直到今天（见附表 X 和 X A）。

与曹洞宗相平行，临济宗在中国也可由圆悟克勤（1063—1135）传承到无准师范（1178—1249），于是再分为两个长支系（见附表 VI）。第一分支自雪岩祖钦（1216—1287）开始，继续传了十五代，到隐元隆琦（1592—1673）去了日本，成为日本黄檗宗的创建人。第二分支自净慈妙伦（1201—1261）开始，连续传了十四代到高庵圆清，开始创建了鼓山系，鼓山系（见附表 VI A）一直兴盛到今天。根据虚云大师（1840—1959）编著的《星灯集》，鼓山系一直传到虚云大师和他的第二代法嗣灵源方丈（1902—   　　），灵源是台湾基隆大觉寺的创建人。

In this book, one photograph was taken when the present author visited Reverend Ling-yuan with Reverend Sheng-yen (Shōgen, 1930-).

From Chart VI, Genyū Shōden (1549-1614) had another disciple, Ten'in Enshū (1575-1635), whose disciple was Gyokurin Tsūshū (1614-1675). Gyokurin Tsūshū was recognized prominent as the founder of Kao-min Temple (Kōmin-ji), Yangchow, Kiangsu. The Kao-min (Kōmin) line leads to Abbot Lai-Ko (Raika, 1881-1953), another prominent Zen Master of the Rinzai School in China. (See Chart VI B).

书中有一照片是本书作者在拜访灵源法师时，与圣严法师在一起的合影留念。

根据附表Ⅵ：幻有正传法师（1549—1614）另有一弟子天隐圆修（1575—1635），天隐有一很卓越的弟子玉琳通琇（1614—1675），是江苏扬州高旻寺的创建人。高旻系传至来果方丈（1881—1953），是临济宗在中国的另一位卓越的禅宗大师（见附表ⅥB）。

CHAPTER 3   THE NANGAKU BRANCH AND THE IGYŌ SCHOOL

Nan-yueh Huai-jang (Nangaku Ejō, 677-744) started the Nangaku Branch of Zen after Hui-neng (Enō), the Sixth Patriarch. R. H. Blyth's *Zen and Zen Classics*, Vol. 3, is devoted to this branch of Zen history, except for the first chapter, which deals with "The Disciples of Tōzan" of the Seigen Branch.

In Chapter 2 above, mention was made about how Ejō instructed Baso concerning *zazen* by comparing sitting in meditation to polishing a tile for a mirror. On another occasion Ejō said to Baso:

> To train yourself in sitting meditation (*zazen*) is to train yourself to be a sitting Buddha. If you train yourself in *zazen*, (you should know that) Zen is neither sitting nor lying. If you train yourself to be a sitting Buddha (you should know that), the Buddha is not a fixed form. Since the Dharma has no (fixed) abode, it is not a matter of making choices. If you (make yourself) a sitting Buddha, this is precisely killing the Buddha. If you adhere to the sitting position, you will not attain the principle (of Zen).

The English translation was taken from *The Way of Zen* by Alan W. Watts, page 110. The Chinese version was quoted in *History of Chinese Zen Masters* by Y. H. Ku, page 58.

Ma-tsu Tao-i (Baso Dōitsu, 709-788) was a native of Shih-fang in the district of Han-chou (now northwest of Cheng-tu, in Szechwan Province). He became a monk when he was twelve years old. Then he traveled to Nan-yueh, in Hunan Province, and studied under Master Huai-jang (Ejō), who had then nine disciples. Of these only Baso received the sacred mind-seal (as heir). According to the *Lamp Records*, six disciples received the Inka. Remember the story about Daruma (See *Daishō Daizōkyō*, Vol. 51, page 151):

> Daruma said: "In Tang-China, there were three persons who

received my Dharma: one received my marrow, one received my bones, and one received my flesh. Hui-ke (Eka) received my marrow, Taoyu received my bones, and Nun Tsung-chih received my flesh."

So in Ejō's case, he remarked:

You six persons all testify to my body, but each takes a road.

⓷ 南岳系和沩仰宗

在六祖慧能之后，南岳怀让（677—744）创建了禅宗的南岳支系。在 R. H. 布莱思《禅与禅宗经典》的第 3 卷中，除了第 1 章叙述青原支系的洞山众弟子外，其余全都专门叙述关于南岳这一支系的禅宗历史。

本书第二章中曾提到怀让在教导马祖时怎样把沉思坐禅比喻为企图磨砖成镜。另外还有一次怀让曾对马祖这样说：

你想通过沉思坐禅来修炼，你就将修成一尊坐佛。你想修炼坐禅，应知禅道非坐非卧。你想修成坐佛，那就应该知道佛无定相。因为佛法本无所住，所以没有什么可以取舍选择的。如果你想修成坐佛，那就完全等于杀佛。如果你执著奉行坐相，那你就根本不可能领悟禅理。

英文译文见艾伦·瓦茨《禅道》第 110 页，而在拙著《禅宗师承记》第 58 页上则引有中文原文。

马祖道一（709—788）是汉州地区什邡（在今四川成都西北）人，12 岁时就出家为僧。东游至湖南南岳衡山，拜在怀让禅师门下。怀让共有弟子九人，只有马祖得其心印，传为法嗣。根据《传灯录》所载，怀让众弟子中只有六人得到了印证。记得关于达摩祖师的下述这一故事（见《大正藏》第 51 卷，第 151 页）：

达摩说："三人得我法。一人得我髓，一人得我骨，一人得我肉。得我髓者慧可，得我骨者道育，得我肉者尼总持。"

同样，怀让也如此讲：

汝等六人同证吾身，各契其一。一人得吾眉，善威仪——

One person (Chang Hao) receives my eyebrows, dignified in appearance. One person (Chih Ta) receives my eyes, swift in looking around. One person (Tan Jan) receives my ears, deft in hearing reason. One person (Shen Chao) receives my nose, well versed in sensing odor (*chi*). One person (Yen Tsin) receives my tongue, able in making speeches. One person (Tao-i) receives my mind or heart, understanding the ancient and the present.

One may note that just as Hui-ke (Eka) became the Second Patriarch, because he received the marrow of Daruma, Baso became the dharma-heir of Ejō, because he received the mind (or heart) of the Master. However, the other five persons did also receive the Inka, and thus became disciples. (See the *Lamp Records*, in *Daishō Daizōkyō*, Vol. 51, pages 240-241). Ejō entered nirvana in 744 A.D., the third year of the Tien-Pao era under the reign of Hsuan-tsung.

From the *Lamp Records*, Professor Chang Chung-yuan had translated the following biographical notes concerning Baso Dōitsu. (See Chang: *Original Teachings of Ch'an Buddhism*, Pantheon Books, 1969, pages 148-152).

> One day the Master spoke to his assembly as follows: "All of you should realize that your own mind is Buddha, that is, this mind is Buddha's Mind. The great Master Bodhidharma came from India to China to transmit the Mahayana Buddhist doctrine of the One Mind in order to enlighten us all."
>
> ...
>
> "Those who seek for the Truth should realize that there is nothing to seek. There is no Buddha but Mind; there is no Mind but Buddha. Do not choose what is good, nor reject what is evil, but rather be free from purity and defilement. Then you will realize the emptiness of sin."
>
> ...
>
> "Whenever you speak about Mind, you must realize that appearance and reality are perfectly interfused without impediment. This is what

the achievement of *bodhi* is."

Then the assembly was asked to hear Master Baso's gāthā:

Anytime you wish to speak about Mind, speak!

In this way, *bodhi* is tranquil.

When appearance and reality are perfectly interfused without
impediment,

常浩；一人得吾眼，善顾盼——智达；一人得吾耳，善听理——
坦然；一人得吾鼻，善知气——神照；一人得吾舌，善谭说——
严峻；一人得吾心，善古今——道一。

可以指出，正像慧可得到了达摩的"髓"而成为禅宗第二祖，
那么马祖道一得到了怀让的"心"就应是南岳系的祖师。不过
其他五人，确实也不同程度地得到了怀让的印证，所以也都是
他的传承弟子（见《传灯录》，《大正藏》第 51 卷，第 240—241
页）。怀让圆寂于公元 744 年，即唐玄宗天宝三年。

根据《传灯录》中有关马祖道一的传记内容，张钟元教授
已把它译成英文。以下这段可参见张氏《佛教禅宗之源》（潘塞
恩图书出版公司，1969 年版）第 148—152 页：

有一天马祖禅师对众人说："你们都应懂得你们自心是佛，
此心即是佛心。当初大祖师菩提达摩自南印度来到中国，传授
上乘一心之法，要使我们一切众生都能开悟。……

"凡求佛法真理的人，要懂得应该别无所求。除心之外别无
佛，除佛之外也无心。既不趋善，也不避恶，洁净和污秽两不
沾边，那么罪性也就空了。……

"不论何时，如果谈到了心，要懂得见色即是见心。外象与
本质、事与理都完全互相渗合，两无所碍。菩提道果，就应该
是这样。"

然后马祖禅师要众人听他读一首诗偈：

关于内心，不论何人要说就说，
这样做，菩提就平静安宁。
相状和本性、事和理完全渗透无碍，

Birth is simultaneously no-birth.

Baso was remarkable in appearance. He strode like an ox and looked around like a tiger. His tongue could be stretched to reach over his nose; two circular marks were imprinted on the soles of his feet.

Baso had many disciples, among them were:

Po-chang Huai-hai (Hyakujō Ekai, 720-814)

Ta-chu Hui-hai (Daishu Ekai)

Yu-lao Hsiao-jan (Gyokurō Kyūnen)

Yen-kuan Chi-an (Enkan Saian, 750?-842)

Kuei-tsung Chih-chang (Kisū Chijō)

Wu-hsieh Ling-mo (Gosetsu Reimoku, 747-818)

Nan-chuan Pu-yuan (Nansen Fugan, 748-834)

Hsi-tang Chih-tsang (Saidō Chizō, 735-814)

Ta-mei Fa-chang (Daibai Hōjō, 752-839)

Po-chang Wei-cheng (Hyakujō Isei)

Pan-shan Pao-tsi (Banzan Hōseki)

Ma-ku Pao-che (Mayoku Hōtetsu)

Lu-tsu Pao-yun (Roso Hōun)

Chang-ching Huai-hui (Shōkei Eki, 756-815)

Go-hu Ta-yi (Gako Daigi, 746-818)

Fu-yung Ta-yu (Fuyō Daiyu)

Hsing-shan Wei-kuan (Kōzen Ikan, 755-817)

Fen-chou Wu-nieh (Bunsō Mugyō, 760-821)

Pang Yun (Hō Kōji, d. 811)

Teng Yin-feng (Tō Impō)

Fu-kuang Ju-man (Bukkō Nyoman)

Po-chang Huai-hai (Hyakujō Ekai, 720-814) became a monk when he was twenty years old. When studying under Baso, Hyakujō came up to the Master for a second time. Baso first used "Kwatz!" (this was later used by Rinzai); he uttered it so loudly that it deafened Hyakujō's ears for three days. At a later date Hyakujō went out attending Baso. A flock of wild geese was flying by. Baso asked: "What are they?" Hyakujō Ekai answered: "They are wild geese." Baso: "Whither are they flying?" Ekai: "They have flown away." Baso suddenly took hold of Ekai's nose and gave it a twist. Hyakujō felt so painful that he cried aloud: "Oh! Oh!" Baso said: "You say that they have flown away. But they have been here from the very beginning." This enlightened Hyakujō suddenly, his back wet with perspiration. This was an example of *satori*, as recorded. (For the English version, see D. T. Suzuki: *Essays in Zen Buddhism*, First Series, 1949, 1961, page 240).

那么"生"同时也就是"不生"。

马祖相貌奇特：行走如牛，环视像虎，伸舌可以过鼻，脚跟下还有两轮斑纹。

马祖有很多弟子，其中有：

百丈怀海（720—814）	麻谷宝彻
大珠慧海	鲁祖宝云
玉姥翛然	章敬怀晖（756—815）
盐官齐安（750？—842）	鹅湖大义（746—818）
归宗智常	芙蓉大毓
五泄灵默（747—818）	兴善惟宽（755—817）
南泉普愿（748—834）	汾州无业（760—821）
西堂智藏（735—814）	庞蕴（？—811）
大梅法常（752—839）	邓隐峰
百丈惟政	佛光如满
盘山宝积	

百丈怀海（720—814）20岁时出家为僧，师从马祖学佛法。当他第二次拜见禅师时，马祖大声呼斥（临济以后也常用棒喝），响声震耳，使百丈聋了三天。后来某一天，百丈侍立马祖身旁，一群野鹅飞过。马祖问："那是什么？"百丈答："那是一群鹅。"马祖问："飞向哪里？"百丈答："他们飞过去了。"马祖忽然捏着百丈的鼻子拧了一把。百丈觉得很痛，高叫"哦，哦！"马祖说："你说他们飞走了，但他们何曾飞去？"这启发了百丈，顿然领悟，汗流浃背。这就是所谓"顿悟"的一例而被记载（参见铃木大拙：《佛教禅宗论文集》系列I，1949、1961年版，第240页）。

On the day following Hyakujō's *satori*, Baso appeared in the preaching hall (zendō), and was about to speak before the assembly. Hyakujō came forward and rolled up the matting. Baso came down from his seat quietly and returned to his room. Baso called Hyakujō to his room and asked him about his behavior. Hyakujō replied: "You twisted my nose yesterday. It was quite painful." Baso said: "Where was your thought wandering then?" Hyakujō said: "It is not painful any more today." Hyakujō, having been enlightened, felt like a "golden-haired lion."

Hyakujō Ekai drew up his set of regulations known as "Regulations in the Zen Monastery" (Hyakujō shingi) in about the middle of the Tang Dynasty. These regulations were preserved today in a compilation by imperial order in the Yuan Dynasty. (See *Daishō Daizōkyō*, No. 2025).

Chang-ching Ta-an (Chōkei Daian, 793-883) asked Hyakujō: "I wish to know about Buddha; what is he?" Hyakujō answered: "It is like seeking for an ox while you are riding on it." Daian: "What shall I do after I know?" Hyakujō: "It is like going home riding on it." Daian: "How can I behave in accordance with the Dharma?" Hyakujō then told him: "You should behave like a cow-herd, who carries a staff and sees to it that his cattle would not wander away into somebody else's rice-fields." This story was referred to frequently in Zen literature, and The Ten Cow-herding Pictures showed the upward steps of spiritual training in a systematic way. These steps are: (1) Looking for the Cow; (2) Seeing the Traces of the Cow; (3) Seeing the Cow; (4) Catching the Cow; (5) Herding the Cow; (6) Coming Home on the Cow's Back; (7) The Cow Forgotten, Leaving the Man Alone; (8) The Cow and the Man Both Gone Out of Sight; (9) Returning to the Origin, Back to the Source; and (10) Entering the City with Bliss-bestowing Hands.

The following anecdote was described by R. H. Blyth in his *Zen and Zen Classics*, Vol. 3, Chapter 4:

> A monk asked Hyakujō, "What is the Buddha?"
> Hyakujō asked the monk, "Who are you?"

The monk said: "I am I."

Hyakujō said: "Do you know this 'I' or not?"

The monk replied: "Clearly."

Hyakujō held up the mosquito flapper and said: "Do you see this?"

"I do," said the monk.

Hyakujō said: "I have no word."

在百丈顿悟的第二天，马祖来到讲经堂上，准备向众人讲经。百丈走向前来，就把席毯卷起。马祖平静地从座上走下来，回到房内，再把百丈叫来，责问他刚才的举止是为什么。百丈答："昨天你拧了我的鼻子，我很疼。"马祖问："那么你内心在想些什么呢？"百丈说："今天我不再疼了。"百丈在开悟了以后，自我感觉就好像一头金毛狮子。

大约在唐代中期，百丈怀海起草了一份"禅寺寺内法规"条例。这些法规条例在元代由朝廷敕令汇编后一直保存到现在，即《敕修百丈清规》。（参见《大正藏》第 2025）。

长庆大安（793—883）问百丈："我想知道，到底什么是佛？"百丈答："你好像是骑在牛背上在找牛。"大安问："我现在知道以后，又该如何去做呢？"百丈说："就好比骑牛回家。"大安问："如何做才能合乎佛法？"于是百丈就告诉他："你要像牧童那样拿了牛鞭，管好你的牛，不要闯入别人家的稻田中。"这一故事在禅宗文献中经常被引用，还有十幅牧牛图，系统地表示了内心修炼的分段步骤，它们是：（1）寻牛，（2）寻到了牛的脚印，（3）见到牛，（4）抓住牛，（5）驯牧牛，（6）骑上牛背回家，（7）留下人来忘掉牛，（8）牛和人全都忘失，（9）返本还源，（10）在尘俗中逍遥。

在 R. H. 布莱思的《禅与禅宗经典》第 3 卷第 4 章中讲述了下面这样的故事：

一僧问百丈："什么是佛？"

百丈问僧："你是什么？"

僧说："我就是我。"

百丈说："你知道这个'我'吗？"

僧答："很清楚。"

百丈拿起一只蚊拍，问："你看见这个吗？"

僧答："我看见了。"

百丈说："我无话可讲了。"

He was a great teacher, as well as a great organizer, emphasizing discipline in a Zen temple. Hyakujō had many excellent disciples, among them:

Kuei-shan Ling-yu (Isan Reiyū, 771-853)

Huang-po Hsi-yun (Ōbaku Kiun, d. 850)

Chang-ching Ta-an (Chōkei Daian, 793-883)

Ta-tzu Huan-chung (Daiji Kanchū, 780-862)

Kuei-shan Ling-yu (Isan Reiyū) and his disciple, Yang-shan Hui-chi (Kyōzan Ejaku, 807-883), were the founders of the Kuei-yang (Ikyō or Igyō) School. Huang-po Hsi-yun (Ōbaku Kiun) was the teacher of Lin-chi I-hsuan (Rinzai Gigen, d. 866), who founded the Lin-chi (Rinzai) School. Kuei-shan (Isan) had other disciples: Hsiang-yen Chih-hsien (Kyōgen Chikan), Ling-yun Chih-chin (Reiun Shigon), and Ching-shan Hung-yin (Keizan Kōin). Ōbaku's other disciples were: Mu-chou Tao-tsung (Bokujū Dōshō), Pei Hsiu, the Prime Minister (Haikyū Shōkoku), O-shih Ling-kuan (Useki Reikan), and Chien-ching Tsu-nan (Senkei Sonan). Mu-chou was also known as Chen Tsun-su (Chin Sonshuku, 780?-877?). Chōkei's disciples were: Ling-shu Ju-min (Reiju Nyobin, d. 918), and Ta-sui Fa-chen (Daizui Hōshin).

Ta-chu Hui-hai (Daishu Ekai) was the author of *Tun-wu Ju-tao Yao-men Lun* (*Tongo Nyūdō Yōmon Ron*)—*On the Essentials for Entering Tao through Sudden Awakening*, edited by Miao-hsieh (Myōkyō), first published in 1374. Yu-lao Hsiao-jan (Gyokurō Kyūnen) was the Zen teacher of the Japanese monk Saichō (767-822), founder of the Tendai School in Japan. Yen-kuan Chi-an (Enkan Saian, 750?-842) was the teacher of I-kung (Gikū) and Tao-chu (Dōjo), both of whom went to Japan. Kuei-tsung Chih-chang (Kisū Chijō) had a disciple, Kao-an Ta-yu (Kōan Daigu). Nan-chuan Pu-yuan (Nansen Fugan, 748-834) had many disciples, among them: Chao-chou Tsung-shen (Jōshū Jūshin, 778-897), Chang-sha Ching-tsen (Chōsha Keijin, 788-868), and Lu Keng (Riku Kō, 764-834). Ta-mei Fa-chang (Daibai Hōjō, 752-839) was the dharma teacher of Hang-chou Tien-lung (Kōshū Tenryū), whose disciple was Chu-chi (Gutei). Fu-kuang Ju-man (Bukkō Nyoman) had a famous disciple—Po Chü-i (Haku Kyoeki), a well-known poet.

Master Kuei-shan (Isan) was a native of Chang-chi in Fuchow (now Fukien Province). In the Chien-shan Monastery (Kenzen-ji) in his native city, he studied under the Vianya master Fa-chang (Hōchō). Later he was ordained at the Lung-hsing Monastery (Ryūkō-ji) in Hangchow. At the age of twenty-three he went to Kiangsi and visited Master Po-chang (Hyakujō). One day Isan was attending Hyakujō who asked him: "Who are you?" "I am Kuei-shan (Isan)," replied Isan. Hyakujō said: "Will you

百丈是大导师，也是大组织者，他十分重视禅寺内的清规戒律。他有很多优秀的弟子，其中有：

　　沩山灵祐（771—853）

　　黄檗希运（？—850）

　　长庆大安（793—883）

　　大慈寰中（780—862）

沩山灵祐和他的弟子仰山慧寂（807—883）是沩仰宗的创建人。黄檗希运的弟子临济义玄（？—866）创建了临济宗。沩山灵祐的其他弟子还有：香严智闲、灵云志勤和径山洪湮。黄檗希运的其他弟子则有睦州道踪、相国裴休、乌石灵观和千顷楚南。睦州道踪的另一名字是陈尊宿，长庆的弟子是灵树如敏和大隋法真。

大珠慧海是《顿悟入道要门论》的作者，由妙叶编纂，1374年初版。玉姥翛然是日本僧人最澄禅师（767—822）的师父，最澄则是日本天台宗的创建人。盐官齐安（750？—842）是义空和道助两人的师父，两人都去了日本。归宗智常有一弟子为高安大愚。南泉普愿（748—834）有许多弟子，其中如赵州从谂（778—897）、长沙景岑（788—868）和陆亘（764—834）。大梅法常（752—839）是杭州天龙的法师，天龙的弟子是俱胝。佛光如满有一著名的弟子白居易，是大诗人。

沩山灵祐禅师是福州长溪（今福建省）人。先在福州当地的建善寺拜律师法常为师，后在杭州龙兴寺受戒。23岁到江西拜见百丈禅师。有一天沩山侍立在禅师旁，师问："你是谁？"答："我是

poke the fire pot and find out whether there is some burning charcoal in it?" Isan did so, and then said: "There is no burning charcoal." Master Hyakujō rose from his seat. Poking deep into the fire pot, he extracted a small glowing piece of charcoal which he showed to Isan, saying: "Is this not a burning piece?" At this, Isan was awakened, and made a profound bow. Hyakujō then quoted the sutra:

> To behold the Buddha-nature one must wait for the right moment and the right conditions. When the time comes, one is awakened as from a dream. It is as if one's memory recalls something long forgotten. One realizes that what is obtained is one's own and not from outside one's self.

The following anecdotes were taken from Professor Chang Chung-yuan's translations (See *Original Teachings of Ch'an Buddhism*, pages 200-208):

> One day Master Kuei-shan Ling-yu (Isan Reiyū) came into the assembly and said:
>
> "The mind of one who understands Ch'an (Zen) is plain and straightforward without pretense. It has neither front nor back and is without deceit or delusion. Every hour of the day, what one hears and sees are ordinary things and ordinary actions. Nothing is distorted. One does not need to shut one's eyes and ears to be non-attached to things. In the early days many sages stressed the follies and dangers of impurity. When delusion, perverted views, and bad thinking habits are eliminated, the mind is as clear and tranquil as the autumn stream. It is pure and quiescent, placid and free from attachment. Therefore he who is like this is called a Ch'annist (Zennist), a man of non-attachment to things."
>
> ...
>
> During an assembly period, the Master (Isan) said:
>
> "When the approach to enlightenment is like the swift thrust of a sword to the center of things, then both worldliness and holiness are completely eliminated and Absolute Reality is revealed. Thus the One and the Many are identified. This is the *Suchness* of Buddha."

Isan's disciple, Yang-shan Hui-chi (Kyōzan Ejaku, 807-883), was a native of Huai-hua in Shao-chou (now Chu-chiang in Northern Kwangtung Province). When he was seventeen, he cut off two fingers and then obtained his parents' permission to leave home and become a monk. He went to Nan-hua Monastery (Nanka-ji), where the Sixth Patriarch was enshrined, to have his head shaved. Later he went to visit Master Isan. Isan asked him: "Are you your own master or not?" Kyōzan answered:

沩山。"百丈说:"你拨一下炉中,看是否还有炭火。"沩山拨后说:"已经没有了。"百丈禅师从座中站起来,深拨炉内有火处,取出一小块还在燃烧的炭给沩山看,说:"这不是炭火吗?"沩山即悟,深深鞠了一躬。百丈就读了一段佛经,经中大意为:

　　要见佛性,当观时节因缘,时节到来时,就像是从迷梦中一觉醒来,也像是忽然想起了久忘之事,于是就能认识到:所获得的原是来自本心而不是来自外界。

下面一些故事引自张钟元译的《佛教禅宗之源》第200—208页:

　　有一天,沩山灵祐禅师来到佛堂,对众人讲:"悟禅之人的心是平静坦然、直率无伪的,既无正面,也无背面。没有欺骗,也没有虚妄。每天时时刻刻所闻所见,都是寻常的事和物,未受扭曲的本来面目。不要闭目塞听,而要做到情不附物。过去许多圣人也都强调要能承受愚蠢和污浊的迷惑和困扰。当终能排除迷妄、邪念、幻想等恶习之时,那么心灵就会像秋水一样清澈宁静,淡泊洁净,像这样的人就可称为禅道中人,即不随附于任何事物之人。"……

　　有一次沩山禅师在佛堂上向众人说法时,说:"启悟之道就像一把利剑直插事物中心,不管世俗还是神圣都完全消失,而真理显露。把一和多统一起来,即是佛性。"

沩山灵祐的弟子仰山慧寂(807—883)是韶州怀化(在今广东番禺东南)人。17岁时,慧寂自断两只手指,表示决心,要求父母允许他出家为僧。他到南华寺落发,寺内供奉着六祖之龛。后来又去参拜沩山禅师。师问:"你有自主吗,还是没有呢?"

"I am." Isan asked: "Where is your own master?" Kyōzan walked away from the west of the hall to the east and stood there. Isan recognized immediately that he was an unusual man (that is, a dharma vessel) and decided to teach him. One day Kyōzan asked the Master: "Where is the abiding place of the real Buddha?" Isan answered:

Imagine the wonder of no-thought and trace it back to the infinity of the light of the spirit. While thoughts are exhausted and returned to their source, nature and appearance are ever abiding. Reality and events are no longer differentiated. Therein is the real *Buddha of Suchness*.

Hearing this, Kyōzan was suddenly enlightened. Kyōzan lived to seventy-seven years of age. He left the following gāthā:

My age, a full seventy-seven.
Even now I am fading away.
Rising and falling, let nature take its course.
In my two arms I hold my bended knee.

Isan had another disciple Hsiang-yen Chih-hsien (Kyōgen Chikan), who was disappointed in the beginning and left. When he arrived at the tomb of National Teacher Nan-yang Hui-chung (Nan'yō Echū Kokushi), he built a hut nearby and stayed there. One day while he was weeding, a piece of rock which he had dislodged struck a bamboo tree. The sound it produced awakened him to laughter and sudden enlightenment. Then a gāthā he made testified to his gratitude to Master Isan.

With one stroke, all previous knowledge is forgotten.
No cultivation is needed for this.
This occurrence reveals the ancient way
And is free from the track of quiescence.
No trace is left anywhere.
Whatever I hear and see does not conform to rules.
All those who are enlightened
Proclaim this to be the greatest action.

慧寂答："有主。"师问："主在哪里？"慧寂从堂西走到堂东，就停步了。沩山禅师立即觉察到他不是寻常人，决心收为弟子并教导他。有一天慧寂问禅师："真佛住在哪里？"沩山禅师回答：

想象"无思"的奇妙，并一直追思到灵光无穷处，思尽了再还归本源，在这里本性和相状都永恒存在，事和理并无区分。真佛即在此。

慧寂听后，就立刻开悟；后于77岁时圆寂，留下一首诗偈：

年满七十七，老去是今日。
任性自浮沉，两手攀屈膝。

沩山另有一弟子香严智闲，起初觉得失望而离去。他到达南阳，见到了国师南阳慧忠之墓，就在附近筑一茅舍住下了。有一天他在除杂草时丢掷的一块瓦砾，击中了一棵竹树，发出声响，正失笑间，忽然省悟。于是就作了一首诗偈，以表示对大师沩山的感谢之心，大意如下：

就是这一击，使过去一切所知都忘却，
更不需任何修炼学习。
此事显示了一条终古大路，
没有什么悄然良机，
也不留任何踪迹，
所闻所见更不合任何仪式。
所有悟道人都称赞说：
这才是最高上上根机。

附原文如下：

一击忘所知，更不假修持。
动容扬古路，不堕悄然机。
处处无踪迹，声色外威仪。
诸方达道者，咸言上上机。

Kyōgen then came to the assembly and said:

> The Tao is attained by one's inner awakening; it does not depend
> upon words. Look at the invisible and boundless. Where can you find
> any intermittances? How can you reach it by the labor of the intellect? It
> is simply the reflection of illumination, and that is your whole daily task.
> Only those who are ignorant will go in the opposite direction.

Answering a monk's question "What is Tao?," Kyōgen remarked: "A
dragon is singing in the decaying woods." The monk did not understand.
So Kyōgen added: "The eyes in the skull."

The above English translations were taken from Professor Chang
Chung-yuan's *Original Teachings of Ch'an Buddhism*, pages 219-228.

The Igyō School did not flourish after four or five generations.
Kyōzan's disciples were:

Hsi-ta Kuang-mo (Saitō Kōboku)

Nan-ta Kuang-yung (Nantō Kōyō)

Lung-chuan Wen-hsi (Ryūsen Bunki, 820-899)

Huo-shan Ching-tung (Kakusan Keitsu)

Shun-chih (Junshi of Korea)

Saitō had one disciple: Tzu-fu Ju-pao (Shifuku Nyohō), whose
disciples were Tzu-fu Chen-sui (Shifuku Teisui) and Pao-tzu Te-shao (Hōji
Tokusho). Pao-tzu had two disciples: San-chueh Chih-chien (Sankaku
Shiken) and Hsing-yang Tzu-to (Kōyō Jitō). Nantō had three disciples:
Pa-chiao Hui-ching (Bashō Esei), Huang-lien I-chu (Ōren Gisho) and
Ching-hua Chuan-fu (Seike Zenfu). Bashō Esei had six disciples: Hsing-
yang Ching-jang (Kōyō Seijō), Yu-ku Fa-man (Yukoku Hōman), Pa-chiao
Ju-yu (Bashō Jigu), Pa-chiao Chi-che (Bashō Keitetsu), Shu-ning Shan-yi
(Junei Zengi), and Chen-tien Tzu-huo (Shōten Jikaku). Shōten's disciple
was Lo-han Chi-tsung (Rakan Keishū).

Besides Hyakujō, Baso had an outstanding disciple, Nan-chuan Pu-
yuan (Nansen Fugan, 748-834). Nansen was a native of Hsin-cheng in
Chengchow (present Honan Province). In 757 A.D., when he was ten years

old, he studied under Nangaku Ejō. After he acquired a thorough knowledge of Buddhist philosophy, he became a disciple of Baso, and achieved sudden enlightenment. The following anecdotes were recorded in the *Lamp Records*, Vol. 8, reprinted in *Daishō Daizōkyō*, Vol. 51, pages 257-259.

One day while Nan-chuan (Nansen) was serving rice gruel to his fellow monks, his Master, Ma-tsu (Baso), asked him: "What is in the

智闲来到佛堂向众人讲：

道由悟达，不在语言。况见密密堂堂，曾无间隔。不劳心意，暂借回光，日用全功，迷徒自背。

在回答一僧"如何是道"的提问时，智闲说："枯木里龙吟。"僧不理解，于是智闲再说："骷髅里眼睛。"

这些内容在张钟元教授《佛教禅宗之源》第219—228页中译成了英文。

沩仰宗在传了四五代之后就不再继续兴盛了。仰山的弟子有：

西塔光穆

南塔光涌

龙泉文喜（820—899）

霍山景通

新罗顺支

西塔光穆有一弟子资福如宝，资福如宝的弟子为资福贞邃和报慈德韶。报慈有二弟子：三角志谦和兴阳词铎。南塔光涌则有三个弟子：芭蕉慧清、黄连义初和清化全怤。芭蕉慧清有六个弟子：兴阳清让、幽谷法满、芭蕉住遇、芭蕉继彻、寿宁善义和承天辞確。承天辞確的弟子是罗汉继宗。

除百丈外，马祖还有一卓越弟子南泉普愿（748—834），是郑州新郑（在今河南省）人。公元757年，在他10岁时，从大慧禅师受业（据《五灯会元》，"唐至德二年依大隈山大慧禅师受业"。南岳怀让[Nangaku Ejō]744年卒，谥大慧禅师，并非同一人），深入学得了佛学哲理后，成为马祖的弟子，并获得了顿悟。下述故事载于《传灯录》第8卷，又载于《大正藏》第51卷，第257—259页。

有一天南泉在为众僧人分粥时，马祖大师问他："桶里是

wooden bucket?" Nan-chuan replied: "This old fellow should keep his mouth shut and not say such words."

In 795 A.D., when he was forty-eight years old, Nansen moved to Chih-yang and built a small temple on the top of Mount Nan-chuan (Nansenzan). He remained there for thirty years, never once coming down. Before the Master passed away, the head monk asked him: "Where are you going after you passed away?" The Master answered: "I am going down the hill to be a water buffalo." The monk continued: "Would it be possible to follow you there?" The Master answered: "If you want to follow me, you must come with a piece of straw in your mouth."

Nansen's famous disciple, Chao-chou Tsung-shen (Jōshū Jūshin, 778-897), was a native of Ho-hsiang in Tsao-chou (present Shantung Province). Before he was ordained, he visited Nansen. He arrived while Nansen was lying down resting. Nansen asked Jōshū: "Where have you just come from?" Jōshū replied: "I have just left the Shui-hsiang Monastery (Zuizō-ji)." Note that "Shui-hsiang" means "auspicious image" and that the Monastery had an image of Buddha. The Master asked: "Have you seen the standing image of Buddha?" Jōshū answered: "What I see is not a standing image of Buddha, but a supine Enlightened One!" The Master asked: "Are you your own master?" Jōshū answered: "Yes, I am." "Where is this master of yours?" asked the Master. Jōshū said: "In the middle of the winter the weather becomes bitterly cold. I wish all blessings on you, Master!" At this, Nansen permitted him to become his disciple. The following anecdotes were taken from Professor Chang Chung-yuan's translation in *Original Teachings of Ch'an Buddhism*, pages 153-163:

> Once Master Nan-chuan (Nansen) remarked:
>
> "In the middle of last night I gave Monju (Manjusri) and Fu-gen (Samantabhadra) each twenty blows and chased them out of my temple."
>
> Chao-chou (Jōshū) challenged him:
>
> "To whom have you given your blows?"

The Master answered:

"Could you tell me where Teacher Wang's mistake was?"

(Nan-chuan's family name was WANG.)

Chao-chou bowed and departed.

...

On one occasion the Master (Nansen) stated:

"Ma-tsu (Baso) of Kiangsi maintained that the Mind is the Buddha.

However, Teacher Wang (meaning Nan-chuan himself) would not say it

什么？"南泉却说："此老汉应该闭他的嘴，不要说这种话。"

公元 795 年，南泉 48 岁时迁居池阳，在当地南泉山巅建了一座小禅寺，就在那里待了三十年，从不下山。在将去世前，首座僧问："大师离此后将去哪里？"师答："我将下山做一条水牛去。"僧再问："我能随师一起去吗？"师答："如果你愿跟我去，必须口衔一枚草。"

南泉有一著名弟子赵州从谂（778—897），是曹州郝乡（在今山东曹县）人。在尚未受戒之前就来参拜南泉禅师，正好禅师在休息，问赵州："你刚才从哪里来？"赵州答："刚才离开瑞像院。"师问："见到了瑞像吗？"赵州答："我未见瑞像，只见卧如来。"师问："你是有主沙弥，还是无主沙弥？"答："是有主沙弥。"师问："主在哪里？"赵州答："早春犹寒，愿师尊万福。"于是南泉就接受他为弟子了。下述故事引自张钟元教授《佛教禅宗之源》第 153—163 页。

有一次南泉禅师这样说："昨天深夜，向文殊和普贤各打二十下，赶出了本院。"

赵州追问师父：

"师父打了谁？"

南泉禅师回答：

"你能告诉我王老师错在哪里呢？"（南泉禅师出家前的俗姓为王）

赵州礼拜而出。……

又有一次南泉禅师说：

"江西马祖说心即是佛，佛即是心。可是王老师（南泉自称）

this way. He would advocate 'Not Mind, not Buddha, not things.' Is there any mistake when I say this way?"

After listening to this, Chao-chou (Jōshū) made a bow and went away. Thereupon a monk followed him (Jōshū), saying, "What did you mean just now, when you bowed and left the Master?" Chao-chou replied: "You will have to ask the Master." The monk went to the Master (Nansen) and said, "Why did Jūshin (Jōshū) behave that way a moment ago?" Nan-chuan exclaimed, "He understood my meaning!"

…

Chao-chou asked:

"Tao is not external to things: the externality of things is not Tao. Then what is the Tao that is beyond things?" Master Nan-chuan struck him. Thereupon Chao-chou took hold of the stick and said, "From now on, do not strike a man by mistake!" The Master said, "We can easily differentiate between a dragon and a snake, but nobody can fool a Ch'an (Zen) monk."

…

One day an elder monk asked Master Nan-chuan (Nansen), "When we say, 'The Mind is the Buddha,' we are wrong. But when we say, 'Not Mind, not Buddha,' we are not correct, either. What is your idea about this?" Master Nan-chuan answered: "You should believe 'The Mind is the Buddha' and let it go at that. Why should you talk about right or wrong? It is just the same as when you come to eat your meal. Do you choose to come to it through the west corridor, or by another way? You cannot ask others which is wrong."

We may remark that Jōshū would not ask such a question as the elder monk did. The most significant conversation (mondō) between Nansen and Jōshū went as follows:

Jōshū: "What is Tao?"

Nansen: "*Everyday-mindedness* is Tao."

Jōshū: "Is it possible to approach it?"

Nansen: "If you intentionally approach it, you will miss it."

Jōshū: "If you do not approach it intentionally, how can you know it?"

Master Nansen then explained to Jōshū: "Tao is not a matter either of knowing or of not-knowing. Knowing is a delusion; not-knowing is indifference. When one has really attained Tao with non-intention, one

却不这样说，而倡导'不是心，不是佛，也不是物'。我这样说有什么错吗？"

赵州听后礼拜而出。有一僧跟随赵州之后，问他："你刚才向师父礼拜，然后就离开了，这是什么意思？"赵州答："你应该去问师父。"于是那僧就去问师父："刚才从谂为什么这样做？"师父惊叹说："他完全领会了我的旨意！"……

赵州从谂问："道不在事物之外，事物之外就不是道。那么事物之外的道是什么呢？"南泉禅师打了他一下。赵州抓住了棒说："今后请不要因任何人错了就打他。"大师说："我们很容易把龙和蛇区分开来，但谁都不能去愚弄一位禅僧。"……

一天，有一老僧问南泉禅师："我们如果说心即是佛，我们就错了。但如果说不是心、不是佛，我们也不对。那么请教师父，究竟应该怎样说呢？"南泉禅师回答："你只要深信心即是佛，那就这样，又何必去议论它是对是错呢？正好像你每次来斋堂就餐时，穿过东廊西廊或其他什么处，不会去问怎样走才是对的或错的。"

我们可以这样说，赵州从谂当然不会像那老僧提这样的问题。在南泉禅师与赵州之间曾有一段很有意义的对话：

赵州问："什么是道？"

南泉答："平常心是道。"

赵州问："能趋近它吗？"

南泉答："如果你故意企求趋近它，那么你就会错过它。"

赵州问："如果不故意企求趋近它，那么又怎能认识它呢？"

于是南泉禅师就向赵州解释说："道并不属于那种可认识或不可认识的事理。认识只是一种幻觉，不认识又是漠然无知。不企求趋近它而确实达到的道，就好像是处于太空中，完全

is as if in the great *VOID*, free from obstruction and limitation. How can any assertion or negation be made?"

Hearing this, Jōshū was awakened. After his ordainment, one day Jōshū returned to Nansen and asked, "Where should one rest after having attained Tao?" The Master replied, "One should become a buffalo down the hill." Then Jōshū thanked the Master for this instruction. Nansen further remarked: "In the middle of last night, the moonlight shone on the window." So Nansen and Jōshū were an ideal pair—Master and disciple.

Jōshū lived to the venerable age of one hundred and twenty years. The recent Chinese Zen Priest Hsu Yun (Kiun, 1840-1959), whom the author had the privilege of meeting at Tsao-chi (Sōkei) and Chungking, lived to one hundred and twenty years.

Chao-chou Tsung-shen (Jōshū Jūshin, 778-897) of the Kuan-yin Monastery in Chao-chou (near present Shih-chia-chuang, Hopei Province) was a native of Ho-hsiang in Tsao-chou (Shantung Province). He became a monk when he was a child. Later he met Nansen, Ōbaku, Hōju, Enkan and Kassan, but received the confirmation from Nansen. From the *Lamp Records*, Vol. 10 (See *Daishō Daizōkyō*, Vol. 51, pages 276-278), there were many anecdotes. Professor Chang Chung-yuan's translation gave the following:

> Jōshū visited Ōbaku, who closed the door of his chamber when Ōbaku saw Jōshū coming. Whereupon Chao-chou (Jōshū) lit a torch in the Dharma Hall and cried out for help. Ōbaku immediately opened the door and grabbed him, demanding, "Speak! Speak!" Chao-chou answered: "After the thief is gone, you draw your bow!"
>
> ...
>
> Jōshū visited Hōju (Pao-shou, a disciple of Rinzai) at his monastery. When Pao-shou (Hōju) saw him coming, he turned around in his seat. Chao-chou unfolded his sitting cloth and bowed. Pao-shou came down from his seat, and Chao-chou immediately left him.

...

Jōshū visited Enkan and said to him, "Watch the arrow!"

Enkan (Yan-kuan) answered, "It is gone!"

Chao-chou said: "It hit the target."

...

无障碍和无界限，又怎能强说肯定或否定呢？"

赵州听后得到了启发而领悟。在受戒之后，赵州有一天回到了南泉禅师处，问："在已得道之后又该去哪里作息呢？"禅师说："应下山去做一条牛。"赵州拜谢了大师的指示。禅师还这样说："昨夜三更时，明月照窗上。"所以南泉和赵州是一对很理想的师徒。

赵州高寿达 120 岁。本书作者曾有幸在曹溪和重庆见到过的近代中国禅师虚云老和尚，同样也享年 120 岁（1840—1959 ）。

赵州从谂（778—897）是曹州（在今山东）人，但是居住在赵州（今河北石家庄附近）观音院。他在童年就出家做了和尚。后来他拜谒和遇见过南泉、黄檗、宝寿、盐官和夹山等众多禅师，见道于南泉。在《传灯录》第 10 卷中（见《大正藏》第 51 卷，第 276—278 页）载有许多有关他的故事，下面一些内容已由张钟元教授译成英文：

赵州去拜访黄檗禅师。黄檗见他来了，却关门不想见他。于是赵州就在法堂内点燃了火炬，并高声呼救。黄檗只得立刻开门抓住了他，要他"快讲！快讲！"赵州回答："等贼走了以后，你方才张弓！"……

赵州来到宝寿（临济的一个弟子）的寺中，要想见他。宝寿见到他来，就在座中转过身去，背向着他。赵州打开坐具并行了礼，然后宝寿方从座中走下来，而赵州却立刻离开他走了。……

赵州访问盐官，向他说："看箭！"盐官回答："箭已经过了！"赵州说："箭已中了靶。"……

Jōshū arrived at Kassan's monastery and went to the Dharma Hall with a staff in his hand. Chia-shan (Kassan) asked him, "What is the staff for?" "To test the depth of the water" was the answer. Chia-shan said, "There is not a drop here. What can you test?" Jōshū leaned on his staff and went away.

...

Jōshū was invited to stay in the Kuan-yin (Kannon) Monastery in his native town of Chao-chou. He came to the assembly and said: "It is as if a transparent crystal were held in one's hand. When a foreigner approaches it, it mirrors him as such. I take a stalk of grass and let it act as a golden-bodied one, sixteen feet high, and I take a golden-bodied one, sixteen feet high and let it act as a stalk of grass. Buddhahood is passion (*klesa*), and passion is Buddhahood."

During this sermon a monk asked him: "In whom does Buddha cause passion?" Jōshū: "Buddha causes passion in all of us." Monk: "How do we get rid of it?" Jōshū: "Why should we get rid of it?"

The following is a famous anecdote:

A monk asked, "Since all things return to One, where does this One return to?" Jōshū replied: "When I was in Tsing-chou, I had a robe made which weighed seven *chin*."

Another incident is also given in Professor Chang's translation:

Someone was walking in the garden with the Master (Chao-chou) and saw a rabbit running away in fright. He asked, "How could the rabbit be frightened and run away from you, since you are a great Buddhist?" To this the Master replied, "It is because I like to kill."

"To kill" might be a figurative speech. When the Master failed to rise from his seat to greet the Prince-General of Chen-ting, the Master explained:

Ever since my younger days
I have abstained from meat.
Now my body is getting old.

Whenever I see my visitors

I have no strength left for coming down from the Buddha-seat.

As vegetarians, all Buddhists in China refrained from any killing of living things. However, the story of the killing of a cat, in which both Nan-chuan and Chao-chou were involved, is almost unbelievable. According to *Wu-men-kuan* (*Mumon-kan*), the episode was related as follows:

赵州到了夹山大师的寺中，拿了手杖来到法堂。夹山问他："拿手杖做什么？"回答："用来探水的深浅。"夹山说："这里连一滴水也没有，你能探到些什么？"于是赵州就倚杖而走了。……

赵州从谂被邀请住进赵州的观音院。他上堂对众人讲："那就像一颗晶莹剔透的明珠被拿在手掌中。胡人来了它就反映出胡人。我拿一株草当作一丈六尺金身用，而一丈六尺金身则当作一株草用。佛是烦恼，烦恼是佛。"一僧问道："不明白佛引起什么烦恼？"赵州答："引起一切人间烦恼。"僧问："怎样方可排除烦恼呢？"赵州答："那又为什么要去排除烦恼呢？"

下面是一个有名的故事：

一僧问："万物都回归为'一'，那么'一'回归到哪里？"赵州说："当我在青州时，我做了一件袈裟布衫重七斤。"

在张钟元教授译文中还有一段故事：

有一客人陪同赵州大师在园中散步，见到一兔子受惊奔逃。客问："你是佛门大禅师，为什么兔子见到你会惊恐奔逃呢？"大师回答："为老僧好杀。"

这里的"杀"可能是象征性的比喻字。有一次，有一真定将军王公贵人来访，大师未从座中起立去迎接，而解释说：

自小持斋身已老，见人无力下禅床。

中国佛教信众一般常吃素（斋），戒杀生。下述涉及南泉和赵州有关杀猫的故事不太可信。根据《无门关》所载，故事如下：

Once in the monastery of Master Nan-chuan, the disciples of the East Hall and of the West Hall had an argument about a cat. Nan-chuan grabbed the cat and, holding it aloft, said: "If any one of you assembled here can say the right thing, the cat will be saved; if not, it will be killed." No one was able to answer. Thereupon Nan-chuan killed the cat. In the evening Chao-chou, who had been away for the day, returned. Nan-chuan turned to him and asked, "What would you have said had you been here?" Chao-chou took off his straw sandals, put them on his head, and walked out. "If you had been here," commented Nan-chuan, "the cat would have been saved."

This is case No. 14, and the English translation is taken from Dumoulin-Peachey, *A History of Zen Buddhism*, page 99. Dumoulin commented:

The saving word lay in the seemingly senseless action, which transcended all affirmation and negation.

There is no logical solution to the "paradoxical words and strange actions" which were introduced into Southern Chinese Zen, especially through Ma-tsu. The paradox discloses itself in the pregnant meaning of meaninglessness, to be found in the concrete situation of enlightenment. Probably the Zen master with the richest record of paradoxical sayings and remarkable actions is Chao-chou. Some of his sayings lend themselves to interpretation, as when he answers a request for instruction about enlightenment by simply saying, "Go wash your bowl." Enlightenment can be found in everyday life...

In the history of Chinese Ch'an (Zen), there were a number of lay disciples who attained great fame, among them were Wang Wei (699-759), the famous poet-painter, and Pang Yun (d. 811), the disciple of Baso.

Wang Wei was a contemporary of Nan-yang Hui-chung (Nan'yō Echū), Shih-tou Hsi-chien (Sekitō Kisen), and Ma-tsu Tao-i (Baso Dōitsu). He took the courtesy name Mu-chi (after *Vimalakirti*). His inscription for the Sixth Patriarch's biographical account indicated the depth of his understanding of Hui-neng's Ch'an teaching:

When there is nothing to give up
One has indeed reached the Source.
When there is no void to abide in
One is indeed experiencing the Void.

有一次在南泉大师寺院中，东西两佛堂的弟子们对一只猫发生了争论。南泉抓住了这只猫，高高举起说："你们中间如果有人说对了，此猫就可得救。否则就杀了此猫。"结果无人能回答，南泉就把猫杀了。当时赵州白天不在，傍晚才回来。南泉就问他："假使你在的话，你会怎样讲？"赵州脱下他的草鞋，放在头上便走了。南泉解释说："如果赵州在这里，此猫就可得救了。"

参见杜慕林著、保罗·披切译《佛教禅宗史》第99页，第14例。杜慕林的评注说：

在这看来几乎毫无意义的行动中，"得救"之辞却超脱了所有的肯定和否定的言辞。

在中国的禅宗南支中，尤其是由马祖禅师所引入的那些"悖论言辞和怪异行动"中，是找不到合逻辑的解答的。在启示领悟的具体情况下，这些悖论却能展示出所孕育的深刻意义。在所有禅师中，要以赵州禅师在悖论言辞和怪异行动上有着最丰富的记录。也有某些言辞却是可以得到解释的。例如在请求对"启示领悟"作指示时，只是简单地回答："洗钵盂去。"这就是说，只要从日常生活中就可以得到领悟……

在中国禅宗历史上，有很多极有名望的居士，例如著名的诗人和画家王维（699—759）及马祖的弟子庞蕴（？—811）。

王维是南阳慧忠、石头希迁和马祖道一等禅师的同时代人。王维字摩诘（源自《维摩诘经》），在他为"六祖传"所撰碑铭中，显示出他对慧能所传禅宗的教旨有很深刻的理解：

当不再剩下什么不可丢弃时，
你就的确到达了源头处。
当不再有任何空间可以居留时，
你就的确认识体会了太空。

> Transcending quiescence is no-action.
>
> Rather it is Creation, which constantly acts.

This translation appeared on page 144 of Chang's *Original Teachings of Ch'an Buddhism*.

Pang Yun (Hō Kōji), his wife, and his daughter, Ling-chao (Reishō), were all devoted to Ch'an (Zen). Pang Yun once remarked:

> How difficult it is!
>
> How difficult it is!
>
> My studies are like dying the fibers of a thousand pounds of flax in the sun by hanging them on the trees!

His wife responded:

> My way is easy indeed!
>
> I found the teachings of the Patriarchs right on the tops of the flowering plants!

Their daughter, Ling-chao (Reishō), said:

> My study is neither difficult nor easy.
>
> When I am hungry I eat.
>
> When I am tired I rest.

The daughter got ahead of her father, while Pang Yun was ready to pass away. See Chang's *Original Teachings of Ch'an Buddhism*, page 145 and pages 174-177.

According to *Dharma Records of Abbot Hsu Yun*, Vol. 8, pages 262-265, he was revered as the Eighth Patriarch of the Igyō School. His disciple, Reverend Hsuan-hua (Senka), then becomes the Ninth Patriarch in the Igyō line. Reverend Hsuan-hua is the Chief Abbot of the Gold Mountain Temple, San Francisco, and the founder of Dharma Realm University, Talmage, California, U.S.A.

超越了宁静，那就不是行动，
而是创造，永远在起作用。

原文为：

> 无有可舍，
> 是达有源。
> 无空可住，
> 是知空本。
> 离寂非动，
> 乘化用常。

参见张钟元《佛教禅宗之源》第 144 页的译文。

庞蕴以及他的妻子和女儿灵照都信奉禅宗。庞蕴曾这样说：

> 这真太难啊！
> 真太难啊！
> 我的钻研就好像要染千斤的麻，
> 悬挂树上，在太阳光下晒！

他的妻子回应说：

> 我行的道实在很简要！
> 我就在开着花朵的树顶上找到了
> 师父的教导。

他们的女儿灵照说：

> 我的钻研不难也不易。
> 饥了我就吃，
> 倦了我就歇。

当庞蕴即将去世时，他的女儿恰巧比他稍早一步抢先走了。参见张钟元《佛教禅宗之源》第 145 页以及第 174—177 页。

根据《虚云和尚法汇》第 8 卷第 262—265 页，他被尊为沩仰宗第八祖，所以他的弟子宣化法师就成为沩仰宗第九祖。宣化法师是美国旧金山市金山寺的住持方丈，是美国塔尔马奇佛法大学的创建人。

CHAPTER 4   THE RINZAI SCHOOL

Huang-po Hsi-yun (Ōbaku Kiun, d. 850 A.D.) was a dharma-heir of Po-chang Huai-hai (Hyakujō Ekai, 720-814), and hence a dharma brother of Kuei-shan Ling-yu (Isan Reiyū, 771-853), Chang-ching Ta-an (Chōkei Daian, 793-883), and Ta-tzu Huan-chung (Daiji Kanchū, 780-862). Huang-po (Ōbaku) became a monk when he was a child. He was confirmed or ordained by Po-chang (Hyakujō). He was then invited to preside over a big temple newly built and named after Huang-po Shan (Mount Ōbaku). His fame was far and wide, and more than one thousand faithful followers gathered around him. He left posterity with his *The Essence of Mind*, recorded and collected by Pei Hsiu the Prime Minister (Haikyū Shōkoku), a great admirer of Ōbaku and also a good friend of Kuei-feng Tsung-mi (Keihō Shūmitsu, 780-841). In Pei Hsiu's Preface, 858 A.D., he recorded how in 843 and in 849 he questioned Master Ōbaku and put down the answers in writing. Some abstracts were taken from R. H. Blyth's *Zen and Zen Classics*, Vol. 3, Chapter 5 as follows:

> The material things before you—that is it. But when the (rational) mind moves, we deny it, we refuse it.
>
> Pei Hsiu (Haikyū) said, "Illusion obstructs the Mind; how can illusion be got rid of?" Huang-po (Ōbaku) said, "Creating illusion, getting rid of illusion—both these are illusion, for illusion has no root; it appears by reason of discrimination. If you do not think of contraries such as ordinary and superior, illusion ceases of itself, and how can you get rid of it? When there is not a hair's breadth of something to rely on, this is called, 'Giving away with both hands, and thus receiving Buddhahood.'" Pei Hsiu (Haikyū) said, "There being nothing to rely on, how can anything be transmitted?" Huang-po (Ōbaku) said, "Mind is transmitted by Mind." Pei Hsiu (Haikyū) said, "If the Mind is transmitted, why do you say there is no such thing as Mind?" Huang-po (Ōbaku) said, "Not receiving the Law (Dharma) is called 'transmission of Mind.' If you understand what this Mind is, this is the No-Mind, the No-Law." Pei

Hsiu (Haikyū) said, "If there's no Mind, and no Law, how can you talk about 'transmitting' something?" Huang-po (Ōbaku) said, "When you hear me say 'transmission of Mind,' you think of there being a 'something' to transmit, so a Patriarch declared:

肆 临济宗

　　黄檗希运（？—850）是百丈怀海（720—814）的法嗣，因此也是沩山灵祐（771—853）、长庆大安（793—883）和大慈寰中（780—862）的师兄弟。黄檗年幼时就出家做和尚，拜百丈为师，并受戒。黄檗山上新建的大禅寺黄檗寺请他去住持说法。他声名远播，有一千多信众前来听他讲道传法。黄檗口述《传法心要》，由相国裴休集记汇编成卷，传与后世。裴休十分崇奉黄檗，也是圭峰宗密（780—841）的好友。裴休在序言中（公元858年）叙述了他在843年与849年是怎样向黄檗大师提问，并把大师的解答用文字记录下来的，以下片段引自R. H. 布莱思《禅与禅宗经典》第3卷第5章：

　　出现在你面前的事物虽是存在，但当此心（理性）运作时，我们就能够否定它，不接受它。裴休问："幻觉掩蔽了心，那么该怎样来消除幻觉呢？"黄檗说："产生幻觉和消除幻觉，两者本身其实都是幻觉。幻觉本无根，只是由于要区分事物，就产生了幻觉。如果不去思考事物之间的矛盾或对立，那么幻觉就停止而且不存在了，你又能怎样去消除它呢？当不存在任何一丝一毫之地可以依赖时，那就'用双手丢弃这一切，这样就能得到佛法。'"裴休说："如果没有什么可以依赖，那么佛法怎样能相传呢？"黄檗说："以心传心。"裴休说："既然心心相传，为什么又说心不存在呢？"黄檗说："不接受'法'就是'传心'。如果你悟解了什么是心，那就是无心和无法。"裴休说："既然无心和无法，那又怎能谈论可以相传些什么呢？"黄檗说："当你听我说心心相传时，你是在想：有某些东西在那里相传。有一位禅师曾这样说：

When you realize the nature of Mind,

You speak of it as a wonderful mystery;

Enlightenment is unattainable;

When attained, you do not describe it as something known.

If I get you to understand this, do you think you could?"

According to the *Lamp Records*, Vol. 12, Ōbaku had thirteen disciples, among them:

(1) Lin-chi I-hsuan (Rinzai Gigen, d. 866)

(2) Mu-chou Tao-tsung (Bokujū Dōshō)

(3) Wei-fu Ta-chueh (Ifu Daikaku)

(4) Chien-ching Tsu-nan (Senkei Sonan)

(5) O-shih Ling-kuah (Useki Reikan)

(6) Lo-han Tsung-che (Rakan Sōsetsu)

(7) Pei Hsiu the Prime Minister (Haikyū Shōkoku)

Mu-chou Tao-tsung was also known as Chen the Elder (Chin Sonshuku), whose disciple was Chen Tsao (Chinsō), prefect of Mu-chou. Mu-chou Tao-tsung (Bokujū Dōshō) used to make straw sandals and secretly put them by the road. He was thus known as "Sandal Chen." Those Ch'an (Zen) learners who were highly endowed with talents greatly respected him. For anecdotes of him, the reader is referred to Professor Chang Chung-yuan's *Original Teachings of Ch'an Buddhism*, pages 107-115, and to R. H. Blyth's *Zen and Zen Classics*, Vol. 3, pages 138-144.

Lin-chi I-hsuan (Rinzai Gigen, d. 866) was the founder of the Lin-chi or Rinzai School. Rinzai was a native of Nanhua in Tsao-chou (Sōshū), now Tsao-Hsien, southwest of Tsining, in Shantung Province. He studied under Ōbaku. One day the head monk Chen the Elder (Chin Sonshuku) suggested that he should go to see Master Ōbaku alone. So Rinzai went to Ōbaku's room and asked him: "What is the real meaning of Bodhidharma (Daruma) coming from the West?" The Master struck him at once. Rinzai visited the Master three times, and each time he received blows. Rinzai was ready to leave, and Master Ōbaku advised him to visit Master Kao-an

Ta-yu (Kōan Daigu), disciple of Kuei-tsung Chih-chang (Kisū Chijō). Kōan Daigu said something which enlightened Rinzai and sent him back to Ōbaku. Rinzai, though he realized Ōbaku's "motherly kindness," was

当你理解心的本性时，
你把它说成是像奇异的奥秘；
那就达不到启示领悟；
如果启悟了，就不会把它描述为
已知的任何事物。
我想帮助你理解它，你认为你能够吗？"

根据《传灯录》第12卷，黄檗有弟子十三人，他们之中有：
（1）临济义玄（？—866）
（2）睦州道踪（陈尊宿）
（3）魏府大觉
（4）千顷楚南
（5）乌石灵观
（6）罗汉宗彻
（7）相国裴休

睦州道踪也被称为"陈尊宿"（受人尊敬的陈姓长者——译者注），睦州刺史陈操是他的弟子。道踪经常自编草鞋，暗地里放置路旁，帮助穿破鞋的行人，所以也被称为"陈蒲鞋"。许多很有才华的学禅人士都非常尊敬他。有关他的故事读者可以参阅张钟元教授《佛教禅宗之源》第107—115页，以及R. H. 布莱思《禅与禅宗经典》第3卷第138—144页。

临济义玄（？—866）是临济宗的创建人，原籍曹州南华（在今山东曹县，济宁的西南方），拜黄檗为师。有一天首座僧陈尊宿建议他应该单独去拜见黄檗禅师。于是他就去禅师房中求教，问："什么是佛法大义？"禅师打了他一下。就这样他前后共三次去拜见禅师，每次都挨了打。于是临济就准备向禅师告辞了。黄檗推荐他去拜见圭宗智常的弟子高安大愚禅师。临济听了高安的一些说教之后，得到了启悟。高安仍叫他回到黄檗处去。临济知道黄檗

ready to slap Master Ōbaku, who cried out: "What a crazy fellow! He is coming to pluck the tiger's beard!" Rinzai immediately cried out: "Kwatz!" As Rinzai attained *satori*, or enlightenment, he was quite a different person. He exclaimed: "There is not much after all in the Buddhism of Ōbaku." (See Suzuki: *Essays in Zen Buddhism*, First Series, page 247.)

Rinzai-roku was a collection of dialogues by Master Rinzai, which revealed his teachings. As translated by Alan W. Watts in *The Way of Zen*, the following passages are illuminating (see pages 101-102):

Why do I talk here? Only because you followers of the Tao go galloping around in search of the Mind, and are unable to stop it. On the other hand, the ancients acted in a leisurely way, appropriate to circumstances (as they arose).

O you followers of the Tao—when you get my point of view you will sit in judgment on top of the... Buddhas' heads. Those who have completed the ten stages will seem like underlings, and those who have arrived at Supreme Awakening will seem as if they had cangues around their necks. The Arhans and Pratyeka-buddhas are like a dirty privy. *Bodhi* and *nirvana* are like hitch-posts for a donkey.

There is no place in Buddhism for using effort. Just be ordinary and nothing special. Relieve your bowels, pass water, put on your clothes, and eat your food. When you're tired, go and lie down. Ignorant people may laugh at me, but the wise will understand... As you go from place to place, if you regard each one as your own home, they will all be genuine, for when circumstances come, you must not try to change them. Thus your usual habits of feeling, which make *karma* for the Five Hells, will of themselves become the Great Ocean of Liberation.

Outside the Mind there is no Dharma, and inside also there is nothing to be grasped. What is it that you seek? You say on all sides that the Tao is to be practiced and put to the proof. Don't be mistaken! If there is anyone who can practice it, this is entirely *karma* making for birth-and-death. You talk about being perfectly disciplined in your six senses and in the ten thousand ways of conduct, but as I see it all this is creating *karma*. To seek the Buddha and to seek the Dharma is precisely making *karma* for the hells.

In Ma-tsu (Baso), Nan-chuan (Nansen), Chao-chou (Jōshū), Huang-po

也很仁慈，却仍准备还击一掌。师惊呼："你真是大狂人，竟敢来捋虎须！"临济也立即高声呼叫而出。临济在得到启悟之后，好像变成另一个人，他声称黄檗所讲的佛法"终究是没有什么的"（参见铃木大拙《佛教禅宗论文集》，系列 I，第 247 页）。

《临济录》是临济禅师语录集，展示了他的一些说教。以下摘录的几段很有启发意义，见艾伦·瓦茨《禅道》第 101—102 页：

我为什么在此说教？就因为你们想要求道，你们到处奔驰不停，想要追逐心灵。但是古来圣人，却是按照合适的环境，悠闲地修行。

各位求道人，你们如果信从我的见解，你们就将会高坐在……众佛头顶上去判断。如果谁要完成了那十个阶段，那他就像是走卒仆从；如果谁要达到超越的觉醒，那也好像是枷锁套上了头颈。阿罗汉以及佛陀好像是肮脏的茅坑，菩提和涅槃好像是蠢驴的套绳。

在佛法中没有什么需要去刻苦追寻，而应保持平常心，不需特殊性。只须正常大小便、穿衣和进食，倦了就去休息。无知者嘲笑我，智者却能理解我……到处为家，随遇而安，一切将是坦率真诚的。任何机缘遭遇来临，切莫妄图变更。若能如此，那么你的日常感觉意识，就不会因烦恼堕入五重地狱，而会得到大海那样的自由解脱。

在心之外别无佛，在它里面也没有什么要去领会掌握，那么你们还有什么要去找寻？你们总是说"道"要实践和求证，切莫这样迷误不醒！谁说能够那样地实践、修行？那完全是生死烦恼妄情。你们说要在六识和万行中进行完全的修炼，在我看来，这全是在为烦恼造业。这样地寻求佛性和佛法，确实就是在为痛苦和地狱烦恼造业。

从马祖、南泉、赵州、黄檗和临济这几位禅师那里，我们

(Ōbaku), and Lin-chi (Rinzai), we can see the "flavor" of Zen at its best. Mr. Watts spoke about the difficulty of translating the records of these masters from colloquial Chinese speech of Tang Dynasty into modern English. So there seems no need of re-translating them, although the original Chinese versions are available.

Rinzai's "Four Kinds of Attitudes" (Shiryōken) can be stated as follows. (See *The Development of Chinese Zen*, by Heinrich Dumoulin, S. J., originally in German; English translation by Ruth Fuller Sasaki, published by The First Zen Institute of America, Inc., New York, 1953, pages 72 and 22-24).

> In some instances I abstract man from the environment; in some instances I abstract the environment from man; in some instances I abstract both man and environment; and in some instances I abstract neither man nor environment.

The translation was made by Sokei-an. On page 22, Ruth Fuller Sasaki's translation reads as follows:

> As to formula, the text depends upon the well-known "four propositions" of Indian Buddhist logic; as to meaning, it corresponds to the four aspects of Reality (Dharmadhatu or hōkkai in Japanese) of the Kegon teaching...
>
> Analogous formulas are the "Fourfold Relations of Guest and Host" (Shihinju) and the "Fourfold Precedence and Subsequence of Light and Activity" (Shishōyū). With all such formulas the technical terms must be understood as symbols. We are concerned with a logical or metaphysical dialectic regarding the relationship of subject and object, relative and Absolute, appearance and Reality, which later will be dealt with somewhat in detail in the example of the "Five Ranks" (goi) of the Sōtō School.
>
> Another of Rinzai's expressions, that regarding the "Three Mysteries and the Three Essentials" (sangen sanyo), is likewise to be found in *Rinzai-roku*. The basic passage states: "Each statement must necessarily

comprise the three mysteries; each mystery must necessarily comprise the three essentials."

According to one such explanation (from commentaries), the three mysteries are:

Taichūgen 体中玄, that is, "what the Buddhas of the three periods and the patriarchs of the historical eras attained in enlightenment"— thus, the content of enlightenment—corresponds to substance (tai 体).

可以领会到禅宗风格的最佳表达。不过瓦茨先生谈及，要把唐代当时的日常通俗汉语译成近代英语确有很大的难度，所以尽管原始的中文版本可用，似乎并不需要重译。

临济提出的"四料简"所述如下（见杜慕林用德语撰写的《中国禅宗的发展》，由罗丝·富勒·佐佐木译成英文，美国第一禅堂出版，纽约，1953 年，第 72 页和第 22—24 页）：

有时我把人从环境中抽出来；有时我把环境从人那里抽出来；有时我把人和环境都抽出来；有时人和环境两者我都不抽。

根据该书第 22 页罗丝·富勒·佐佐木的译文，大意如下所述：

在程式上，这种文句来自著名的印度佛教的"四命题"逻辑；在意义上则相当于《华严经》教旨中关于"实在"的四个方面……

类似的程式还有"四宾主"和"四照用"。在所有这些程式中引用的术语都应理解为表达符号。所涉及的命题都是有关主观和客观、相对和绝对、外观和实体在逻辑上或形而上学上的辩证对立关系。这在以后有关曹洞宗的"五位"中较详细地再讨论。

在《临济录》中还可找到另一个临济表达方式是"三玄三要"。其基本表达字句这样说："每一陈述必须有三个玄秘，每一玄秘必须有三个要点。"

根据注解中解释如下，所谓"三玄"，是：

体中玄：三世佛和列代祖师达到的启悟——启悟内容相当于"体"。

Kuchūgen 句中玄, that is, "what the patriarchs in the historical eras manifest as enlightenment"—the distinctive features of enlightenment—corresponds to characteristics (sō 相).

Genchūgen 玄中玄, that is, "how the Buddhas of the three periods and the patriarchs of the historical eras transmit (enlightenment)"—thus, the operation of enlightenment—corresponds to activity (yū 用).

Substance, characteristics, and activity are inseparably interfused and one. Each of the three mysteries comprises the three essentials, which are not different from one mystery, in the meaning of the doctrine of the *Avatamsaka-sutra* (*Kegon kyō*) regarding unity in differentiation.

In R. H. Blyth's *Zen and Zen Classics*, Vol. 3, pages 152-153, "man" was replaced by "person," and "environment" was replaced by "thing." The following passages were taken from Blyth's:

Kokufu came forward and asked,

"What is this taking away the person, not the thing?"

Rinzai answered:

"When the sun shines, the earth is covered with brocade;

The baby's hair hangs down, white as silk."

Kokufu asked:

"How about taking away the thing, not the person?"

Rinzai answered:

"The Emperor's command is performed throughout the country;

The smoke and dust of war at an end, the general leaves the fortress."

Kokufu asked, "How about when both person and thing are taken away?"

Rinzai answered:

"When all relations are broken, we are really alone."

Asked Kokufu, "And when neither person nor thing is taken away?"

Rinzai answered:

"The Emperor ascends the jewelled throne,

And the old rustics sing."

In the Kegon School, there are Four Aspects of Reality:

1) Illusion departs from the subject;

2) Illusion departs from the object;

3) Both subject and object are denied, but their differentiation continues to exist;

4) When the transcending of the opposition of subject and object has been confirmed, the confrontation of subject and object ceases completely.

句中玄：列代祖师显示的启悟——启悟的显著特性，相当于"相"。

玄中玄：三世佛和历代祖师怎样传道（启悟）——即启悟的运用——相当于"用"。

本体、特性和运用是不可分割、相互渗透的整体。三个玄秘中的每一个都包含三个要点。但它们都统一为同一个"玄"则无区别，这就是《华严经》中关于把区别和分化统一成为整体的教旨。

在 R. H. 布莱思《禅与禅宗经典》第 3 卷第 152—153 页也有与佐佐木相类似的译文。以下片段即引自该书：

克符前来并问："如果把人而不是把物抽去，那将是什么呢？"

临济答："阳光照射时，织锦铺满地；童发垂下白似丝。"

克符问："如果把物而不是把人抽去，那将怎样呢？"

临济答："君王下令，全国执行；战争烟尘消散，将军辞别堡垒归来。"

克符问："如果把人和物都抽去，又将是怎样呢？"

临济答："如果把所有相关的都断开，我们就真正孤单。"

克符问："如果人和物都不抽去，那又将怎样呢？"

临济答："君王升上宝座，乡老齐声欢唱。"

根据华严宗，"实体"的四个方面是：

（1）虚幻离开主体；

（2）虚幻离开客体；

（3）主客体都否定，但其区别还在；

（4）肯定了主客体对立面的超越性，那么主客体之间的对抗就完全停止。

Rinzai's way of expressing himself against *falsehood* can be best exemplified by the following passages (see Suzuki: *Essays in Zen Buddhism*, First Series, pages 347-348):

> O you, followers of Truth, if you wish to obtain an orthodox understanding (of Zen), do not be deceived by others. Inwardly or outwardly, if you encounter any obstacles, lay them low right away. If you encounter the Buddha, slay him; if you encounter the Patriarch, slay him; if you encounter the Arhat or the parent or the relative, slay them all without hesitation: for this is the only way to deliverance. Do not get yourselves entangled with any object, but stand above, pass on, and be free. As I see those so-called followers of Truth all over the country, there are none who come to me free and independent of objects. In dealing with them, I strike them down any way they come. If they rely on the strength of their arms, I cut them right off; if they rely on their eloquence, I make them shut themselves up; if they rely on the sharpness of their eyes, I will hit them blind. There are indeed so far none who have presented themselves before me all alone, all free, all unique. They are invariably found caught by the idle tricks of the old masters. I have really nothing to give you; all that I can do is to cure you of the diseases and deliver you from bondage.
>
> O you, followers of Truth, show yourselves here independent of all objects, I want to weigh the matter with you. For the last five or ten years I have waited in vain for such, and there are no such yet. They are all ghostly existences, ignominious gnomes haunting the woods or bamboo-groves; they are selfish spirits of the wilderness. They are madly biting into all heaps of filth. O you, mole-eyed, why are you wasting all the pious donations of the devout! Do you think you deserve the name of a monk, when you are still entertaining such a mistaken idea (of Zen)? I tell you, no Buddhas, no holy teachings, no discipling, no testifying! What do you seek in a neighbor's house? O you, mole-eyed! You are putting another head over your own! What do you lack in yourselves? O you, followers of Truth, what you are making use of at this very moment

is none other than what makes a Patriarch or a Buddha. But you do not believe me, and seek it outwardly. Do not commit yourself to an error. There are no realities outside, nor is there anything inside you may lay

以下一段是临济大师在反对"虚妄"上的最佳表达（见铃木大拙《佛教禅宗论文集》，系列 I ，第347—348页）：

众位求道者，你们要想领悟正宗禅道，当心不要受人蒙骗。不论在内在外，如果遇到任何障碍，立刻把它们放下。如果遇到佛就把他宰了，如果遇到宗师也把他宰了，如果遇到阿罗汉或任何亲友也不需犹豫，统统都宰了，这是要得到拯救的唯一道路。不要被任何事物所困扰，要站在事物之外，走过越过后完全自由自在。我看全国这些所谓求道者来见我的没有任何人能自由自在地解脱于事物之外。对待这些人，我就要给他们当头一棒，不管他们是从哪里来的。如果认为还可凭借他们强壮的臂力，我就立刻把他们的臂断开。如果认为可以凭借他们的滔滔口才，我就叫他们闭嘴莫谈。如果认为可以凭借他们的目光敏锐，我可以一击叫他们瞎了眼。直到现在，实在没有任何人到我这里来，能够独立解脱和自由自在。他们全都是被那些老法师们的无聊花招所迷惑，所以我也实在没有什么好向你们讲解。所有我能做的首先是要治好你们的病态，要把你们的束缚都解开。

众位求道者，在这里，你们对一切事物都应该丢得开。我要着重向你们讲解，最近五年或十年，我是白白地在等待，等不到真正的醒悟者。他们都是像幽灵那样地存在，像可鄙的魔鬼出没在森林和竹林内。他们都是荒野里的自私幽灵，在疯狂地啃所有的垃圾堆。你们啊，就是那么鼠目寸光，都在浪费虔诚者的热心捐献！你们对禅道竟怀着这样的错误信念！你们还称得上是僧人吗？我说你们没有佛性，没有圣训，没有教规，也没有体认！你们却找到别人的屋里去，你们真是鼠目寸光！把别人的头放上了自己的身。难道你们自身还缺少什么不成？你们啊，众位求道人，此时此刻对你们真正有用的也只有自己的心，成为宗师或成佛，更无其他门好进。可是你们对我不相信，偏向外界去追寻。不要再犯错误了，应知外界并无实体，

your hands on. You stick to the literal meaning of what I speak to you, but how far better it is to have all your hankerings stopped, and be doing nothing whatever.

Rinzai said to the monks, "Sometimes 'Kwatz' is like the treasured sword of the Vajra King; sometimes like a golden-haired lion crouching on the ground; sometimes the shadow of a sounding-stick on the grass; and sometimes not a shout at all. How do you understand this?" The monks hesitated. Rinzai shouted "Kwatz!"

The Rinzai School was transmitted in the following manner:

(1) Lin-chi I-hsuan (Rinzai Gigen, d. 866)

(2) Hsing-hua Tsun-chiang (Kōke Zonshō, 830-888)

(3) Nan-yuan Hui-yu (Nan'in Egyō, d. 952)

(4) Feng-hsueh Yen-chao (Fuketsu Enshō, 896-973)

(5) Shou-shan Sheng-nien (Shuzan Shōnen, 926-993)

The sixth generation had several disciples, among them:

(6a) Fen-yang Shan-chao (Fun'yō Zenshō, 947-1024)

(6b) Ku-yin Yun-tsung (Koku'in Unsō, 965-1032)

(6c) Yeh-hsien Kuei-sin (Yōken Kisei)

(6d) Shen-ting Hung-yin (Jintei Kō'in)

(6e) Chen-tien Chih-sung (Chōten Chisū)

(6f) Kuang-hui Yuan-lien (Kō'e Genren, 951-1036)

Fen-yang's dharma-heirs were:

(7a) Shih-shuang Tsu-yuan (Sekisō Soen, 986-1039)

(7b) Lang-ya Hui-chueh (Rōga Ekaku)

(7c) Fa-hua Chuan-chu (Hōka Zenkyo)

(7d) Ta-yu Shou-chi (Daigu Shushi, d. 1057)

Ku-yin's dharma-heirs were:

(7e) Chin-shan Tan-ying (Kinzn Don'ei, 989-1060)

(7f) Li Tsun-hsu (Ri Junkyoku, d. 1038)

Chin-shan had a disciple Hsi-yu Kung-chen (Seiyo Kōshin). Li Tsun-hsu was the author of *Tien-sheng Kuang-teng Lu* (*Tenshō Kōtōroku*), dated 1036.

Yeh-hsien's dharma heir was:

里面也没有什么可以凭依。你们对我所讲的只从字面上来了解其意义。最好是什么也不要做，把你们苦苦在追求的，全都休止和停息。

临济对众和尚说："有时一喝，如金刚宝剑；有时一喝，如踞地金毛狮子；有时一喝，如探竿影草；有时一喝，不作一喝用。大家是否都能明白？"大家都很犹豫，深感莫测，于是临济大师就大声吆喝。

临济宗的世系传承如下：

（1）临济义玄（？—866）

（2）兴化存奖（830—888）

（3）南院慧颙（？—952）

（4）风穴延沼（896—973）

（5）首山省念（926—993）

（6a）汾阳善昭（947—1024）

（6b）谷隐蕴聪（965—1032）

（6c）叶县归省

（6d）神鼎洪湮

（6e）承天智嵩

（6f）广慧元琏（951—1036）

汾阳善昭的法嗣有：

（7a）石霜楚圆（986—1039）

（7b）琅琊慧觉

（7c）法华全举

（7d）大愚守芝（？—1057）

谷隐蕴聪的法嗣有：

（7e）金山昙颖（989—1060）

（7f）李遵勖（？—1038）

金山昙颖有一弟子为西余拱辰。李遵勖著有《天圣广灯录》，1036年成书。

叶县的法嗣是：

(7g) Fu-shan Fa-yuan (Fuzan Hō'en, 991-1067). Fu-shan was also known as Yuan-chien Ta-shih (Enkan Daishi), who was responsible for picking Tou-tzu I-ching (Tōsu Gisei, 1032-1083) as the dharma heir of Ta-yang Ching-yuan (Daiyō Keigen, 943-1027) in the Tsao-tung (Sōtō) School.

For the eighth generation, Shih-shuang Tsu-yuan (Sekisō Soen), better known as Tzu-ming Ta-shih (Jimyō Daishi) had the following dharma-heirs:

(8a) Huang-lung Hui-nan (Ōryū Enan, 1002-1069)

(8b) Yang-chi Fang-hui (Yōgi Hō'e, 992-1049)

(8c) Ta-nin Tao-kuan (Dainei Dōkan)

(8d) Ching-su (Shōso Jisha)

Ta-yu Shou-chi (Daigu Shushi) had one dharma-heir:

(8e) Yun-feng Wen-yueh (Umpō Monyetsu, 997-1062)

Jimyō Daishi had two other disciples:

(8f) Tsui-yen Ko-chen (Suigan Keshin, d. 1064)

(8g) Tao-wu Wu-chen (Dōgo Goshin)

Ōryū Enan was the founder of the Ōryū Sect, and Yōgi Hō'e was the founder of the Yōgi Sect. These sects are presented in Chapter 5.

From Lin-chi I-hsuan (Rinzai Gigen, d. 866) to Shih-shuang Tsu-yuan (Sekisō Soen, 986-1039), we have seven generations in the Lin-chi (Rinzai) School. In R. H. Blyth's *Zen and Zen Classics*, Vol. 3, pages 165-167, some anecdotes were recorded concerning Hsing-hua Tsun-chiang (Kōke Zonshō, 830-888) and his dharma brother San-sheng Hui-jan (Sanshō Enen).

> A monk asked Sanshō, "What is the meaning of Daruma coming from the West?" Sanshō answered, "Stinking meat attracts flies." The monk brought this up to Kōke, who said, "I wouldn't have said that." The monk asked, "What is the meaning of Daruma coming from the West?" Kōke answered, "There are enough blue-bottles on a broken-down donkey."

Sanshō said, "If someone comes, I go out to meet him, but not for his sake." Kōke said, "If someone comes, I don't go out. If I do go out, I go out for his sake."

Kōke was head monk at various temples. He visited Yun-chu Tao-ying (Ungo Dōyō) of the Sōtō School. But he became Lin-chi's (Rinzai's)

（7g）浮山法远（991—1067）。又称圆鉴大师，由他负责挑选了投子义青（1032—1083）作为曹洞宗大阳警玄（943—1027）的法嗣。

关于临济宗的第八代，则有石霜楚圆（多被称为慈明大师），众法嗣如下：

（8a）黄龙慧南（1002—1069）

（8b）杨岐方会（992—1049）

（8c）大宁道宽

（8d）清素（侍者）

大愚守芝有一法嗣是：

（8e）云峰文悦（997—1062）

石霜楚圆即慈明另有两弟子：

（8f）翠岩可真（？—1064）

（8g）道吾悟真

黄龙慧南是黄龙宗创建人，杨岐方会则是杨岐宗创建人。关于此两宗将于第五章再谈。

临济宗自临济义玄（？—866）到石霜楚圆（986—1039）一共传了七代。在 R. H. 布莱思《禅与禅宗经典》第 3 卷第165—167 页，载有临济第二代法嗣兴化存奖与其师兄三圣慧然之间的一些故事，如下：

学僧问三圣禅师："如何是祖师西来意？"三圣答："臭肉来蝇。"学僧告诉兴化，兴化说："我则不然。"学僧："如何是祖师西来意？"兴化："破驴脊上足苍蝇。"

三圣道："我逢人即出。出则不为人。"兴化道："我逢人即不出。出则便为人。"

兴化存奖曾是许多寺院的首座僧，他也访谒过曹洞宗的云居道膺，但后来还是侍从临济，成为临济的法嗣。有一天，

attendant and dharma-heir. One day Emperor Chuang-tsung of Late Tang told Master Kōke that he got a priceless pearl and nobody has given an estimate of its value. Master Kōke asked to see the pearl. The Emperor showed him the pearl. Then the Master said: "Who dares to bid a price on the Emperor's treasure?" Kōke received a horse from the Emperor Chuang-tsung as a reward for his teaching. He rode away on it, fell off, and broke his leg. Returning to his temple, he got the head monk to make some crutches and went along the corridor. He asked a monk, "Do you know me?" The monk replied, "Why shouldn't I know you?" Kōke said, "Here's somebody who explained the Dharma, and can't walk as a result of it." These anecdotes testified that Kōke was a National Teacher (Kokushi). Emperor Chuang-tsung reigned 923-925, and Kōke entered nirvana in 925. Chuang-tsung was succeeded by Ming-tsung in 926, the year Shou-shan Sheng-nien (Shuzan Shōnen) was born.

Kōke's famous disciple was Nan-yuan Hui-yu (Nan'in Egyō, d. 952), who was also known as Pao-yin Ho-shan (Hō'ō oshō). He passed away in the second year of the Kuang-shen (Kōjun) era under the reign of Chou Tai-tsu. Some anecdotes were given by R. H. Blyth in his *Zen and Zen Classics*, Vol. 3, pages 167-169.

> Nan'in asked the monk in charge, "What sutra is your Reverence lecturing on?" He replied, "The *Yuima Sutra*." Nan'in pointed to the Zen seat and said, "You understand?" "I don't," replied the monk. Nan'in said to the attendant, "Bring in some tea."
>
> A monk said to Nan'in, "What is the Great Meaning of Buddhism?" Nan'in said, "The origin of a myriad diseases." The monk said, "Please cure me!" Nan'in said, "The World Doctor folds his hands."

Blyth commented: "This is unusually poetical, and of a melancholy grandeur. It also happens to be true. Buddhism is both the cause and effect of an unsound mind in an unsound body. Note that greediness, stupidity, maliciousness and so on are not illnesses, for animals have them. Illness means thinking you are ill. And who can cure the illness which Doctor Buddha and Doctor Christ have caused?"

A monk asked Nan'in, "What is your special teaching?" Nan'in said, "In autumn we reap; and in winter we store."

后唐庄宗告诉兴化说，他得到一颗无价之宝的明珠，但到底值多少，无人能对它估价。兴化要求能亲眼看一下，庄宗给他看了。兴化说："谁有胆量敢对君王的宝珠进行估价呢？"庄宗赐了一匹马给兴化，以答谢他所作的说教。他骑马辞去，但从马上跌下来，摔断一腿。回到寺内后，叫首座僧替他做了根拐杖。他拄着拐杖，在走廊里走着，遇见一僧，问："你还认识我吗？"僧答："为什么不呢？"兴化说："这个人讲解佛法，但得到的结果却是不能走路了。"这段故事说明兴化曾经是朝廷国师。后唐庄宗在位是923—925年（按另作923—926），而兴化的圆寂也是在925年。庄宗之后由明宗继位于926年，而首山省念出生也在这一年。

兴化有一著名的弟子是南院慧颙，也被称为宝应和尚，于后周太祖广顺二年（952）逝世。在布莱思《禅与禅宗经典》第3卷第167—169页中讲述了关于他的一些故事：

南院问主管僧："大师在讲什么经？"僧答："《维摩诘经》。"南院指着禅座并问："你真懂吗？"僧答："我不懂。"南院对侍从说："请倒杯茶来。"

一僧问南院："什么是佛教大意？"南院说："千万疾病之源。"僧说："请救治我的病吧！"南院说："天下医生束手无策。"

布莱思对上文的注解说："这里具有很不寻常的诗意，也含有很伤感的庄严，恰巧这也确是真实的。佛教是身心不健的因和果，我也提请注意，贪愚和恶意等都不能算是病，因为所有动物都有。如果在思想上自己就认为自己生了病，那么由救世医者的佛祖或基督所导致的思想疾病又有谁能来医治呢？"

一僧问南院："什么是你的特别教导？"南院答："秋天收获，冬天藏好。"

A monk asked Nan'in, "What is the Way (Tao)?" Nan'in answered, "A kite flies across the great sky; nothing remains there."

A monk asked Nan'in, "What about a seamless stupa?" Nan'in said, "Seven flowers, eight tearings." "How about the man in the tower?" "He doesn't comb his hair or wash his face."

Nan-yuan (Nan'in) had two well-known disciples: Ying-chiao An (Eikyo-an) and Feng-hsueh Yen-chao (Fuketsu Enshō, 896-973). Ying-chiao An was sitting by the fire when an official asked him, "How can one get out of the burning in the Three Worlds?" Ying-chiao An picked up the incense-tongs and showed him some embers, saying, "Officer! Officer!" The Official was enlightened. Feng-hsueh (Fuketsu) lived to seventy-eight years old and passed away in the sixth year of the Kai-Pao (Kaihō) era under the reign of Tai-tsu (Taiso), the first Emperor of Sung Dynasty. Blyth gave the dates as 896-973, based on *Ku-tsun-su Yulu* (*Kosonshuku goroku*), which are different from what was given in the *Lamp Records*, *Daishō Daizōkyō*, Vol. 51, pages 302-303.

Many anecdotes were given in Y. H. Ku's *History of Chinese Zen Masters*, pages 158-164, based upon the *Lamp Records*.

Feng-hsueh (Fuketsu) was asked by a monk, "When speech and silence are both inadmissible, how can one pass without error?" Feng-hsueh replied: "I always remember Kiang-nan in the third moon—the cry of the partridge, the fragrance of the wild flowers."

This was cited in Alan W. Watts' *The Way of Zen*, pages 182-183. There were some interesting questions and answers in the *Lamp Records*:

Question: "How is the host in the guest?"

Fuketsu answered, "A blind man enters the city."

Question: "How is the guest in the host?"

Fuketsu answered, "The Emperor returns with sun and moon shining anew."

Question: "How is the guest in the guest?"

Answered Fuketsu, "From the eyebrows arise the white clouds."

Question: "How is the host in the host?"

Fuketsu answered: "Grind the three-feet knife. Ready to kill the 'unfair' fellow."

一僧问南院:"什么是道?"南院答:"一只风筝飞越长空后,什么痕迹都不留。"

一僧问南院:"什么是无缝塔?"南院答:"七朵花,撕成八。"僧问:"那么塔中人呢?"南院答:"他既不洗脸,也不理发。"

南院有两个有名的弟子:颖桥安和风穴延沼(896—973)。正当颖桥安坐在炉旁时,有一长官问他:"三界着火,应怎样才能逃脱?"颖桥安拿起了焚香钳给他看,钳上有余烬,说:"长官长官,你请看!"那长官就得到了启发。风穴延沼享年78岁,于宋太祖开宝六年(973)圆寂。布莱思根据《古尊宿语录》给出其生卒年份为896—973年,但这与《传灯录》中所列的年份(887—973)不一致,见《大正藏》第51卷第302—303页。

在拙著《禅宗师承记》第158—164页中,依据《传灯录》所载,引有一些有关故事如下:

一僧问风穴:"如果高谈阔论和默默无语两者都不许,那么怎样才能不犯错误?"风穴答:"常忆江南三月里,鹧鸪啼处野花香。"

在艾伦·瓦茨《禅道》第182—183页中也曾引了这一诗句。在《传灯录》中还引有一些很有意义的问答词句如下:

问:"主在客中会怎么样?"

风穴答:"盲人进入闹市中。"

问:"客在主中又怎么样?"

风穴答:"君王回驾,日月照明一新。"

问:"客在客中又将怎样?"

风穴答:"眉间起白云。"

问:"那么主在主中呢?"

风穴答:"磨砺三尺刃,准备宰杀不公正的人。"

Feng-hsueh (Fuketsu) had three famous disciples, of whom Shou-shan Sheng-nien (Shuzan Shōnen, 926-993) was the greatest.

> A monk asked Shou-shan (Shuzan): "What is the special teaching of your family?"
>
> Shuzan said: "One sentence cuts across the mouth of a thousand rivers; Before a cliff of ten thousand yards, one finds the mystery."
>
> The monk asked: "How is Shuzan's Kyō (outlook and inlook)?"
>
> Shuzan said: "Let all the people see."
>
> The monk asked: "How is the person in the Kyō (outlook)?"
>
> Shuzan said: "Have you received the blows?"
>
> The monk saluted the Master.

These anecdotes were recorded in the *Lamp Records, Daishō Daizōkyō*, Vol. 51, pages 304-305. (See also Y. H. Ku, *History of Chinese Zen Masters*, pages 165-168.) Fuketsu was the first generation Abbot at Shuzan-ji. He was also the third-generation Abbot of Nan-yuan of Pao-yin Yuan (Hō'ō-in). He lived to sixty-eight years old.

Fen-yang Shan-chao (Fun'yō Zenshō, 947-1024) was Shuzan's dharma-heir. Some questions and answers (mondō) were given below:

> A monk asked: "What is the source of the Great Tao (Dō)?"
>
> Fun'yō answered: "Dig the earth and find the heaven."
>
> Question: "How is the guest in the guest?"
>
> Fun'yō answered: "Fold your hands before the temple and ask Buddha."
>
> Question: "How is the host in the guest?"
>
> Fun'yō answered: "Facing you on the opposite side, there were no comrades."
>
> Question: "How is the guest in the host?"
>
> Master said: "Clouds and clouds across the sea; Draw your sword and disturb the Dragon-gate!"
>
> Question: "How is the host in the host?"
>
> Master said: "Three heads and six arms hold up heaven and

earth; Angry No-cha (a legendary figure) attacks the Imperial Court-bell."

Fen-yang (Fun'yō) had four famous disciples, mentioned above, among them Tzu-ming Tsu-yuan (Jimyō Soen, 986-1039) was the greatest. Shih-shuang Tsu-yuan (Sekisō Soen) became a monk when he was twenty-two years old. His mother encouraged him to travel and seek

风穴有三个弟子很有名，其中最卓越的是首山省念（926—993）。

一僧问首山："请问什么是尊系的特有教导？"
首山答："一言截破千江水，万仞峰前始得玄。"
僧问："首山境色怎样？"
首山答："让所有人都可见此境。"
僧问："那么怎样将是境中人？"
首山说："你吃了棒棍不曾？"
僧向大师施礼致谢。

这些故事载于《传灯录》，见《大正藏》第 51 卷第 304—305 页（或见拙著《禅宗师承记》第 165—168 页）。风穴是首山寺的第一代方丈，也是宝应寺南院的第三代方丈，在 68 岁时圆寂。

首山的法嗣是汾阳善昭（947—1024），有关他的一些问答辞如下：

一僧问："什么是大道的源和根？"
汾阳答："挖地把天寻。"
僧问："怎样是客在客中？"
汾阳答："举手合掌，庙前问佛尊。"
僧问："怎样是主在客中？"
汾阳答："面向你的背，没有同路人。"
僧问："怎样是客在主中？"
师答："浮云朵朵飘过海，拔剑捣龙门。"
僧问："怎样是主在主中？"
师答："三头六臂擎天地，忿怒哪吒扑帝钟。"

汾阳善昭有著名弟子四人。如上所述，其中以慈明楚圆最为卓越（即石霜楚圆，986—1039）。石霜在 22 岁时出家

learned masters. He served under Fen-yang Shan-chao (Fun'yō Zenshō) for two years, but he was not allowed to enter the Master's room. Sekisō was so disappointed that he planned to leave. One evening he grumbled about not receiving the Master's instructions. The Master held up his stick in anger, and the disciple (Sekisō) tried to defend himself. Suddenly the Master used his hands to "blind-fold" Sekisō's eyes. Sekisō was greatly enlightened and understood that Rinzai's teachings are "common sense." He attended to Fen-yang (Fun'yō) for seven more years and then left.

There were many anecdotes which appeared in the *Lamp Records* (see *Daishō Daizōkyō*, Vol. 51, pages 482-484; and also Y. H. Ku, *History of Chinese Zen Masters*, pages 175-185).

> When a monk asked him, "What is the meaning of Daruma (the First Patriarch) coming from the west?" Sekisō answered: "Three days of wind and five days of rain."

Master Tzu-ming (Jimyō Daishi) was a good friend of two high officials: Yang Ta-nien (Yō Dainen) and Li Tsun-hsu (Ri Junkyoku, d. 1038). In 1038 A.D., Li sent an invitation to Master Tzu-ming, saying that Yang already passed away, and he wished to meet with the Master before his own death. The Master took a boat and went to the Capital. Master Tzu-ming wrote the following gāthā:

> The Yangtze River is endless.
> When can I reach the Capital?
> The boat is receiving cool wind as a help.
> There is no need of using the oars.

After meeting with the Master, Li Tsun-hsu passed away a little over a month later. Master Tzu-ming (Jimyō Daishi) left posterity with his dharma-heirs, most notably Huang-lung Hui-nan (Ōryū Enan, 1002-1069), founder of the Oryū Sect, and Yang-chi Fang-hui (Yōgi Hō'e, 992-1049), founder of the Yōgi Sect. From Ōryū, the lineage leads to Myōan Eisai, founder of the Rinzai School in Japan. On the other hand, the Yōgi

Sect produced many masters that would influence the development of Zen in Japan. Enji Ben'en, founder of Tōfuku-ji, was Mujun Shihan's disciple, and so was Mugaku Sogen, founder of Engaku-ji. Rankei Dōryū, founder of Kenchō-ji, was Mumyō Esei's disciple. Mukan Fumon, founder of Nanzen-ji, was the disciple of Jōji Myōrin (Mujun's disciple), as well as the dharma-heir of Enji Ben'en. Daikyū Shōnen, founder of Jōchi-ji,

为僧，其母鼓励他云游四方，寻求名师。他曾经师事汾阳达两年，仍未蒙师父准许入室，感到很失望而打算离去。某一天晚上，他因得不到师父指教而口出怨言，师父大怒，举起了手杖，石霜力图自卫。师父忽举起手来，蒙住石霜的双眼，石霜突然大受启发，顿悟了临济宗的教旨就是"寻常心态"。他继续师事汾阳七年，然后离开。

在《传灯录》中有很多相关故事（见《大正藏》第51卷，第482—484页和拙著《禅宗师承记》第175—185页），略如下述：

一僧问石霜："祖师达摩自西方来，意义究竟何在？"石霜答："三日风，五日雨。"

慈明大师是两位高官杨大年和李遵勖（？—1038）的好友。公元1038年，李遵勖写信邀请慈明大师说：杨大年已经去世，很希望在自己尚未去世之前还能见大师一面。于是慈明大师就坐船去了京城，并写了一首诗偈：

长江行不尽，帝里到何时？
既得凉风便，休将栌棹施。

李遵勖在见到慈明大师后一个多月便去世了，慈明大师于1040年圆寂，衣钵传给了法嗣，最著名的即黄龙宗的创建人黄龙慧南（1002—1069）及杨岐宗的创建人杨岐方会（992—1049）。黄龙宗世系传到了明庵荣西，就是日本临济宗的创建人。另一方面杨岐宗也造就了很多大师，对日本的禅宗发展有很大的影响。例如东福寺创建人圆尔辨圆，是无准师范的弟子，同样还有圆觉寺的创建人无学祖元。建长寺的创建人兰溪道隆是无明慧性的弟子。南禅寺的创建人无关普门是净慈妙伦（无准的弟子）的弟子，同时也是圆尔辨圆

was Sekikei Shingetsu's dharma-heir. Nampo Jōmyō was Kidō Chigu's dharma-heir. Nampo's disciple Shūhō Myōchō became the founder of Daitoku-ji. Note that Rankei, Kidō, and Sekikei were dharma cousins, as they were Shōgen Sūgaku's dharma grandsons. So many Zen Masters in Japan, whether they came to China from Japan, or they went to Japan from China, were from the Yōgi Sect. Even Shinchi Kakushin, the dharma grandfather of Bassui Tokushō and Jiun Myō'i, founders of Kōgaku-ji and Kokutai-ji respectively, was the dharma-heir of Mumon Ekai. Ha'an Sosen (Mujun Shihan's dharma teacher), Shōgen Sūgaku, and Mumon Ekai were all the fifth-generation dharma descendants of Goso Hō'en, who was the dharma grandson of Yōgi. So far as the Rinzai School was concerned, the Yōgi Sect flourished both in China and in Japan.

The Ōryū and Yōgi Sects are presented in Chapter 5.

的法嗣。净智寺的创建人大休正念是石溪心月的法嗣。南浦绍明是虚堂智愚的法嗣，而南浦的弟子宗峰妙超则是大德寺的创建人。注意到兰溪、虚堂和石溪三人应是师兄弟，因为他们都是松源崇岳的第二代法嗣。所以许多日本禅师，不论是由日本来过中国的，或是由中国去日本的，都属于杨岐宗世系。即使是拔队得胜和慈云妙意的师祖心地觉心也是无门慧开的法嗣，而拔队和慈云两人则分别是洪岳寺和国泰寺的创建人。无门慧开以及破庵祖先（无准师范的师父）、松源崇岳都是五祖法演的第五代法嗣，而五祖法演则是杨岐的第二代法嗣。作为临济宗的支系，杨岐宗在中日两国都很兴盛繁荣。

第五章将专门介绍黄龙宗和杨岐宗。

CHAPTER 5   THE ŌRYŪ AND YŌGI SECTS

Huang-lung Hui-nan (Ōryū Enan, 1002-1069) was the founder of the Ōryū Sect in the Rinzai School in China. The lineage from Ōryū to Myōan Eisai, founder of the Rinzai School in Japan, is given below:

(1) Huang-lung Hui-nan (Ōryū Enan, 1002-1069)

(2) Hui-tang Tsu-hsin (Kaidō Sōshin, 1025-1100)

(3) Ling-yuan Wei-ching (Reigen Isei, d. 1117)

(4) Chang-ling Shou-cho (Chōrei Shutaku, 1065-1123)

(5) Wu-shi Kai-shen (Muji Kaijin, 1080-1148)

(6) Hsin-wen Tan-fen (Shinbun Donfun)

(7) Hsueh-an Chun-chin (Setsu'an Jūkin, 1117-1200)

(8) Hsu-an Huai-chang (Ki'an Eshō)

(9) Ming-an Yung-si (Myōan Eisai, 1141-1215)

Eisai was the eighth-generation dharma descendant of Ōryū Enan. Ōryū's other disciples were:

(2a) Yun-an Ko-wen (Un'an Kokumon, 1025-1102)

(2b) Yun-kai Shou-chih (Ungai Shuchi, 1025-1115)

(2c) Lau-tan Hung-yin (Rokutan Kō'in, 1012-1070)

(2d) Yang-shan Hsing-wei (Kyōzan Kō'i, 1018-1080)

(2e) Tung-lin Chang-chung (Tōrin Chōsō, 1025-1091)

(2f) Shang-lan Shun (Jōran Jun)

Yun-an Ko-wen or Pao-feng Ko-wen (Hōbō Kokumon) had three disciples:

(3a) Tou-shuai Tsung-yueh (Tosotsu Jūetsu, 1044-1091)

(3b) Chan-tang Wen-chun (Tandō Bunjun, 1061-1115)

(3c) Chueh-fan Hui-hung (Kakuhan Ekō, 1071-1128)

Tung-lin (Tōrin) had a famous disciple, Su Tung-po (Sotōba, 1036-1101), a literary genius. Shang-lan (Jōran) was probably older than Tōrin; but he was a friend of Su Tung-po's father, and became the dharma teacher of Su Che (So Tetsu), Su Tung-po's younger brother.

In becoming the disciple of Tōrin, Su Tung-po composed the

following gāthā (poem):

The sound of the brook is the wide and long tongue. Is the view of
the mountain not the body of purity? In the night I can have eighty-four

伍 黄龙和杨岐两宗派

黄龙慧南（1002—1069）是中国临济宗支系黄龙宗的创建人。
从慧南开始直到日本临济宗创建人明庵荣西的世系嗣承如下：

（1）黄龙慧南（1002—1069）

（2）晦堂祖心（1025—1100）

（3）灵源惟清（？—1117）

（4）长灵守卓（1065—1123）

（5）无示介谌（1080—1148）

（6）心闻昙贲

（7）雪庵从瑾（1117—1200）

（8）虚庵怀敞

（9）明庵荣西（1141—1215）

荣西是黄龙慧南的第八代法嗣。黄龙慧南的其他弟子还有：

（2a）云庵克文（1025—1102）

（2b）云盖守智（1025—1115）

（2c）泐潭洪英（1012—1070）

（2d）仰山行伟（1018—1080）

（2e）东林常总（1025—1091）

（2f）上蓝顺

云庵克文或宝峰克文，有三个弟子：

（3a）兜率从悦（1044—1091）

（3b）湛堂文准（1061—1115）

（3c）觉范慧洪（1071—1128）

东林常总有一非常有名的弟子苏东坡（1036—1101），是天才文
学家。至于上蓝顺的年龄很可能比东林大，他是苏东坡父亲的
好友，是苏东坡之弟苏辙的师父。

作为东林的弟子，苏东坡写了一首偈诗：

溪声便是广长舌，山色岂非清净身。

thousand gāthās. In the days to come how can I tell the others?

This poem was quoted by Dōgen Kigen, founder of the Sōtō School in Japan, in his treatise: *Shōbōgenzō*. Su Che was a good friend of Yun-an Ko-wen, and he wrote a Preface for the Dialogues of Yun-an Ko-wen.

Hui-tang (Kaidō) had other disciples besides Reigen. They were:

(3d) Tsao-tang Shan-ching (Sōdō Zensei, 1037-1142)

(3e) Ssu-hsin Wu-sin (Shishin Goshin, 1043-1114)

Tsao-tang (Sōdō) had a disciple Hsueh-feng Hui-kung (Seppō Ekū, 1096-1158). Ssu-hsin (Shishin) had a disciple Chao-tsung Hui-fang (Chōsō Ehō).

Reigen had another disciple:

(4a) Fu-hsin Pen-tsai (Butsushin Honsai), whose disciples were: Shan-tang Tsu-shun (Sandō Sojun) and Pien-feng Tsu-chin (Betsuhō Sochin).

Muji Kaijin had other disciples:

(6a) Tzu-han Liao-po (Jikō Ryōboku)

(6b) Tai-an Sien (Tai'an Sen)

Jikō's disciple was Hsueh-feng Seng-yen (Seppō Sō'en).

From Ōryū to Myōan Eisai, we had altogether nine generations. Many masters and lay disciples were produced. However, it remains for the Yōgi Sect to flourish even more after the nine generations.

The lineage from Yōgi to Mujun Shihan (1178-1249) is given below:

(1) Yang-chi Fang-hui (Yōgi Hō'e, 992-1049)

(2) Pai-yun Shou-tuan (Haku'un Shutan, 1025-1072)

(3) Wu-tsu Fa-yen (Goso Hō'en, 1024?-1104)

(4) Yuan-wu Ko-chin (Engo Kokugon, 1063-1135)

(5) Hu-chiu Shao-lung (Kokyū Shōryū, 1077-1136)

(6) Yin-an Tan-hua (Ō-an Donka, 1103-1163)

(7) Mi-an Hsien-chieh (Mittan Enketsu, 1118-1186)

(8) Pu-an Tsu-sien (Ha'an Sosen, 1136-1211)

(9) Wu-chun Shih-fan (Mujun Shihan, 1178-1249)

Note that Enji Ben'en (1202-1280) was Mujun's disciple, and hence he was the ninth-generation dharma descendant of Yōgi. (In Japan, Enji Ben'en was Myōan Eisai's dharma grandson.)

Starting from Goso Hō'en, another lineage can be established:

夜来八万四千偈，他日如何举似人。

日本曹洞宗的创建人道元希玄在他的论著《正法眼藏》中也引了这首诗偈。苏辙是云庵克文的好友，他为云庵克文的"对话集"写了一篇序。

晦堂祖心的弟子，除灵源惟清外还有两人：

（3d）草堂善清（1037—1142）

（3e）死心悟新（1043—1114）

草堂善清有一弟子为雪峰慧空（1096—1158），死心悟新有一弟子为超宗慧方。

灵源惟清的另一弟子为：

（4a）佛心本才。佛心的弟子则有山堂僧洵和别峰祖珍。

无示介谌的其他弟子有：

（6a）慈航了朴

（6b）退庵先

慈航的弟子是雪峰僧彦。

从黄龙慧南到明庵荣西，总共传了九代，已造就了许多禅师以及更多的俗家弟子。但从第九代以后，更为兴盛繁荣的则是杨岐宗。

从杨岐方会到无准师范的世系传承如下：

（1）杨岐方会（992—1049）　（2）白云守端（1025—1072）

（3）五祖法演（1024？—1104）（4）圆悟克勤（1063—1135）

（5）虎丘绍隆（1077—1136）　（6）应庵昙华（1103—1163）

（7）密庵咸杰（1118—1186）　（8）破庵祖先（1136—1211）

（9）无准师范（1178—1249）

注意：圆尔辨圆（1202—1280）是无准的弟子，所以应是杨岐的第九代法嗣。（在日本，圆尔辨圆也是黄龙宗明庵荣西的第二代法嗣。）

自五祖法演开始，又建立另一世系如下：

(3) Wu-tsu Fa-yen (Goso Hō'en, 1024?-1104)

(4a) Kai-fu Tao-ning (Kaifuku Dōnei, 1053-1113)

(5a) Yueh-an Shan-ko (Gettan Zenka, 1079-1152)

(6a) Ta-hung Tsu-chen (Daikō Soshō)

(7a) Yueh-lin Shih-kuan (Getsurin Shikan, 1143-1217)

(8a) Wu-men Hui-kai (Mumon Ekai, 1183-1260)

(9a) Hsin-ti Chueh-hsin (Shinchi Kakushin, 1207-1298)

Note that Kohō Kakumyō (1271-1361) was Shinchi Kakushin's disciple. Kohō's two disciples, Bassui Tokushō (1327-1387) and Jiun Myō'i (1273-1345), were the founders of Kōgaku-ji and Kokutai-ji in Japan respectively. Bassui had a disciple: Shun'ō Reizan (1344-1408).

Besides Yuan-wu Ko-chin (Engo Kokugon) and Kai-fu Tao-ning (Kaifuku Dōnei), Wu-tsu Fa-yen (Goso Hō'en) had other famous disciples:

(4b) Lung-men Ching-yuan (Ryūmon Sei'on, 1067-1120)

(4c) Tai-ping Hui-chin (Taihei Ekin, 1059-1117)

(4d) Ta-sui Yuan-ching (Daizui Genjō, 1065-1135) or Nan-tang Tao-
hsin (Nandō Dōkō, 1065-1135)

(4e) Hung-fu Tzu-wen (Kōfuku Shimon)

Lung-men (Ryūmon) had three disciples:

(5b) Mo-an Fa-chung (Boku'an Hōchū, 1084-1149)

(5c) Hsueh-tang Tao-hsing (Setsudō Dōkō, 1089-1151)

(5d) Cho-an Shi-kuei (Chikuan Shiki, 1083-1146)

Boku'an's disciple was: Pu-an Yin-shu (Fu'an Inshuku, 1115-1169). Setsudō's disciples were: Hui-an Hui-kuang (Kai'an Ekō) and Cho-an Shu-jen (Katsuan Shujin). Kai'an's disciples were: Hsueh-feng Yuan-shao (Seppō Genshō), Ching-shan Yuan-chun (Keisan Gensō), and Pao-en Chih-in (Hō'on Chi'in).

Yuan-wu Ko-chin (Engo Kokugon) had other disciples:

(5e) Ta-hui Tsung-kao (Daie Sōkō, 1089-1163)

(5f) Fu-hai Hui-yuan (Bukkai E'on, 1103-1176)

(5g) Fu-hsin Fa-tai (Bussei Hōtai)

(5h) Hu-kuo Ching-yuan (Gokoku Keigen, 1094-1146)

Ta-hui's disciples were:

(6b) Fu-chao Te-kuang (Busshō Tokkō, 1121-1203)

(6c) Lan-an Ting-hsi (Raian Teiju, 1092-1153)

Fu-chao's disciples were:

(7b) Kung-shu Tsung-in (Kūshū Sō'in, 1148-1211)

(7c) Po-chien Chu-chien (Hokkan Koken, 1164-1246)

（3）五祖法演（1024？—1104）（4a）开福道宁（1053—1113）

（5a）月庵善果（1079—1152）（6a）大洪祖证

（7a）月林师观（1143—1217）（8a）无门慧开（1183—1260）

（9a）心地觉心（1207—1298）

注意：心地觉心的弟子是孤峰觉明（1271—1361），而孤峰则有两个弟子——拔队得胜（1327—1387）和慈云妙意（1273—1345），两人分别为日本向岳寺和国泰寺的创建人。拔队得胜有一弟子为峻翁令山（1344—1408）。

五祖法演的弟子除圆悟克勤和开福道宁之外，其他有名弟子为：

（4b）龙门清远（1067—1120）（4c）太平慧勤（1059—1117）

（4d）大随元静，即南堂道兴（1065—1135）（4e）洪福子文

龙门清远有弟子三人：

（5b）牧庵法忠（1084—1149）（5c）雪堂道行（1089—1151）

（5d）竹庵士珪（1083—1146）

牧庵的弟子是普庵印肃（1115—1169），雪堂的弟子是晦庵惠光和且庵守仁，而晦庵惠光的弟子则有雪峰元笔、径山元聪和报恩智因。

圆悟克勤的其他弟子有：

（5e）大慧宗杲（1089—1163）（5f）佛海慧远（1103—1176）

（5g）佛性法泰;（5h）护国景元（1094—1146）

大慧宗杲的弟子有：

（6b）拙庵德光（佛照）（1121—1203）

（6c）懒庵鼎需（1092—1153）

拙庵德光的弟子有：

（7b）空叟宗印（1148—1211）

（7c）北涧居简（1164—1246）

Lan-an's disciples were:

(7d) Mo-an An-yun (Boku'an An'ei)

(7e) Po-tang Nan-ya (Hakudō Nanka)

Fu-hai Hui-yuan (Bukkai E'on) had two disciples:

(6d) Tsi-tien Tao-tsi (Saiten Dōsai, 1148-1207)

(6e) Chueh-er (Kaku'ō)

Kaku'ō came from Mount Hiei, Japan, and became enlightened on hearing the sound of drums by the Yangtze River. He went up Mount Hiei after his return to Japan, and never came down. So it was Myōan Eisai (1141-1215), the dharma descendant of the Ōryū Sect, who founded the Rinzai School in Japan. However, many masters in the Japanese Rinzai School came from the Yōgi Sect.

In the rest of this Chapter, we continue on with the Yōgi Sect. Starting from (4) Yuan-wu Ko-chin, (5) Hu-chiu Shao-lung, (6) Yin-an Tan-hua, and (7) Mi-an Hsien-chieh, we have parallel transmission as follows:

(8) Pu-an Tsu-sien (Ha'an Sosen, 1136-1211)

(8b) Sung-yuan Chung-yueh (Shōgen Sūgaku, 1132-1202)

(8c) Tsien-fu Tao-sen (Senfuku Dōsei)

(9) Wu-chun Shih-fan (Mujun Shihan, 1178-1249)

(9b) Yun-an Pu-yen (Un'an Fugan, 1156-1226)

(9c) Chi-zei Tao-chung (Chizetsu Dōchū, 1169-1250)

(10) Wu-hsueh Tsu-yuan (Mugaku Sogen, 1226-1286)

(10b) Hsu-tang Chih-yu (Kidō Chigu, 1185-1269)

(10c) Wan-chi Hsing-mi (Gankyoku Kōmi)

Note that after (7) Mi-an Hsien-chieh (Mittan Enketsu), we have three parallel lines: the first line goes through Pu-an Tsu-sien (Ha'an Sosen), Wu-chun Shih-fan (Mujun Shihan), to Wu-hsueh Tsu-yuan (Mugaku Sogen), who went to Japan and became the founder of Engaku-ji. Mujun Shihan's other disciples were:

(10d) Hsueh-yen Tsu-ching (Seggan Sokin, 1216-1287)

(10e) Ge-an Pu-ning (Gottan Funnei, 1197-1276)

(10f) Miao-chien Tao-yu (Myōken Dōyū, 1201-1256)

(10g) Zing-tzu Miao-lun (Jōji Myōrin, 1201-1261)

(10h) Huan-chi Wei-i (Kankei I'itsu, 1202-1281)

Note that Gottan Funnei and Huan-chi's disciple, Ching-tang Chueh-yuan (Kyōdō Kaku'en, 1244-1306) went to Japan. Zing-tzu Miao-lun's disciple Mukan Fumon (1212-1291) went back to Japan and became

懒庵鼎需的弟子则有：

（7d）木庵安永

（7e）柏堂南雅

佛海慧远有弟子两人：

（6d）济颠道济（1148—1207）

（6e）觉阿

觉阿来自日本比睿山，在中国听到了扬子江的击鼓声而启悟。回日本后上了比睿山，从此就不再下山了。因此，创建日本临济宗的明庵荣西（1141—1215）是黄龙宗的传嗣，不过日本临济宗的许多禅师则是来自杨岐宗。

本章以下部分将继续叙述杨岐宗。始自（4）圆悟克勤，（5）虎丘绍隆，（6）应庵昙华，（7）密庵咸杰，另有一平行世系如下：

（8）破庵祖先（1136—1211）　（8b）松源崇岳（1132—1202）

（8c）荐福道生　　　　　　　（9）无准师范（1178—1249）

（9b）运庵普岩（1156—1226）（9c）痴绝道冲（1169—1250）

（10）无学祖元（1226—1286）（10b）虚堂智愚（1185—1269）

（10c）顽极行弥

注意：在（7）密庵咸杰之后共有三个平行世系，第一世系经过破庵祖先和无准师范传到无学祖元。后来无学去了日本，是圆觉寺的创建人。无准师范的其他弟子有：

（10d）雪岩祖钦（1216—1287）（10e）兀庵普宁（1197—1276）

（10f）妙见道佑（1201—1256）（10g）净慈妙伦（1201—1261）

（10h）环溪惟一（1202—1281）

注意兀庵普宁和环溪惟一的弟子镜堂觉圆（1244—1306）去了日本，而净慈妙伦的弟子无关普门（1212—1291）回到日本后成为南禅寺

the founder of Nanzen-ji. Myōken Dōyū also came to Sung-China from Japan. His disciple, Wu-kung Ching-nien (Gokū Keinen, 1217-1272), also studied in China.

Pu-an Tsu-sien (Ha'an Sosen) had another disciple, Shih-tien Fa-hsun (Sekida Hōkun, 1171-1245), whose disciple was Yu-chi Chih-hui (Gukyoku Chi'e). Gukyoku's disciple, Ching-cho Cheng-cheng (Seisetsu Shōchō, 1274-1339), went to Japan.

After (7) Mi-an Hsien-chieh, the (b) line started from Sung-yuan (Shōgen), went through Yun-an Pu-yen to (10b) Hsu-tang Chih-yu (Kidō Chigu, 1185-1269). Kidō's disciple, Nampo Jōmyō (1235-1308), was a great Rinzai Master well-known by his honored title, Daiō Kokushi (National Teacher). Nampo's disciple was Shūhō Myōchō (1281-1336), well-known by his honored title, Daitō Kokushi. Shūhō's disciple was Kanzan Egen (1277-1360). So Kidō was the spiritual leader of both the Daitoku-ji and Myōshin-ji in Japan. Kidō had another disciple, Chu-shan Chih-yuan (Kyōsan Shigen), who came from Japan. Kidō's dharma brother, Shih-fan Wei-yen (Sekihan I'en), had a disciple, Shi-chien Tzu-tan (Saikan Sudon, 1249-1306), who went to Japan and became the dharma teacher of Sung-shan Chu-chung (Sūsan Kyochū, 1278-1346).

After (7) Mi-an Hsien-chieh, the (c) line started from Tsien-fu (Senfuku), went through Chi-zei Tao-chung to (10c) Wan-chi Hsing-mi (Gankyoku Kōmi). Wan-chi's disciple, I-shan I-ning (Issan Innei, 1247-1317), went to Japan and became the dharma teacher of Hsueh-tsen Yu-mei (Sesson Yūbai, 1290-1346).

Mi-an's disciple (8b) Sung-yuan Chung-yueh (Shōgen Sūgaku) had great influence in the Rinzai School in Japan, not only because Kidō was Shōgen's dharma grandson, but also because another dharma grandson, Lan-chi Tao-lung (Rankei Dōryū, 1213-1278), was the founder of Kenchō-ji. Besides Yun-an Pu-yen (Unan Fugan), Sung-yuan had the following disciples and descendants:

(9d) Wu-ming Hui-shin (Mumyō Esei, 1162-1237)

(9e) Yen-an Shan-kai (En'an Zenkai)

(9f) Wu-ai Chueh-tung (Mugai Kakutsu)

(9g) Mi-on Wen-li (Metsu'ō Bunri, 1167-1250)

(10d) Lan-chi Tao-lung (Rankei Dōryū, 1213-1278)

(10e) Shih-chi Hsin-yueh (Sekikei Shingetsu, d. 1282)

(10f) Hsu-chou Pu-tu (Kishū Fudo, 1199-1280)

(10g) Huen-chuan Ju-kung (Ō-kawa Nyokyō, 1221-1289)

的创建人。妙见道佑是在南宋时期从日本来到中国的，他的弟子悟空敬念（1217—1272）也来到中国修道学佛。

（8）破庵祖先另有一弟子石田法薰（1171—1245），石田弟子是愚极智慧，愚极弟子清拙正澄（1274—1339）则去了日本。

在（7）密庵咸杰之后的一支系，从松源崇岳开始，经运庵普岩传到（10b）虚堂智愚（1185—1269）。虚堂的弟子南浦绍明（1235—1308）是一位卓越的临济宗禅师，以其尊号"大应国师"而著称。南浦的弟子宗峰妙超（1281—1336），也以其尊号"大灯国师"而著称。宗峰的弟子是关山慧玄（1277—1360），所以虚堂就成为日本大德寺和妙心寺在名义上或精神上的祖师了。虚堂另有一弟子巨山志源来自日本，虚堂的师兄弟石帆惟衍则有一弟子西涧子昙（1249—1306）去了日本，并成为嵩山居中（1278—1346）的宗师。

在（7）密庵咸杰之后的另一支系从荐福道生开始，经痴绝道冲传到（10c）顽极行弥。顽极的弟子一山一宁（1247—1317）去了日本，并成为雪村友梅（1290—1346）的宗师。

密庵的弟子（8b）松源崇岳对日本临济宗有很大影响，不仅因为虚堂智愚是松源的第二代弟子，而且因为松源还另有一个第二代弟子兰溪道隆（1213—1278）是建长寺的创建人。松源的其他弟子和传嗣，除云庵普岩外还有：

（9d）无明慧性（1162—1237）（9e）掩庵善开（金山）

（9f）无碍觉通（华藏）（9g）灭翁文礼（天目）（1167—1250）

（10d）兰溪道隆（1213—1278）（10e）石溪心月（？—1282）

（10f）虚舟普度（1199—1280）（10g）横川如珙（1221—1289）

Lan-chi Tao-lung (Rankei Dōryū) had many dharma heirs: among them were Nampo Jōmyō and Yaku'ō Tokuken (1245-1320), both of whom went to Sung-China. Yaku'ō's disciple, Jakushitsu Genkō (1290-1367), also went to China and became later the founder of Eigen-ji.

Shih-chi (Sekikei) had two important disciples: one was Mushō Jōshō (1234-1306), who came to Sung-China; and the other was Ta-hsiu Cheng-nien (Daikyū Shōnen, 1215-1289), who went to Japan and became the founder of Jōchi-ji.

Hsu-chou Pu-tu (Kishū Fudo) had two important disciples: Hu-yen Zing-fu (Kogan Jōfuku) and Shōrin Kyūrin, who came from Japan. Hu-yen (Kogan) had several disciples: Ming-chi Tsu-tsun (Myōkyoku Soshun, 1262-1336), who went to Japan; Chi-hsiu Chih-liao (Sokukyū Keiryō, d. 1350), whose disciple Guchū Shūkyū (1323-1409) came to China and later became the founder of Fotsu-ji.

Huen-chuan Ju-kung (Ō-kawa Nyokyō) had a disciple: Ku-lin Ching-mu (Korin Seimo), who had three famous disciples: Cho-sien Fan-sien (Jikusen Bonsen), who went to Japan; Yueh-lin Tao-chao (Getsurin Dōkyō, 1293-1351); and Shih-shih Shan-chiu (Sekishitsu Zenkyū, 1294-1389). Both Getsurin and Sekishitsu went to Yuan-China and then returned to Japan.

Wu-chun Shih-fan (Mujun Shihan) had many disciples, among them were Enji Ben'en, who came from Japan, and later became the founder of Tōfuku-ji; and Wu-hsueh Tsu-yuan (Mugaku Sogen), who was invited to Japan to be the founder of Engaku-ji. Mugaku's disciples were:

Kōhō Kennichi (1241-1316)

Ki'an So'en (1261-1313)

Kennichi's disciple Musō Soseki (1275-1351) was most influential in Japan and became the founder of Tenryū-ji and Shōkoku-ji. Musō Kokushi (National Teacher) had many disciples: (1) Shun'oku Myōha (1311-1388); (2) Mukyoku Shigen (1282-1359); (3) Zekkai Chūshin (1336-1405), who went to Ming-China; (4) Gidō Shūshin (1325-1388); and (5) Seisan Ji'ei (1302-1369).

Hsueh-yen Tsu-chin (Seggan Sokin, 1216-1287) had many disciples, among them were: (1) Kao-feng Yuan-miao (Kōhō Gemmyō, 1238-1295); (2) Hsuko Hsi-lin (Kikoku Keryō, 1247-1322); (3) Ti-niu Ju-ting (Tetsugo Jitei, 1240-1303); (4) Ling-shan Tao-yin (Reisan Dō'in, 1255-1325), who went to Japan; and (5) Tao-chang An-shin (Dōjō Anshin).

兰溪道隆有许多法嗣，其中如南浦绍明和约翁德俭（1245—1320），两人在宋朝时都来过中国。约翁的弟子寂室元光（1290—1367）也曾来过中国，以后成为永源寺的创建人。

石溪心月有两个重要弟子，其一是无象静照（1234—1306），也在宋朝时到中国来；另一人则是大休正念（1215—1289），在去日本后成为净智寺的创建人。

虚舟普度有两名重要弟子：虎岩净伏和胜林琼林（来自日本）。虎岩有几个弟子如：去了日本的明极楚俊（1262—1336）以及即休契了（？—1350）。即休的弟子愚中周及（1323—1409）则由日本来到中国，以后成为佛通寺的创建人。

横川如珙有一弟子为古林清茂，古林有著名弟子三人：竺仙梵仙去了日本，月林道皎（1293—1351）及石室善玖（1294—1389）两人则在元朝时来过中国，后再回到日本。

无准师范有很多弟子，其中如圆尔辨圆来自日本，后为东福寺的创建人，还有无学祖元则被邀请去了日本，是圆觉寺的创建人。无学祖元的弟子有：

高峰显日（1241—1316）

规庵祖圆（1261—1313）

高峰显日的弟子梦窗疏石（1275—1351）在日本非常有影响，成为天龙寺和相国寺的创建人。梦窗还是国师，有许多弟子：（1）春屋妙葩（1311—1388）；（2）无极志玄（1282—1359）；（3）绝海中津（1336—1405），在明朝时来到中国；（4）义堂周信（1325—1388）；以及（5）青山慈永（1302—1369）。

雪岩祖钦（1216—1287）有许多弟子，其中如：（1）高峰原妙（1238—1295）；（2）虚谷希陵（1247—1322）；（3）铁牛持定（1240—1303）；（4）灵山道隐（1255—1325），后去日本；（5）道场庵信。

Kao-feng Yuan-miao's lineage went down to Yin-yuan Lung-chi (Ingen Ryūki, 1592-1673) as follows:

(1) Kōhō Genmyō (1238-1295)

(2) Chūhō Myōhon (1263-1323)

(3) Sengan Genchō (1284-1357)

(4) Manhō Jijō (1303-1381)

(5) Hōzō Fuji

(6) Kihaku Egaku (1372-1441)

(7) Kaishū Eiji (1393-1461)

(8) Hōhō Myōken (d. 1472)

(9) Tenki Honzui

(10) Mubun Shōsō (1450-1512)

(11) Getsushin Tokuhō (1512-1581)

(12) Genyū Shōden (1549-1614)

(13) Mitsu'un Engo (1566-1642)

(14) Hi-in Tsuyō (1593-1661)

(15) Ingen Ryūki (1592-1673) (See Chart VI).

Note that Yin-yuan Lung-chi (Ingen Ryūki) was the fifteenth generation dharma descendant of Hsueh-yen Tsu-chin (Seggan Sokin), and became the founder of Ōbaku School in Japan.

Hsu-ko Hsi-lin (Kikoku Keryō) had a disciple Pien-chuan Miao-yin (Betsuden Myō'in), whose disciple was Yu-kang Tsang-chin (Gyoku'oka Zōchin, 1315-1395). Ti-niu Ju-ting (Tetsugo Jitei) had a disciple Zei-hsueh Shih-chen (Zetsugaku Sesei, 1260-1332), whose disciple was Ku-mei Cheng-yu (Kobai Shōyū, 1285-1352). Ku-mei's disciple was Wu-wen Yuan-hsuan (Mumon Gensen, 1323-1390), who was the founder of Hōkō-ji in Japan. Tao-chang An-shin (Dōjō Anshin) had a disciple Shih-ou Ching-kung (Seki'oku Seikyō, 1272-1352).

Kao-feng Yuan-miao (Kōhō Gemmyō) had other disciples: Dangai Ryōgi (1263-1334); Haku'un I'ka (d. 1336); and Daikaku Soyō.

Chung-feng Ming-pen (Chūhō Myōhon) had other disciples: Muin

Genkai (d. 1358), Kosen Ingen (1295-1374), Myōshū Seitetsu (d. 1347), Fuku'an Sōki (1280-1358), Onkei Soyū (1286-1344), Gyōkai Honjō (d. 1352), and Kansai Ginan. All these seven priests came from Japan and went back to spread the teachings of Chūhō Myōhon.

从高峰原妙到隐元隆琦的传承世系如下：
（1）高峰原妙（1238—1295）
（2）中峰明本（1263—1323）
（3）千岩元长（1284—1357）
（4）万峰时蔚（1303—1381）
（5）宝藏普持
（6）虚白慧岳（1372—1441）
（7）海舟永慈（1393—1461）
（8）宝峰明瑄（？—1472）
（9）天奇本瑞
（10）无闻正聪（1450—1512）
（11）月心德宝（1512—1581）
（12）幻有正传（1549—1614）
（13）密云圆悟（1566—1642）
（14）费隐通容（1593—1661）
（15）隐元隆琦（1592—1673）（见表Ⅵ）
注意：这里隐元隆琦是雪岩左钦的第十五代传嗣，成为日本黄檗宗的创建人。
虚谷希陵有一弟子别传妙胤，别传的弟子是玉冈藏珍（1315—1395）。铁牛持定有一弟子绝学世诚（1260—1332），再传弟子为古梅正友（1285—1352），又传弟子为无文元选（1323—1390），是日本方广寺的创建人。道场庵信有一弟子为石屋清珙（1272—1352）。
（1）高峰原妙的其他弟子有：断崖了义（1263—1334）、白云以假（？—1336）和大觉祖雍。
（2）中峰明本的其他弟子有：无隐元晦（？—1358），古先印元（1295—1374），明叟齐哲（？—1347），复庵宗已（1280—1358），远溪祖雄（1286—1344），业海本净（？—1352），及关西义南。此七人全都来自日本，回日本后传播中峰明本的教义。

Sengan Genchō's other disciples were: Daisetsu Sonō (1313-1377), who came from Japan; Hō'on Baikei, whose disciple Shōsō Nichigan came from Japan; and Muyō Shuki (1286-1361).

(4) Manhō Jijō had another disciple Kaishū Fuji (1355-1450).

(9) Tenki Honzui had two other disciples: Musō Jō, and Daisen Kō.

(12) Genyū Shōden (1549-1614) was also known as Ryūchi (Dragon Pond). He had two important disciples: Mitsu'un (Tendō) Engo (1566-1642) and Ten'in Enshū (1575-1635). Mitsu'un had the following disciples: Hi-in Tsuyō (1593-1661), Gohō Nyogaku (1585-1633), Hōka Tsunin (1604-1648), Ryūchi Tsubi (1594-1657), Tendō Dōbun (1596-1674), Konan Tsumon (1599-1671), Tsugen Tsuki (1595-1652), Hasan Kaimyō (1597-1666), Kinzoku Tsujō (1593-1638), Setchō Tsu'un (1594-1663), Hō'on Tsuken (1593-1667), and Tōjō Hōzō. Ten'in Enshū's disciples were: Kassan Honyo (d. 1646), Hō'on Tsushū (1614-1675), Ri'an Tsumon (1604-1655); Shōsai Tsuju (1593-1642), and Sanshi Tsusai (1608-1645).

At the end of this Chapter we shall trace the lineage from Zing-tzu Miao-lun (Jōji Myōrin, 1201-1261) to Han-shan Te-ching (Kansan Tokusei, 1546-1623). Note that Jōji Myōrin was a dharma brother of Mugaku Sogen and Seggan Sokin.

(1) Jōji Myōrin (1201-1261)

(2) Zuigan Bunhō (d. 1335)

(3) Kachō Sento (1265-1334)

(4) Fukurin Chito (1304-1370)

(5) Kosetsu Shōshun

(6) Musai Myōgo

From Musai Myōgo on we have three parallel branches: (a), (b), and (c).

(7a) Hōgetsu Tan

(8a) Tennei Sen

(9a) Kichi'an So

(10a) Hōshū Dōsai (1487-1560)

(11a) Unkoku Hō'e (1500-1579)

(12a) Kansan Tokusei (1546-1623)

(13a) Gǔ'eki Chikyoku (1599-1655)

（3）千岩元长的其他弟子有：来自日本的大拙祖能（1313—1377）以及报恩梅溪。报恩的弟子为正宗日颜，也来自日本，还有无用守贵（1286—1361）。

（4）万峰时蔚的另一弟子是海舟普慈（1355—1450）。

（9）天奇本瑞另有两弟子：无相成和大川洪。

（12）幻有正传（1549—1614），又名龙池，有两名重要弟子：密云圆悟（1566—1642）及天隐圆修（1575—1635）。密云的弟子有：费隐通容（1593—1661），五峰如学（1585—1633），宝华通忍（1604—1648），龙池通微（1594—1657），天童道忞（1596—1674），古南道门（1599—1671），通玄通奇（1595—1652），破山海明（1597—1666），金粟通乘（1593—1638），雪窦通云（1594—1663），报恩通贤（1593—1667），以及邓尉法藏。天隐圆修的弟子则有：夹山本豫（？—1646），报恩通琇（1614—1675），理安通问（1604—1655），松际通授（1593—1642），以及山茨通际（1608—1645）。

本章以下部分将跟踪自净慈妙伦（1201—1261）到憨山德清（1546—1623）的传承世系。这里应注意，净慈妙伦也是无学祖元和雪岩祖钦的师兄弟。

（1）净慈妙伦（1201—1261）

（2）瑞岩文宝（？—1335）

（3）华顶先睹（1265—1334）

（4）福林智度（1304—1370）

（5）古拙昌俊

（6）无际明悟

自无际明悟开始，共有三个平行分支（a）、（b）和（c），分列如下：

（7a）宝月潭

（8a）天宁宣

（9a）吉庵祚

（10a）法舟道济（1487—1560）

（11a）云谷法会（1500—1579）

（12a）憨山德清（1546—1623）

（13a）藕益智旭（1599—1655）

Han-shan Te-ching (Kansan Tokusei, 1546-1623) was a great friend of Tzu-po Cheng-ko (Shihaku Shinka, 1543-1603) and Lien-chi Chih-hung (Renchi Shukō, 1535-1615). By the end of Ming Dynasty, these three priests and Ngo-i Chih-hsueh (Gū'eki Chikyoku, 1599-1655) were the four great masters. We have designated Gū'eki as the dharma-heir of Kansan. (See Rev. Chang Sheng-yen Litt. D., *Chinese Buddhism near the End of Ming Dynasty*, page 99.)

The (b) branch is given below:

(7b) Tai'oka Chō

(8b) Gihō Nei (d. 1491)

(9b) Temmoku (Hōhō) Shin

(10b) Ya'ō Egyō

(11b) Mushu Nyokū (1491-1580)

(12b) Mugen Seichū (1540-1611)

(13b) Kōzen Ekō (1576-1620)

(14b) Fumyō Myōyō (1587-1642)

(15b) Kōan Ensei (Kozan line)

Note that Kōan Ensei was an Abbot at Kozan-ji, Foochow. The Kōan line or the Kozan line went down to Abbot Hsu Yun (Kiun, 1840-1959) and beyond. (See Chart VI A). The author is indebted to Reverend Ling-yuan (Reigen, 1902-) of Daikaku-ji, Keelung, Taiwan, for obtaining the *Star-Lamp Records*, edited by Abbot Hsu Yun, whom the author had the privilege to know in person in 1941-1942 . (See Chart VI A).

The (c) branch started from Sosan Shōki and then was further divided.

(7c) Sosan Shōki (1404-1473)

(8c) Katsudō Soyū

(9c) Tentsu Ken

(10c) Getsusen Hōshu (1492-1563)

Designating the sub-branch of (c) as (d), there are:

(8d) Kokei Kakuchō (d. 1473)

(9d) Dokuhō Kizen (1443-1523)

Note that (10a) Hōshū Dōsai (1487-1560), (11b) Mushu Nyokū (1491-1580), and (10c) Getsusen Hōshu (1492-1563) were contemporaries. Also note that Ingen Ryūki (1592-1673) and (13a) Gū'eki Chikyoku (1599-1655) were contemporaries.

憨山德清（1546—1623）是紫柏真可（1543—1603）和莲池袾宏（1535—1615）的挚友。这三位大师再加上藕益智旭是明代末年的四大禅师。不过如上所列，藕益应是憨山的法嗣（见圣严法师：《明末中国佛教之研究》，第 99 页）。

分支（b）的传承世系如下：

（7b）太冈澄　　　　　　　（8b）夷峰宁（？—1491）

（9b）天目进（宝芳）　　　（10b）野翁慧晓

（11b）无趣如空（1491—1580）（12b）无幻性冲（1540—1611）

（13b）兴善慧广（1576—1620）（14b）普明德用（1587—1642）

（15b）高庵圆清（鼓山系）

按：高庵圆清即是福州鼓山寺的方丈。高庵系亦即鼓山系一直传到虚云禅师（1840—1959）及其后嗣（见附表 VI A）。本书作者感谢台湾基隆大觉寺灵源方丈（1902—　）所提供的《星灯集》，由虚云禅师编纂成集。作者于 1941—1942 年有幸亲自认识虚云方丈（见附表 VI A）。

分支（c）的传承世系如下：

（7c）楚山绍琦（1404—1473）

（8c）豁堂祖裕

（9c）天通显

（10c）月泉法聚（1492—1563）

用（d）来表示（c）的分支则有：

（8d）古溪觉澄（？—1473）；（9d）毒峰季善（1443—1523）；注意：（10a）法舟道济（1487—1560）、（11b）无趣如空（1491—1580）及（10c）月泉法聚（1492—1563）都是同时代人。又可注意：（15）隐元隆琦（1592—1673）及（13a）藕益智旭（1599—1655）也是同时代人。

128

The Kōan or Kozan line can be given below:

(1) Kōan Ensei

(2) Honchi Myōkaku

(3) Shikaku Shinke (1543-1603)

(4) Tankyoku Nyokō

(5) Junketsu Shōki

(6) Jiun Kaishun

(7) Tetsushin Jakubun

(8) Tan'en Shōka

(9) Chigan Fumyō

(10) Taikyō Tsūshō

(11) Goshū Shinkū

(12) Kōka Gengo

(13) Shōsei Kōshō

(14) Shudō Zokusen

(15) Shōgaku Honchō

(16) Eishō Kakujō

(17) Hōrai Shō'on

(18) Katsugo Ryūsen

(19) Ichō Nōsan

(20) Kiryō Jinhan

(21) Myōren Shōka

(22) Teihō Kajō

(23) Zenji Shōkai

(24) Entetsu Tokusei (Kiun, 1840-1959)

(25) Kan'in Butsu'e

(26) Kōmyō Reigen (1902-)

(27) Itei Chishin

(27a) Ijū Chigō

Reverend Reigen was Founder and Abbot of Daikaku-ji, Keelung, Taiwan. Among his many disciples are: Itei Chishin, present Abbot of Daikaku-ji, Keelung; and Ekū Shōgen (1930-), Litt.D., former Abbot of Daikaku-ji, New York City, N.Y., U.S.A., who was given the name Ijū Chigō.

The author wishes to acknowledge his deep indebtedness to Reverend Ling-yuan (Reigen) for supplying the above lineage from *Star-Lamp Records*. Note that *Star-Lamp Records* was reprinted in *Dharma Records of Abbot Hsu Yun*, Vol. 8, pages 246-262.

Now we shall trace the lineage of the Kao-min Temple (Kōmin-ji) line from Hō'on (Gyokurin) Tsūshū to Abbot Lai-Ko (Raika, 1881-1953). (See Chart VI B).

(1) Gyokurin Tsūshū (1614-1675)

(2) Sei'un Kōgaku (1614-1666)

(3) Nankoku Chō'ei

(4) Reiju Meisei (1657-1722)

(5) Ten'e Jitsutetsu

(6) Ryōhan Saishō (1700-1756)

高庵系亦即鼓山系的传承世系如下：

（1）高庵圆清　　　　（2）本智明觉

（3）紫柏真可（1543—1603）

（4）端旭如弘　　　　（5）纯洁性奎

（6）慈云海俊　　　　（7）质生寂文

（8）端员照华　　　　（9）其岸普明

（10）弢巧通圣　　　　（11）悟修心空

（12）宏化源悟　　　　（13）祥青广松

（14）守道续先　　　　（15）正岳本超

（16）永畅觉乘　　　　（17）方来昌远

（18）豁悟隆参　　　　（19）维超能灿

（20）奇量仁繁　　　　（21）妙莲圣华

（22）鼎峰果成　　　　（23）善慈常开

（24）演彻德清（虚云，1840—1959）

（25）宽印佛慧　　　　（26）宏妙灵源（1902—？）

（27）惟定知生　　　　（27a）惟柔知刚（圣严）

灵源法师是台湾基隆十方大觉寺的创建人和方丈，他的众多弟子中有：惟定知生，是当今基隆大觉寺的方丈；以及慧空圣严（1930—　），是美国纽约大觉寺的前方丈，其法名即是惟柔知刚。

本书作者愿在此深切感谢灵源法师根据《星灯集》提供了上述的传承世系。该《星灯集》已收入《虚云和尚法汇》第8卷中（第246—262页）。

以下将跟踪从报恩玉琳通琇到来果方丈（1881—1953）的高旻系的传承世系（见附表 VI B）：

（1）玉琳通琇（1614—1675）

（2）栖云行岳（1614—1666）

（3）南谷超颖

（4）灵鹫明诚（1657—1722）

（5）天慧实彻

（6）了凡际圣（1700—1756）

(7) Shōgetsu Ryōtei (1729-1785)

(8) Hōrin Tatsuchin

(8a) Nyokan Tatsuchō

(9) Hōshu Gosei

(10) Dōgen Shinjin

(11) Tokūji Kū'en

(12) Ōgen Ri

(13) Rōki Riji

(14) Getsurō Zentei

(14a) Sozen Zenshin

(15) Meiken Saizui

(16) Myōju Raika (1881-1953)

(17) Myōge

The lineage from Gyokurin to Sozen Zenshin was taken from Mōgetsu Shinkyō's *Bukkyō Dainen Hyō*, 4th edition, page 52. The author wishes to thank Reverend Lun-tsan of Hong Kong and Reverend Yen-chih of Hua-lien Buddhist Lotus Institute, Taiwan, for supplying information concerning the lineage of Reverend Lai-Ko (Raika).

（7）昭月了贞（1729—1785）

（8）宝林达珍

（8a）如鉴达澄

（9）方聚悟成

（10）道源真仁

（11）德慈空演

（12）应元理

（13）朗辉事融

（14）月朗全定

（14a）楚禅全振

（15）明轩西瑞

（16）妙树来果（1881—1953）

（17）妙解

以上从玉琳通琇到楚禅全振的传承世系摘自望月信亨编《佛教大年表》第4版第52页。本书作者愿在此感谢香港伦参法师及台湾花莲佛教莲社的严持法师，由他们提供了有关来果法师的传承资料。

CHAPTER 6   THE SEIGEN BRANCH

Ching-yuan Hsing-ssu (Seigen Gyōshi, d. 740) started the Seigen Branch of Zen after Hui-neng (Enō), the Sixth Patriarch. R. H. Blyth's *Zen and Zen Classics*, Volume 2 and the first chapter of Volume 3, depicted this branch of Zen history. The Seigen Branch produced the Tsao-tung (Sōtō) School, the Yun-men (Ummon) School, and the Fa-yen (Hōgen) School.

Although Ho-tse Shen-hui (Kataku Jinne, 670-762) made tremendous effort to establish Hui-neng (Enō) as the Sixth Patriarch and to make Tsao-hsi (Sōkei) the principal seat of Zen Monastery, Ching-yuan (Seigen) carried on the dharma lineage parallel to Nan-yueh Huai-jang (Nangaku Ejō, 677-744), who was the founder of the Nangaku Branch.

In Chapter 2, mention was made of Hui-neng's FIVE important disciples: (1) Ho-tse Shen-hui (Kataku Jinne, 670-762); (2) Nan-yang Hui-chung (Nan'yō Echū, d. 775); (3) Yung-chia Hsuan-chueh (Yōka Genkaku, 665-713); (4) Nan-yueh Huai-jang (Nangaku Ejō, 677-744); and (5) Ching-yuan Hsing-ssu (Seigen Gyōshi, d. 740). Shen-hui's line went as far as Kuei-feng Tsung-mi (Keihō Shūmitsu, 780-841), who became the Fifth Patriarch of the Hua-yen (Kegon) School. Yung-chia (Yōka) left posterity with his "Cheng-tao-ke" ("Shōdka") and other writings. Hui-chung (Echū), the National Teacher (Kokushi), lived long, and became an old dharma uncle to the younger masters of the different schools.

The transmission of the "Lamp" was carried on in two parallel branches: the Seigen Branch and the Nangaku Branch. In Chapter 3, the Nangaku Branch was presented, together with a brief review of the Igyō School founded by Kuei-shan (Isan) and his disciple Yang-shan (Kyōzan). In Chapter 4, the Lin-chi (Rinzai) School, founded by Lin-chi I-hsuan (Rinzai Gigen, d. 866), was presented. The Rinzai School, after six generations, branched out into the Huang-lung (Ōryū) Sect and the Yang-chi (Yōgi) Sect. These two Sects were presented in Chapter 5.

The Seigen Branch was as promising as the Nangaku Branch in the transmission of the "Lamp." Ching-yuan (Seigen) himself was a devoted disciple of Enō, and he left Tsao-hsi (Sōkei) to reside at Zing-chu Temple, Ching-yuan Mountain (Mt. Seigen), in Chi-chou (Kichishū). When the Sixth Patriarch was about to enter nirvana, Shih-tou Hsi-chien (Sekitō Kisen, 700-790) asked Master Enō whom should he seek as his teacher. The Sixth Patriarch instructed him to seek "ssu" (in Chinese it means "thinking"). So Sekitō later sat quietly and kept on "thinking." Then a monk reminded Sekitō that "Hsing-ssu," his dharma older brother, had

陆 青原系

青原行思（？—740）开创了六祖慧能之后禅宗的青原系。R. H. 布莱思的《禅与禅宗经典》第 2 卷和第 3 卷第 1 章都描述了禅宗历史的这一系。由青原系产生了曹洞宗、云门宗和法眼宗。

虽然荷泽神会（670—762）在奠定慧能的六祖地位和促使曹溪成为禅宗寺院的首座方面作出了巨大的努力，但青原却继承了与南岳系创建人南岳怀让（677—744）平行的禅法衣钵。

在第二章中曾提到慧能的五大弟子：（1）荷泽神会（670—762），（2）南阳慧忠（？—775），（3）永嘉玄觉（665—713），（4）南岳怀让（677—744）和（5）青原行思（？—740）。荷泽神会一支传到圭峰宗密（780—841），后者成为华严宗的五祖。永嘉的传世之作有《证道歌》等。南阳慧忠国师寿长，因而成为各个不同宗派年轻禅师们的佛门师叔。

法灯的传承由两个平行的派系分别进行，即青原系和南岳系。第三章介绍了南岳系，同时简要概述了沩山灵佑及其弟子仰山慧寂建立的沩仰宗。第四章介绍了临济义玄建立的临济宗。临济宗经过六传之后，分支为黄龙宗和杨岐宗两派，这两宗派都在第五章中作了介绍。

同南岳系一样，青原系在法灯传承中是大有作为的。青原本人是慧能的虔诚弟子，后来他离开曹溪，移居吉州青原山静居寺。当六祖即将进入涅槃之际，石头希迁问六祖慧能，他应寻找何人为师？六祖教导他寻"思"。因此石头后来就静坐深"思"。其后，有一僧人提醒石头，其法门师兄青原行思的名字中有"思"，

the name "ssu," and suggested that Shih-tou (Sekitō) should visit Seigen according to the Six Patriarch's wishes. So the Sixth Patriarch must have thought highly of Seigen, and Seigen might have received the Sixth Patriarch's special teachings.

Shih-tou (Sekitō) became the dharma-heir of Seigen. The Nangaku Branch had the second-generation heir Ma-tsu Tao-i (Baso Dōitsu, 709-788), who was a powerful teacher, revered by his followers as Master Ma. Sekitō left Seigen Mountain for Heng-shan (Hunan), and built a small hermitage on a stone terrace. Hence he got the name, Shih-tou (Sekitō), meaning "stone." It was said at that time, "West of the Great River (Kiangsi), Ta-chi (Daijaku) is the Master; south of the Lake (Hunan), Shih-tou (Sekitō) is the Master." According to the *Lamp Records*, Vol. 14, Sekitō had twenty-one dharma-heirs, among them were:

(1) Tien-huang Tao-wu (Tennō Dōgo, 748-807)

(2) Tan-hsia Tien-jan (Tanka Tennen, 739-834)

(3) Yueh-shan Wei-yen (Yakusan Igen, 751-834)

(4) Tan-chou Chang-tze Kuang (Tanshū Chōshi Kō)

(5) Chao-chou Ta-tien Pao-tung (Chōshū Daiten Hōtsu, 732-824)

(6) Tan-chou Ta-chuan (Tanshū Daisen)

The first four had the title Zen-shi (Zenji), while the other two had the title Ho-shan (oshō), meaning Chief Priest.

Sekitō was the author of *Tsan-tung-chi* (*Sandōkai*), which was handed down to the followers of the Seigen Branch, and later to the Sōtō School, the Ummon School, and the Hōgen School. In the Sōtō School, Tung-shan Liang-chieh (Tōzan Ryōkai, 807-869) constructed the doctrine of the Five Ranks upon the foundation of the dialectic of Sekitō Kisen and other earlier Zen Masters. (See *The Development of Chinese Zen*, by Heinrich Dumoulin, S. J., English translation by Ruth Fuller Sasaki. The First Zen Institute of America Inc., 1953, page 25.)

Sekitō first served under Enō, the Sixth Patriarch, when he was very young. After Enō's passing he became the dharma-heir of Seigen. The following anecdotes were taken from the English translations by R. H. Blyth in his *Zen and Zen Classics*, Vol. 2, pages 20-21:

A monk asked Sekitō, "What is the inner significance of Daruma's coming to (from) the West?" Sekitō said, "Go and ask the outside post of the Hall!" The monk said, "I don't know what you mean." "Nor do I," said Sekitō.

并建议石头应按照六祖遗言拜见青原。由此可见,六祖一定相当重视青原,而青原也很可能得到六祖的特别指点。

　　石头希迁成为青原的禅法传人。南岳系的第二代传人马祖道一(709—788)则被其信徒尊奉为马大师,是一位具有深远影响的禅师。石头离开青原山去湖南衡山,在一石台上造了一个小庵,由此得名"石头"。当时人称:"江西主大寂(即马祖道一);湖南主石头。"根据《传灯录》第14卷记载,石头有21位法嗣,其中有:

　　(1)天皇道悟(748—807)

　　(2)丹霞天然(739—824)

　　(3)药山惟俨(751—834)

　　(4)潭州长髭旷

　　(5)潮州大颠宝通(732—824)

　　(6)潭州大川

上列前四位拥有禅师头衔,其他两位则具有和尚称号。

　　石头是《参同契》的作者,该书先是传给青原系的信徒,其后传给曹洞宗、云门宗和法眼宗。曹洞宗的洞山良价(807—869)在石头希迁及其他几位早期禅宗大师的论辩语录的基础上创立了五位学说。(参见海因立希·杜慕林著《中国禅宗的发展》,罗丝·富勒·佐佐木的英译本,美国第一禅堂出版,1953年版,第25页。)

　　石头年少时先在六祖慧能门下服役。慧能圆寂后,石头成为青原系的法嗣。下列轶事引自布莱思的《禅与禅宗经典》第2卷,第20—21页:

　　一僧人问石头:"达摩西来的深邃意义何在?"石头答:"去问大厅外面的柱子!"僧人说:"我不明白你的意思。"石头说:"我也不明白。"

When Hōun (Pang Yun) met Sekitō for the first time, he asked, "Who is he who does not accompany all things?" Sekitō put his hand over Hōun's mouth. Hōun came to a realization.

One day Sekitō was walking in the hills with his disciple Sekishitsu (Shihshih meaning "stone house"), and, seeing more branches obstructing the path, asked him to cut them away. "I didn't bring a knife," said Sekishitsu. Sekitō took out his own and held it out, blade-end first, to Sekishitsu, who said, "Please give me the other end." "What would you do with it?" asked Sekitō, and Sekishitsu came to a realization.

Note that Sekishitsu was later a disciple of Chōshi Kō of Tanshū. Other anecdotes were given in the *Lamp Records*, Vol. 14 (*Daishō Daizōkyō*, Vol. 51, page 309). See also Y. H. Ku's *History of Chinese Zen Masters*, pages 74-76. The following translation illustrates the conversation between Sekitō and Tennō Dōgo.

Tennō Dōgo asked Sekitō: "Who received the teachings of Tsao-hsi (Sōkei)?" Sekitō answered: "One who understands the dharma of Buddha received it." Dōgo asked: "Did Master receive it?" The Master answered: "I do not understand the dharma of Buddha." A monk asked: "How to be liberated?" Sekitō answered: "Who binds you?" A monk asked: "What is the Pure Land?" Sekitō said: "Who makes you dirty?" A monk asked: "What is nirvana?" Sekitō said: "Who gives you life and death?"

Sekitō, in his teachings, emphasized "The Buddha is the Mind; the Mind is the Buddha."

The Sixth Patriarch entered nirvana in 713 A.D. and left his "body" to posterity. The "body" was enshrined at Nan-hua (Nanka) Temple at Shao-kuan. [The present writer did visit the Nan-hua Temple, while Abbot Hsu Yun (Kiun, 1840-1959) was in charge of the Temple.] Similarly, Sekitō's "body" was well preserved from 790 A.D. to the present. About sixty years ago, Sekitō's "body" was secretly transported to Japan. When the Sōtō School in Japan was celebrating the Six Hundred and Fiftieth Anniversary of Keizan Shōkin's passing, this "body" of Sekitō was recognized by some

Chinese Buddhists at the Zen Exhibition. So in 1975 (650 years after Keizan's passing), Sekitō's "body" was enshrined at Sōji-ji near Yokohama. Some faithful followers revered Sekitō as the Eighth Patriarch of the Sōtō School. Whether Shen-hui (Jinne) was accepted as the Seventh Patriarch of Zen was an open question, although Abbot Hsu Yun respected Shen-hui with this title bestowed on him by the Emperor Te-tsung in 796 A.D.

庞蕴初次见石头时问:"不与万事为伴者是何人?"石头将手掩住庞蕴的口,庞蕴终于悟道。

一天,石头同弟子石室善道在山中行走,看到许多树枝拦阻道路,就令他砍断树枝。石室善道说:"我没有带刀。"石头拿出自己的刀,把刀刃一头向前交给石室善道,石室说:"请把另一头给我。"石头问:"你用另一头干什么?"石室于是悟道。

按:石室后来是潭州长髭旷的弟子。《传灯录》卷14(见《大正藏》第51卷,第309页)中载有其他一些故事,也可参见拙著《禅宗师承记》第74—76页。下列译文描绘了石头和天皇道悟之间的一段对话:

天皇道悟问石头:"何人得到曹溪的教导?"石头回答:"了解佛法的人得到它。"天皇道悟问:"大师您得到了吗?"石头回答:"我不了解佛法。"一僧人问:"如何得解脱?"石头回答:"何人捆住你?"一僧人问:"什么是净土?"石头说:"何人把你弄脏?"一僧人问:"什么是涅槃?"石头说:"何人给你生和死?"

石头在他的教义中强调了"佛即是心,心即是佛"。

六祖慧能于公元713年进入涅槃,并将"肉身"传给后人。"肉身"供奉在韶关南华寺内(本书作者曾参观南华寺,当时虚云和尚任该寺方丈)。同样,石头的"肉身"也从公元790年起被妥善地保存到现在。大约六十年前,石头的"肉身"被秘密运往日本。当1975年日本曹洞宗庆颂莹山绍瑾圆寂650周年时,几位中国僧侣在禅宗展览仪式上认出了石头的"肉身"。因此,石头的"肉身"被送到横滨附近的总持寺供奉。某些虔诚的信徒把石头看作是曹洞宗的八祖。但荷泽神会是否被公认为禅宗的七祖却仍是一个公开的疑问,尽管虚云和尚是用这一称号来尊崇神会的,而这一称号是唐德宗于公元796年赐封的。

We have mentioned six prominent disciples of Sekitō before. The first line leads from Tien-huang Tao-wu (Tennō Dōgo, 748-807) to Hsueh-feng I-tsun (Seppō Gizon, 822-908).

(1) Tien-huang Tao-wu (Tennō Dōgo, 748-807)

(2) Lung-tan Chung-hsin (Ryūtan Sūshin)

(3) Te-shan Hsuan-chien (Tokusan Senkan, 782-865)

(4) Hsueh-feng I-tsun (Seppō Gizon, 822-908)

Hsueh-feng's two famous disciples were: (5a) Yun-men Wen-yen (Ummon Bun'en, 864-949), founder of the Ummon School; and (5b) Yuan-sha Shih-pei (Gensha Shibi, 835-908), founder of the Gensha School. However, Gensha was over-shadowed by his dharma grandson, Fa-yen Wen-i (Hōgen Bun'eki, 885-958), so that the Gensha School was replaced by the Hōgen School. Note that Hōgen Bun'eki was the disciple of Lo-han Kuei-chen (Rakan Keijin, 867-928).

Sekitō line two begins with Tan-hsia Tien-jan (Tanka Tennen, 739-824) to Tou-tze Kan-wen (Tōsu Kan'on).

(1) Tan-hsia Tien-jan (Tanka Tennen, 739-824)

(2) Tsui-wei Wu-hsueh (Suiba Mugaku)

(3) Tou-tze Ta-tung (Tōsu Daidō, 819-914)

(4) Tou-tze Kan-wen (Tōsu Kan'on)

Tou-tze Ta-tung's other disciples were: Niu-tou Wei (Gyūtō Bi), Tien-fu (Tenfuku), Chao-fu (Shōfuku), and Hsiang-shan Cheng-chao Ta-shih (Kōsan Chōshō Daishi). More names appeared in the *Lamp Records*, Vol. 15.

Sekitō line three starts from Yueh-shan Wei-yen (Yakusan Igen, 751-834) to Tsao-shan Pen-chi (Sōzan Honjaku, 840-901) and his dharma brothers.

(1) Yueh-shan Wei-yen (Yakusan Igen, 751-834)

(2) Yun-yen Tan-sheng (Ungan Donjō, 782-841)

(3) Tung-shan Liang-chieh (Tōzan Ryōkai, 807-869)

(4) Tsao-shan Pen-chi (Sōzan Honjaku, 840-901)

(4a) Chiu-feng Pu-man (Kyūhō Fuman Daishi)

(4b) Yun-chu Tao-ying (Ungo Dōyō, d. 902)

(4c) Lung-ya Chu-tun (Ryūga Koton, 835-923)

(4d) Su-shan Kuang-jen (Sozan Kōnin, 837-909)

我们已在前面提到石头的六位知名弟子。石头的第一支系弟子是从天皇道悟（748—807）到雪峰义存（822—908）：

（1）天皇道悟（748—807）

（2）龙潭崇信

（3）德山宣鉴（782—865）

（4）雪峰义存（822—908）

雪峰有两位著名的弟子：

（5a）云门文偃（864—949），是云门宗的创建人。

（5b）玄沙师备（835—908），是玄沙宗的创建人，但玄沙被他的法孙法眼文益（885—958）超越了，玄沙宗因而被法眼宗所取代。按：法眼文益则是罗汉桂琛（867—928）的弟子。

石头的第二支系弟子从丹霞天然到投子感温：

（1）丹霞天然（739—824）

（2）翠微无学

（3）投子大同（819—914）

（4）投子感温

投子大同的其他弟子有：牛头微、天福、招福及香山澄照大师。其他人名见《传灯录》卷15。

石头的第三支系弟子是从药山惟俨到曹山本寂及其师兄弟：

（1）药山惟俨（751—834）

（2）云岩昙晟（782—841）

（3）洞山良价（807—869）

（4）曹山本寂（840—901）

（4a）九峰普满大师

（4b）云居道膺（？—902）

（4c）龙牙居遁（835—923）

（4d）疏山光仁（837—909）

Note that Tōzan Ryōkai and Sōzan Honjaku were the cofounders of the Tsao-tung (Sōtō) School. Sōzan's disciple was Tsao-shan Hui-hsia (Sōzan Eka), whose disciple was Hua-yen Cheng-hui (Kegon Shō'e). Ungo Dōyō had two important disciples: Tung-an Tao-pei (Dōan Dōhai, 889-955) and Yun-chu Huai-yueh (Ungo Egaku). However, according to the *Lamp Records*, Vol. 23 (*Daishō Daizōkyō*, Vol. 51, page 388), Yun-chu Huai-yueh had five disciples: Yuen-shan Chung-yen (Yakusan Chūgen), Feng-hua Ling-chung (Fuka Ryōsū), Tze-chou Lung-chuan (Shishū Ryūsen), Yun-chu Ji-yuan (Ungo Jūen), and Yun-chu Ji-man (Ungo Jūman); but Tung-an Tao-pei had *none*. Kyūhō Fuman's disciple was Tung-an Wei (Dōan I) of Hung-chou (Kōshū), according to the *Lamp Records*, Vol. 20 (See *Daishō Daizōkyō*, Vol. 51, page 365). Then in the *Lamp Records*, Vol. 23, Tung-an Wei (Dōan I) had two disciples: Chung Tung-an Kuan-chih (Chū Dōan Kanshi) and Chen-chou Shih-ching (Chinshū Sekikyō). According to the *Lamp Records*, Vol. 24 (See *Daishō Daizōkyō*, Vol. 51, p. 398), Tung-an Kuan-chih (Dōan Kanshi) had two disciples: Liang-shan Yuan-kuan (Ryōsan Enkan) and Chen-chou Ling-tung (Chinshū Reitsū). Now Liang-shan Yuan-kuan (Ryōsan Enkan) was the dharma teacher of Ta-yang Ching-yuan (Daiyō Keigen, 943-1027); thus the lineage of the Chinese Sōtō School was firmly established. (Note that Tung-an Chih was the same as Tung-an Kuan-chih, the dharma heir of Tung-an Wei, but not the dharma heir of Tung-an Tao-pei.)

According to *Chuan-fa Cheng-tsung Chi* (*Denhō Shōsō Ki*) by Chi-sung (Kaisū, 1007-1072), Vol. 7, Daikan (Enō) had seventh-generation dharma heirs: Ungo Dōyō, Sōzan Honjaku, Kyūhō Fuman, etc. Ungo Dōyō had 28 dharma heirs; Sōzan Honjaku had 14 dharma heirs; and Kyūhō Fuman had one disciple: Dōan I of Kōshū. In Vol. 8, Ungo Egaku (Ungo Dōyō's dharma heir) had five dharma heirs; Sōzan Eka (Sōzan Honjaku's dharma heir) had three dharma heirs; and Dōan I (Kyūhō Fuman's dharma heir) had two dharma heirs: Chung Tung-an Chih (Chū Dōan Shi) and Chen-chou Shih-ching (Chinshū Sekikyō). For Daikan's

(Enō's) ninth-generation dharma heirs, Dōan Shi had two dharma heirs: Liang-shan Yuan-kuan (Ryōsan Enkan) and Chen-chou Ling-tung (Chinshū Reitsū). These records could be easily found in *Daishō Daizōkyō*, Vol. 51, pages 755-756; 759-761.

Sekitō line four starts with Tan-chou Chang-tze Kuang (Tanshū Chōshi Kō). Tanshū Chōshi had one disciple: Shihshih Shan-tao (Sekishitsu Zendō). The line five Chao-chou Ta-tien (Chōshū Daiten,

要指出的是，洞山良价和曹山本寂是曹洞宗的共同创建人。曹山本寂的弟子是曹山慧霞，后者的弟子是华严正慧。云居道膺有两位重要弟子：同安道丕（889—955）和云居怀岳。然而根据《传灯录》卷23（《大正藏》第51卷，第388页），云居怀岳有五位弟子：药山忠彦、风化令崇、梓州龙泉、云居住缘和云居住满；但同安道丕却后继无人。根据《传灯录》卷20（见《大正藏》第51卷，第365页）记载，九峰普满的弟子是洪州同安威。又据《传灯录》卷23，同安威有两位弟子：中同安观志和陈州石镜。据《传灯录》卷24（见《大正藏》第51卷，第398页），同安观志有两位弟子：梁山缘观和陈州灵通。梁山缘观是大阳警玄（943—1027）的师父；就这样确立了中国曹洞宗的传承世系。（按：同安志就是同安观志，是同安威的法嗣，但并非同安道丕的法嗣。）

根据契嵩（1007—1072）的《传法正宗记》第7卷，大鉴大师慧能的第七代法嗣有：云居道膺、曹山本寂、九峰普满等人。云居道膺有二十八位法嗣；曹山本寂有十四位法嗣；九峰普满只有一位弟子洪州同安威。在《传灯录》卷8中，云居怀岳（云居道膺的法嗣）有五位法嗣；曹山慧霞（曹山本寂的法嗣）有三位法嗣；同安威（九峰普满的法嗣）有两位法嗣：中同安观志和陈州石镜。作为慧能的第九代法嗣，同安观志有两位法嗣：梁山缘观和陈州灵通。上述记载均可在《大正藏》第51卷，第755—756、759—761页中找到。

石头的第四支系弟子从潭州长髭旷开始。潭州长髭旷有一位弟子石室善道，第五支系弟子潮州大颠（732—824）有一

732-824) had one disciple: San-ping I-chung (Sanhei Gichū). Daiten oshō met the Confucian scholar Han Yu on his exile, and Daiten was able to convince, if not to convert, Han Yu that there were similar approaches to human nature, if not human virtue, in Buddhism and Confucianism.

Sekitō line six starts with Tan-chou Ta-chuan (Tanshū Daisen). Daisen had two disciples: Sien-tien (Senten) and Pu-kuang (Fukō) of Foochow.

In line two, Suiba had other disciples: Ching-ping Ling-tsen (Seihei Reijun), Tao-chang Ju-nei (Dōjō Nyototsu), and Pai-yun Yo (Haku'un Yaku).

In line three, Yakusan had two other disciples: Tao-wu Yuan-chih (Dōgo Enchi, 769-835) and Chuan-tze Te-cheng (Sensu Tokusei). Dōgo Enchi's disciple was Shih-shuang Ching-chu (Sekisō Keisho, 807-888). Sensu Tokusei's disciple was Chia-shan Shan-hui (Kassan Zenne, 805-881).

(1) Yueh-shan Wei-yen (Yakusan Igen, 751-834)

(2a) Tao-wu Yuan-chih (Dōgo Enchi, 769-835)

(3a) Shih-shuang Ching-chu (Sekisō Keisho, 807-888)

(4a) Chiu-feng Tao-chien (Kyūhō Dōken)

(1) Yueh-shan Wei-yen (Yakusan Igen, 751-834)

(2b) Chuan-tze Te-cheng (Sensu Tokusei)

(3b) Chia-shan Shan-hui (Kassan Zenne, 805-881)

(4b) Shao-shan Huan-pu (Shōzan Kanfu)

Dōgo Enchi had another disciple, Chien-yuan Chun-hsin (Zengen Chūkō). Sekisō Keisho had other disciples: Nan-tsi Seng-i (Nansai Sō'itsu), Ta-kuang Chu-hui (Daikō Gokai), and Chih-hsien Huai-yu (Saiken Eyū). Kassan had many disciples, among them: Lo-pu Yuan-an (Rakufu Gen'an), Shan-lan Ling-chao (Jōran Ryōchō), Huang-shan Yueh-lun (Ō'san Getsurin), Siao-yao Huai-chung (Shōyō Echū), and Pan-lung Ko-wen (Benryū Ke'bun).

Returning to line one, Tennō Dōgo's dharma grandson was Tokusan

Senkan. Tokusan had other disciples besides Seppō Gizon (822-908). These were: Yen-tou Chuan-huo (Gantō Zenkatsu, 828-887), Jui-lung Hui-kung (Zuiryū Ekū), Kao-ting Chien (Kōtei Ken), and Kan-tan Tsu-kuo (Kantan Shikoku). Gantō's disciples were: Lo-shan Tao-hsien (Rasan Dōkan), Ling-yen Hui-chung (Reigan Eshū), Hsuan-chuan Yen (Gensen Gen), and Jui-yen Shin-yen (Zuigan Shigen). Rasan had several disciples

弟子三平义忠。大颠和尚遇见贬谪中的儒家学者韩愈。大颠当时曾使韩愈相信（虽非改信），佛教和儒家学说对于人性（虽然不是人的德性）有相似的看法。

石头的第六支系从潭州大川开始。大川有两位弟子：仙天和福州普光。

在第二支系中，翠微无学还有其他弟子：清平令遵、道场如讷、白云约。

在第三支系中，药山惟俨还有两位弟子：道吾圆智和船子德诚。道吾圆智的弟子是石霜庆诸，船子德诚的弟子是夹山善会：

（1）药山惟俨（751—834）

（2a）道吾圆智（769—835）

（3a）石霜庆诸（807—888）

（4a）九峰道虔

（1）药山惟俨（751—834）

（2b）船子德诚

（3b）夹山善会（805—881）

（4b）韶山寰普

道吾圆智还有一位弟子渐源仲兴。石霜庆诸还有其他弟子：南际僧一、大光居诲和栖贤怀佑。夹山善会有许多弟子，其中有：乐普元安、上蓝令超、黄山月轮、逍遥怀忠和盘龙可文。

再回到第一支系，天皇道悟的法孙是德山宣鉴。德山宣鉴的弟子除了雪峰义存（822—908）外，还有岩头全豁（828—887）、瑞龙慧恭、高亭简和感潭资国。岩头全豁的弟子是：罗山道闲、灵岩慧宗、玄泉彦和瑞岩师彦。罗山道闲有多位弟子，

among them: Ming-chao Te-chien (Meishō Tokuken) and Ching-ping Wei-kuang (Seihei I'kō). Kantan had one disciple: Po-chao Chih-yuan (Hakuchō Shien), whose disciple was Ta-lung Chih-hung (Dairyū Chikō).

The Tsao-tung (Sōtō) School will be presented in Chapter 7. The Yun-men (Ummon) School and the Fa-yen (Hōgen) School will be presented in Chapter 8.

In the rest of the Chapter, we shall follow the three lines represented by Tennō Dōgo, Tanka Tennen, and Yakusan Igen.

Tennō Dōgo wanted to be a monk when he was fourteen years old. He stopped eating three meals a day in order to convince his parents about his wishes. When he was twenty-five years old, he was ordained at the Cho-lin Temple (Chikurin-ji), Hangchow. Then he went to Yu-hang and paid his respects to Master Kuo-i (Koku-itsu Zenji) at Ching-shan, and remained there for five years. Later he visited Nanking (then called Chungling) and spent two years under Ma-tsu (Baso). Then he became a disciple of Shih-tou (Sekitō). So Tennō got the benefit of dharma teachings from both the Nangaku Branch and the Seigen Branch. (Even today, dharma descendants of Tennō Dōgo claimed that they are the dharma descendants of both Baso and Sekitō.) However, Tennō's sudden enlightenment came under Sekitō's probing.

> Sekitō said to Tennō Dōgo: "I know where you came from." Dōgo said: "How can you say that?" Sekitō said: "You know yourself." Dōgo: "Let it be. But how to tell the posterity?" Sekitō: "You tell me who are the posterity!" Then Tennō Dōgo became suddenly enlightened. He understood now how the two great Masters (Baso and Sekitō) enlighten his mind and start him on the right tracks.

See the *Lamp Records*, Vol. 14 (*Daishō Daizōkyō*, Vol. 51, pages 309-310; Y. H. Ku: *History of Chinese Zen Masters*, pages 77-78).

Tennō's dharma heir was Lung-tan Chung-hsin (Ryūtan Sūshin). Ryūtan had been with the Master for three years. He grumbled about the Master's not teaching him anything. Tennō said: "Ever since you came here, when have I not taught you?" Ryūtan said: "What have you taught me?" Then Tennō explained: "When you brought me tea, I received it. When you brought me my meal, I received that from you too. When you bowed to me, I nodded to you. When did I not teach you?" Ryūtan was then enlightened.

其中有：明招德谦和清平惟旷。感潭资国有一位弟子：白兆志圆。后者的弟子是大龙智洪。

本书将在第七章介绍曹洞宗，第八章介绍云门宗和法眼宗。

在本章其余部分，我们将介绍天皇道悟、丹霞天然和药山惟俨为代表的三个支系。

天皇道悟14岁时就想出家为僧。他每天三餐绝食，企图使父母相信他的愿望的真实性。他25岁时，在杭州竹林寺正式受戒出家。其后他去余杭径山参拜国一禅师，并在径山留居五年。后又到南京（当时名钟陵），在马祖道一门下修禅两年。之后他成为石头的弟子。所以天皇道悟得到了南岳系和青原系两系的禅法教益。（即使到今天，天皇道悟的禅法传人也都宣称他们既是马祖又是石头的法嗣。）不过，天皇道悟的豁然开悟却是由于石头的启发：

石头对天皇道悟说："我知道你的来处。"道悟说："您怎么会这样说？"石头说："你自己知道。"道悟说："虽然如此，但是怎样告诉后人呢？"石头说："你告诉我，后人是谁？"于是天皇道悟顿时开悟。他终于明白两位大师（马祖和石头）是如何启迪他的悟性并使他走上正道的。

见《传灯录》卷14（《大正藏》第51卷，第309—310页）和拙著《禅宗师承记》第77—78页。

道悟的法嗣是龙潭崇信。龙潭崇信追随道悟三年之久。他抱怨师父一点不教导他。道悟说："从你到这里来后，我什么时候没有教过你？"龙潭崇信说："您教我什么？"于是道悟解释道："当你给我端茶时，我接茶。当你给我送饭时，我也从你手中接饭。当你向我行礼时，我向你点头。我什么时候没有教导你？"龙潭崇信于是得悟。

Te-shan Hsuan-chien (Tokusan Senkan, 782-865) visited Ryūtan and asked the Master: "Where is the dragon? Where is the pool?" (Ryūtan means "Dragon pool" or "Dragon abyss.") Ryūtan said: "You have seen the 'dragon-pool' right now." Tokusan bowed and left. Ryūtan persuaded Tokusan to stay. One evening, Tokusan was sitting in meditation outside the room. Ryūtan asked: "Why don't you come in?" Tokusan replied: "It's dark in the room." Ryūtan lighted a candle and gave it to Tokusan. As Tokusan was about to hold the candle, the Master blew it off. Tokusan saluted the Master. Ryūtan asked him: "What have you seen?" Tokusan replied: "From now on, nobody can doubt the tongue of an old Ho-shan (oshō) in the universe." So this is the story of how darkness can enlighten a disciple. Tokusan was born in 782 A.D., and entered nirvana in 865 A.D. at the age of eighty-four. He endured great difficulties when Wu-tsung of Tang Dynasty attempted to suppress all Buddhists. He had many disciples, among them were Hsueh-feng I-tsun (Seppō Gizon, 822-908), Yen-tou Chuan-huo (Gantō Zenkatsu, 828-887), and Kan-tan Tsu-kuo (Kantan Shikoku). (See Y. H. Ku, *History of Chinese Zen Masters*, pages 275-278).

Seppō Gizon (822-908) was a native of Nan-an in Chuan-chou (Fukien Province). He accompanied his father to visit the Yu-chien Temple (Gyokukan-ji) at Pu-tien when he was twelve years old, and saluted the Vinaya Master Ching-hsuan (Keigen Rissui) as his teacher. He had his head shaved at the age of seventeen, after serving under Ching-hsuan (Keigen) for five years. Then he went to visit Master Chang-chao (Jōshō) at Fu-yung (Fuyō) Mountain. Later he visited the Pao-sh'a Monastery (Hōsechi-ji) at Yu-chou (southwest of Peking, in present Hopei Province). He was later ordained by Tokusan and found spiritual affinity with Tokusan. Seppō resided in Fukien for more than forty years, and his followers numbered more than fifteen hundred. Emperor I-tsung (r. 860-873) bestowed upon him the purple robe and the honored title of Chen-chueh Ta-shih (Shinkaku Daishi). He lived to eighty-seven years of age. He has many disciples, among them:

Ummon Bun'en (864-949), Gensha Shibi (835-908), Kyōsei Juntoku Daishi (Ryūsaku Dōfu), Chōkei Eryō (854-932), Ankoku Kōtō, Hofuku Jūten (d. 928), Taigen Fu, Kozan Jin'an (Kokushi, 863-939), and Suigan Reisan.

Ummon was the founder of the Ummon School. Gensha's disciple was Rakan Keijin (867-928). Rakan's disciple was Hōgen Bun'eki (885-958), founder of the Hōgen School.

Tanka Tennen (739-824) learned Zen first from Baso, and then went

德山宣鉴（782—865）谒见龙潭崇信时问师父道："龙在何处？潭在何处？"龙潭说："你正是现在见到了龙潭。"德山宣鉴于是下拜，要离去。龙潭劝德山留下。一个晚上，德山正在室外打坐，龙潭问道："你为什么不进来？"德山答道："室内黑暗。"龙潭点了一支蜡烛给德山。德山正准备接蜡烛，师父却吹熄了蜡烛。德山即向师父下拜。龙潭问："你见到什么？"德山回答："从今以后，没有人会怀疑大千世界中一位老和尚的辩才了。"这就是黑暗能够使一位弟子明心见性的故事。德山宣鉴84岁时涅槃。在唐武宗力图废佛教时，他经受了巨大的苦难。他有许多弟子，其中有雪峰义存（822—908）、岩头全豁（828—887）和感潭资国（见拙著《禅宗师承记》第275—278页）。

雪峰义存（822—908）是泉州南安（在今福建省）人。12岁时随父游莆田玉涧寺，参拜庆玄律师为师。他在庆玄门下侍奉五年，于17岁削发，再去芙蓉山谒见常照大师，其后去幽州（在今河北省）宝刹寺。由德山宣鉴为他施具足戒，并且得到德山宣鉴的印证。雪峰义存在福建住了四十多年，其信众超过一千五百人。唐懿宗（在位860—873，按另作859—873）赐他紫袈裟，敕封真觉大师。他寿达87岁。他有许多弟子，其中有云门文偃（864—949）、玄沙师备（835—908）、镜清顺德（龙册道怤）、长庆慧稜（854—932）、安国弘瑫、保福从展（？—928）、太原孚、鼓山神晏（863—939）和翠岩令参。

云门文偃是云门宗的创建者。玄沙师备的弟子是地藏桂琛（867—928）。地藏桂琛的弟子是法眼宗的创建者法眼文益。

丹霞天然（739—824）先是从马祖道一学禅，后去石头门下。

to Sekitō. According to the *Lamp Records* (*Daishō Daizōkyō*, Vol. 51, pages 310-311; Y. H. Ku, *History of the Chinese Zen Masters*, pages 84-87), Tanka started as a Confucian scholar, went to Chang-an (now Sian, Shensi Province), and waited to take the examination in a small hotel. He dreamed of "white light" filling his room. A Zen guest asked him: "Where are you going?" Tanka replied: "I want to take the civil service examination in order to be an official." The Zen guest said: "You choose to be an official! Why not choose to be a Buddha?" Tanka asked: "Where should I go if I choose to be a Buddha?" The Zen guest said: "Master Ma in Kiangsi is the right place to go." So Tanka went to Baso's temple. But Baso told him that Sekitō of Nangaku (Heng-shan) would be his teacher. (In Zen history, there were many instances that if there was a lack of spiritual affinity, the young monk should be sent to some other Master's place.)

> Tanka served under Sekitō for three years. One day Sekitō told the assembly that the next day everybody should do weeding of the grass in front of the Temple Hall. When the time came, everybody brought shovels for weeding, but Tanka was washing his head in a water pan and knelt before the Master. Sekitō smiled and shaved Tanka's head and told him the admonitions. Tanka closed his ears and left for Kiangsi. He did not salute Baso and went to the zendo... Baso entered the Hall and said: "Naturally you!" Tanka saluted Baso and thanked the Master for giving him the name Tennen (meaning "natural"). Baso asked: "Where did you come from?" Tanka said: "From Sekitō." Baso said: "The stone road is slippery. Did you fall?" Tanka said: "If I fell, I will not come here."

Tanka went to the Tendai Mountain and stayed for three years at Hua-ting Feng (Kachō Peak). Then he visited Kuo-i Zen Master at Ching-shan, Yu-hang. Later he went to Lo-yang and resided at Hsiang-shan, Lung-men (Kōzan, Ryūmon), with his close friend Fu-niu Ho-shan (Fukugyū oshō). When he was at the Hui-lin Temple (Erin-ji) in severe winter, he burned the wooden image of Buddha. People ridiculed him. Tanka said: "I want to get 'shari' (bones of Buddha)." People said: "How can you get 'shari' from wood?" Tanka said: "Then you shouldn't blame me."

Tanka went to call on Nan'yō Echū Kokushi, and asked his attendant if Kokushi was in. The attendant said: "Even he is in, he will not receive any guest." Tanka said: "This is too deep for me." The attendant said: "Even the Buddha's eye cannot see." Tanka said: "Dragon gives birth to

根据《传灯录》(《大正藏》第51卷，第310—311页）和拙著《禅宗师承记》第84—87页，丹霞原先是一位儒生，曾去长安（今陕西西安），在一小旅舍中等待考试。他梦见白光满室。有一禅客问他"何处去？"丹霞回答："我要应举考试做官去。"禅客说："您要选官，为何不选佛？"丹霞天然问："如果我要选佛，应该上何处去？"禅客说："江西马祖大师那儿即是好去处。"于是丹霞去了马祖道一的寺庙，但马祖却告诉他南岳的石头是他的师父。（在禅宗历史上有许多例子，说明如果缺乏心灵印证，就应该打发年轻的僧人到其他禅师处去。）

丹霞在石头门下侍奉三年。一天石头吩咐全体僧众第二天都到寺院大厅前除草。到时大家都带了铁铲来除草，唯独丹霞在一水盆中洗头，并跪在师父面前。石头微笑，为丹霞剃发，并为他说戒法。丹霞掩住双耳就离开，到江西去。他没有朝拜马祖，便去禅堂……马祖进入大堂说道："我子天然！"丹霞参拜马祖，感谢师父赐他"天然"之法号。马祖问道："你从何处来？"丹霞说："从石头处来。"马祖说："石头路滑，你跌倒没有？"丹霞说："如果我跌倒，我就不会来这里了。"

丹霞去天台山华顶峰住了三年，并到余杭径山谒见国一禅师。后到洛阳与挚友伏牛和尚同住在龙门香山。当他在慧林寺适逢严冬时，便焚烧木佛。人们讥笑他。丹霞说："我要取舍利。"人们说："你怎能从木头中取得舍利？"丹霞说："那么你们不该责备我。"

丹霞去拜谒南阳慧忠国师，问侍者国师在否。侍者说："即使他在，也不会接见任何客人。"丹霞说："这对我太深远了。"侍者说："连佛眼也看不见。"丹霞说："龙生龙子，凤生凤儿。"

dragon-son; phoenix gives birth to phoenix child." When Kokushi woke up, the attendant told him the story. Kokushi gave the attendant thirty blows. Tanka heard about this and said: "He deserves to be the National Teacher." Tanka saluted Kokushi the next day...

Tanka lived to eighty-six years old. At nirvana, he wore a "kasa" (bamboo hat), held a stick and had his shoes put on. He passed away with one foot lifted off the ground. His disciple was Suiba Mugaku, and Suiba's disciples were Tōsu Daidō and Seihei Reijun.

Yakusan Igen (751-834), the dharma grandfather of Tōzan Ryōkai, became a monk at the age of seventeen. He was enlightened under Sekitō. The following anecdotes were taken from R. H. Blyth's *Zen and Zen Classics*, Vol. 2, pages 79-80.

Yakusan asked a monk, "Where have you come from?" The monk replied, "From the Southern Lake." Yakusan asked: "Has the lake overflowed the banks?" "Not yet," answered the monk. Then Yakusan said: "So much rain, and the lake not yet full?" The monk was silent.

...

A monk asked Yakusan, "Did the essence of Buddhism exist before Daruma came?" "It did," said Yakusan. "Then why did he come, if it already existed?" "He came," said Yakusan, "just because it was here already."

...

Yakusan had not ascended the rostrum for quite a long time, and one day the superior (head monk) came and said, "The congregation of monks are thinking about your preaching a sermon." Yakusan said, "Ring the bell!" The superior banged away at the bell, and the monks all gathered. But Yakusan went back to his own room. The superior followed him, and said, "The Master was going to give a talk, and the monks are ready; why didn't you say anything to them?" Yakusan said, "There are sutra priests for the sutras, and sastra priests for the sastras; why do you question my goings-on?"

Blyth commented by telling the story between Sekitō and Yakusan:

One day, Yakusan was doing *zazen*. Sekitō asked him, "What are you doing?" "Not a thing," replied Yakusan. "Aren't you sitting blankly?" said Sekitō. "If I were sitting blankly, I would be doing something," retorted Yakusan. Sekitō said, "Tell me what is that you are not doing?" Yakusan replied, "A thousand sages could not answer that question."

当国师睡醒，侍者告诉他这件事。国师打了侍者三十杖。丹霞听说后，道："他的确不愧是国师。"第二天丹霞便去参拜国师……

丹霞寿达86岁。涅槃时，他头戴竹笠，手拿禅杖，脚穿僧鞋。圆寂时垂一足未及地。他的弟子是翠微无学，翠微无学的弟子是投子大同和清平令遵。

药山惟俨（751—834）是洞山良价的禅法师祖。他17岁时为僧，在石头处悟禅。下列轶事引自布莱思的《禅与禅宗经典》第2卷，第79—80页：

药山问一僧人："您从何处来？"僧人回答："从南湖来。"药山问："湖水漫上岸了吗？"僧人回答："还没有。"于是药山说："雨水这么多，湖还没有满？"僧人无言。

一僧人问药山："佛教的真谛是否在达摩来此之前就有？"药山说："有。""既然此地已有，那达摩为何要来？"药山说："正是因为佛的真谛已经在此，所以达摩才来。"

药山很久没有登坛讲禅，一天，上座来说："众僧都想请您上堂宣讲。"药山说："敲钟！"上座大声撞钟，僧众全都集合。但药山却回到自己的房间。上座跟随他进来，说："师父准备讲经，众僧都已集合，为何您一言不说？"药山说："经有经师，论有论师，为什么你质问我？"

布莱思在评议时叙述了石头和药山之间的故事：

一天，药山正在坐禅，石头问他："你在做什么？"药山答："不做什么。"石头说："你不是白坐吗？"药山反驳说："如果我是白坐，我就是在做什么啊。"石头说："告诉我什么是你的不做什么？"药山答："一千个圣人也不能回答这个问题。"

Yakusan passed away in 834 A.D., at the age of eighty-four. His disciple, Ungan Donjō (782-841), was the disciple of Hyakujō for twenty years, but got enlightened under Yakusan. Ungan's disciple was Tōzan Ryōkai, who, with Sōzan Honjaku, founded the Sōtō School of Zen. Yakusan's other disciples were Dōgo Enchi (769-835) and Sensu Tokusei.

Anecdotes concerning Ungan Donjō appeared in the *Lamp Records*, Vol. 14 (*Daishō Daizōkyō*, Vol. 51, pages 314-315; Y. H. Ku, *History of Chinese Zen Masters*, pages 90-92). Blyth in his *Zen and Zen Classics*, Vol. 2, page 81, gave the following:

> One day Ungan was ill and Dōgo Enchi asked him a question: "When you are separated from your bag-o'-bones, where can I meet you again?" Ungan replied, "Where there is no birth, no dying." Dōgo said, "Don't say that! Say, where there is not any no birth and no dying, and we don't desire to meet each other again."

Ungan met with Isan and there were conversations between them recorded in the *Lamp Records*. The following was translated from the *Lamp Records*, Vol. 14:

> Master Ungan was making shoes. Tōzan Ryōkai asked the Master for "eyeballs." Master: "Whom did you give your eyeballs?" Tōzan: "I did not." Master: "You did. Where can you find them?" Tōzan kept silent. Ungan: "Were the eyes asking for the eyeballs?" Tozan: "Not the eyes." The Master scolded him.

Tōzan was a great Zen Master. We shall return to Tōzan in Chapter 7.

Dōgo Enchi (769-835) was Ungan's dharma brother. Dōgo was asked by a monk, "What is the deepest?" Dōgo came down from his seat, made obeisance in the manner of women, and said, "You have come from far, and I have no answer for you." Sekisō Keisho (807-888) was Dōgo's disciple. The following story was taken from Blyth's translation:

> Sekisō Keisho asked Dōgo Enchi, "After a hundred years, if someone asks about the absolute meaning of the universe, what shall I say to

him?" Dōgo called boy-attendant, who came, and told him to fill up the water-bottle. Dōgo waited a while, and then to Sekisō, "What was it you asked just now?" Sekisō repeated the question. Dōgo thereupon went back to his room. At this, Sekisō became enlightened.

公元 834 年，药山在 84 岁时圆寂。他的弟子云岩昙晟（782—841）曾经是百丈怀海的弟子，跟了他 20 年，却在药山处悟禅。云岩昙晟的弟子是洞山良价，洞山和曹山本寂共同创建了禅宗的曹洞宗。药山的其他弟子还有道吾圆智（769—835）和船子德诚。

有关云岩昙晟的轶事见《传灯录》卷 14（《大正藏》第 51 卷，第 314—315 页）和拙著《禅宗师承记》第 90—92 页。布莱思在其《禅与禅宗经典》第 2 卷第 81 页提到下列轶事：

一天云岩生病，道吾圆智问他一个问题："当您与您的躯壳分离后，我在何处可以再见到您呢？"云岩答道："不生不灭之处。"道吾说："别说这个！请说何处是没有什么不生不灭而且我们也不想互相再见的地方。"

云岩曾遇见沩山灵祐，《传灯录》中记载了他们之间的对话。下文译自《传灯录》卷 14：

云岩禅师正在做鞋，洞山良价向云岩禅师讨"眼珠"，云岩说："你把自己的眼珠给了谁了？"洞山说："我没有给。"云岩说："你是给了。你能在哪里找到它们呢？"洞山沉默不语。云岩说："是眼睛在讨眼珠？"洞山说："不是眼睛。"于是云岩责骂他。

洞山是一位大禅师。我们将在第七章介绍洞山。

道吾圆智（769—835）是云岩昙晟的禅法师弟。一僧人问道吾："如何是和尚家风？"道吾从禅床下来，作妇女屈膝礼，并说："你从远处来，我不回答你。"石霜庆诸（807—888）是道吾的弟子。下列故事引自布莱思的译文：

石霜庆诸问道吾圆智："百年之后，要是有人问大千世界的至深意义，我该对他说什么？"道吾传唤一少年侍者进来，叫他把净瓶的水加满。道吾等了一会，对石霜说："你刚才问的是什么？"石霜再说了一遍刚才的问题。道吾随即回到自己的房间。于是石霜得到了启悟。

Blyth commented: "This kind of thing shows a genius above even that of Plato or Michelangelo, or Bach himself."

Sensu Tokusei was also a disciple of Yakusan. After he left the Master, he used to ferry a small boat across the river—from this his name "Boatman." He tried to teach Zen to those boarding the ferryboat. He often lifted his oar, and said, "Do you understand?" He passed on the dharma line to Kassan. Kassan Zenne (805-881) became a monk when young, and was enlightened under Sensu. The following anecdotes were taken from the English translation of R. H. Blyth in his *Zen and Zen Classics*, Vol. 2, Chapter 12.

> A monk asked Kassan, "How about when we clear away the dust, and see the Buddha?" Kassan said, "You must wield a sword! If you don't, it's a fisherman living in a nest!" The monk brought the matter to Sekisō (Kassan's dharma cousin), and asked, "How about when we clear away the dust and see the Buddha?" Sekisō answered, "He is not in the country, how can you meet him?" (He must have meant that Buddha was in India.) The monk went back and told Kassan what Sekisō said. Kassan ascended the rostrum and announced, "As for measures for those not yet enlightened, there is no one like me, but as for deep speaking of the absolute, Sekisō is a hundred paces beyond me."
>
> ...
>
> Kassan was doing *zazen* when Tōzan came and asked him. "How about it?" Kassan answered, "Just like this."
>
> ...
>
> A monk came back and interviewed Kassan, and said, "You have an especial understanding of Zen. How is it you didn't reveal this to me?" Kassan said, "When you boiled rice, didn't I light the fire? When you passed round the food, didn't I offer my bowl to you? When did I betray your expectations?" The monk was enlightened.
>
> ...
>
> A monk asked Kassan, "What is Tao (the Way)?" Kassan answered,

"The sun overflows our eyes; for ten thousand leagues (*li*'s) not a cloud hangs in the sky." "What is the Real Form of the Universe?" asked the monk. Kassan replied, "(Even) the fishes at play in the clear-flowing water make their mistakes."

...

Kassan said to the monks, "Find me in the tips of a hundred grasses; recognize the Prince in a noisy market!"

布莱思评议道:"这件事所表明的天才甚至超越了柏拉图或米开朗其罗或巴赫。"

船子德诚也是药山惟俨的弟子。他离开师父后,经常划一艘小船摆渡,由此得名"船子"。他试图给乘坐渡船的客人讲禅。他常常举起桨说:"你们懂吗?"他的禅法传人是夹山善会(805—881)。夹山善会青年时为僧,在船子德诚处悟道。下列轶事引自布莱思的《禅与禅宗经典》第2卷第12章:

一僧人问夹山:"当我们清除了俗尘见到佛祖时,该如何呢?"夹山说:"你应该挥剑!如果你不挥剑,那就是住在网中的渔夫!"僧人将这一问题带到石霜庆诸(他是夹山的堂房师兄弟)那里,问道:"当我们清除了俗尘见到佛祖时,该如何呢?"石霜庆诸回答道:"他不在本国,你怎能见到他?"(他必是指佛祖在印度。)僧人回去把石霜的回答告诉夹山。夹山登上讲坛宣称:"对于要点化那些还没有悟道的人来说,没有人能够像我一样,但是谈论绝对真理的深邃语言时,石霜超过我一百步。"

夹山正在坐禅,洞山良价进来问他:"怎么样?"夹山回答:"就是这样。"

一僧人回来与夹山谈论,说:"您对禅法有一种特别的悟解,为什么不给我点启示呢?"夹山说:"你烧饭时,我没有点火吗?你分派饭菜时,我没有给你碗吗?我什么时候辜负你的期望了呢?"僧人顿时启悟。

一僧人问夹山:"什么是道?"夹山回答:"太阳光充满在我们眼前;空中万里无云。"僧人问:"大千世界的真相是什么?"夹山答道:"在清澈流动的水中游玩的鱼也会犯错。"……

夹山对僧众说:"在百草尖找到我;在闹市上认出僧王!"

Kassan's disciple Shōzan Kanfu left the following anecdotes:

A monk said to Shōzan, "What is the sphere of Shōzan's mind?" Shōzan said, "From olden times up to now, monkeys and birds lifted up their voices; thin blue mist covered all things."

...

A monk asked, "What is Shōzan's special Zen ('family wind')?" Shōzan replied, "On the top of a mountain, rootless grass; the leaves moving, though there is no wind."

夹山的弟子韶山寰普留下下列轶话：

一僧人对韶山说："韶山的禅心范围是什么？"韶山说："从古到今，猿猴和禽鸟高声鸣叫，蓝色薄雾笼罩万物。"……

一僧人问："韶山的独有禅法（"家风"）是什么？"韶山答："无根之草，在山顶上；尽管无风，树叶自动。"

CHAPTER 7   THE SŌTŌ SCHOOL

Tung-shan Liang-chieh (Tōzan Ryōkai, 807-869) was a native of Kuai-chi in present Chekiang Province. He was advised to go to Mount Wu-hsieh (Gosetsu San) to study under Zen Master Ling-mo (Reimoku Zenji). He went there and had his head shaved. At the age of twenty-three, he was ordained at Mount Sung (Sū San), after which he traveled by foot all over the country. He first visited Nan-chuan (Nansen), when Nansen was conducting the annual memorial service for Ma-tsu (Baso). Nansen said: "When we serve food for Master Baso tomorrow, I wonder whether he will come or not." Tōzan came forth from the crowd and said, "As soon as he has company he will come." Next he went to visit Master Kuei-shan (Isan) and said to him: "I have heard that Dharma may also be taught by non-sentient things and that this is practiced by the National Teacher Nan-yang Hui-chung (Nan'yō Echū Kokushi). I have not yet understood its real meaning." Isan replied: "I teach it here too. But I have not found the proper person." Tōzan urged Isan to tell him about it. Isan said: "I inherited my mouth from my parents, but I never dare to say a word." Isan suggested that Tōzan should visit Yun-yen Tan-sheng (Ungan Donjō, 782-841).

When Tōzan arrived at Yun-yen (Ungan, meaning "Cloud Cliff"), he asked Master Ungan, "What kind of man is able to hear the teaching of Dharma through non-sentient things?" Master replied, "The Dharma taught by non-sentient things can be heard by non-sentient things." Tōzan asked, "Can you hear it?" Ungan said, "If I can hear it, you will not hear my teaching the Dharma." Tōzan said, "If this is so, it means that I do not hear you teaching the Dharma." Ungan then said, "When I taught the Dharma, even you did not hear it. How can you expect to be taught by non-sentient things?" Tōzan composed a gāthā and presented it to Master Ungan:

> It is strange indeed!
> It is strange indeed.

Dharma taught by non-sentient things is unthinkable.

Listening through your ears you cannot hear the sound;

But you will understand if you listen by your eyes.

Tōzan left the Master. Ungan asked, "Where are you going?" Tōzan said, "Though I am leaving you, I have not known where to go." Ungan:

柒 曹洞宗

　　洞山良价（807—869）是浙江会稽人。有人向他建议到五泄山灵默禅师门下学习。他去后即剃发，23岁时在嵩山具戒，其后徒步云游四方。他先谒见南泉普愿大师，当时南泉正在为马祖作周年斋。南泉说："明天我们给马祖供斋，不知道他会来否？"洞山从僧众中走出说："只要有伴他就会来。"后来洞山去拜见沩山灵祐大师，对他说："我听说，通过无情之物可以传授禅法，这点已得到南阳慧忠国师的实践。但我还是不明白它的真谛。"沩山灵祐答道："我正在这里传法，但我还没有找到恰当的人。"洞山恳求沩山灵祐告诉他禅法。沩山说："我的嘴是父母传给我的，但我不敢说一个字。"沩山建议洞山应去谒见云岩昙晟（782—841）。

　　洞山来到云岩，他问云岩禅师："哪一种人能够通过无情之物听到佛法的启导？"禅师回答："无情之物可以听到无情之物传授的佛法。"洞山问："您能听到吗？"云岩说："如果我能听到，你就听不到我传授的佛法了。"洞山说："如果这样，这就是说，我听不到您传授的佛法了。"云岩于是说："我教佛法，连你也听不见。你怎能希望听到无情之物启导的佛法呢？"洞山作一偈语呈给云岩禅师：

　　　　也大奇！

　　　　也大奇。

　　　　无情说法不思议。

　　　　若将耳听终难会，

　　　　眼处闻时方得知。

　　洞山要离开云岩禅师，云岩问："何处去？"洞山说："我虽要离去，但不知道去何处。"云岩说："你要去湖南吗？"洞山说：

"Are you going to Hunan?" Tōzan: "No!" Ungan: "Are you going home?" Tōzan: "No!" Ungan: "You will come back sooner or later." Tōzan: "If the Master has an abiding place, I will come." Ungan: "It would be difficult to meet after your departure." Tōzan: "It would be difficult not to meet again." Tōzan said further: "After one hundred years (meaning after the Master's passing), people ask me how my Master looks, I don't know how to answer." Ungan: "Just tell them what it is like." Tōzan hesitated a long while. Ungan said: "You have to be careful about such things." Tōzan kept his doubts. Later when he was crossing the water and saw his image reflected, he suddenly understood the teaching of Ungan. Then he composed the following gāthā:

> You should not search through others,
> Lest the Truth recede farther from you.
> When alone I proceed through myself,
> I meet him wherever I go.
> He is the same as me,
> Yet I am not he!
> Only if you understand this
> Will you identify with Tathata.

The English translation of the above gāthā was taken from Professor Chang Chung-yuan's *Original Teachings of Ch'an Buddhism*, 1969. The Chinese version appeared in the *Lamp Records*, Vol. 15, *Daishō Daizōkyō*, Vol. 51, pages 321-323; Y. H. Ku, *History of Chinese Zen Masters*, pages 222-230.

Tōzan passed away at the age of sixty-three. He had many disciples, among them:

Tsao-shan Pen-chi (Sōzan Honjaku, 840-901)

Yun-chu Tao-ying (Ungo Dōyō, d. 902)

Chiu-feng Pu-man (Kyūhō Fuman)

Lung-ya Chu-tun (Ryūga Koton, 835-923)

Wa-ou Neng-kuang (Ga'oku Nōkō, d. 933), from Japan

Tung-shan Tao-chuan (Tōzan Dōzen, d. 894)

Ching-lin Shih-chien (Seirin Shikan, d. 904)

Hua-yen Shu-zing (Kegon Kyujō)

Yu-hsi Tao-yu (Yūsai Dōyū)

Pai-ma Tun-ju (Hakuba Tonju)

Tien-tung Hsien-chi (Tendō Kankei)

Pai-sui Pen-jen (Hakusui Honjin)

Su-shan Kuang-jen (Sosan Kōnin)

Chin-shan Wen-sui (Kinsan Bunsui)

King-chao Hsien-tze (Keichō Kenshi)

"不！"云岩说："你要回故乡吗？"洞山说："不！"云岩说："你迟早会回来。"洞山说："如果师父有住处，我就来。"云岩说："自此一去难得相见。"洞山说："也难得不相见。"洞山接着说："师父百年之后，如有人问吾师容貌如何，我不知如何回答。"云岩说："你只要告诉他们本来面目。"洞山迟疑很长一会儿。云岩说："你必须仔细关心这些事。"洞山还是怀疑。后来，当他渡过河水看到自己的倒影，突然领悟云岩的教导。于是他作了下列偈语：

> 切忌从他觅，迢迢与我疏。
>
> 我今独自往，处处得逢渠。
>
> 渠今正是我，我今不是渠。
>
> 应须恁么会，方得契如如。

上列偈言的英文译文选自张钟元教授的《佛教禅宗之源》1969年版，中文见《传灯录》卷 15，《大正藏》第 51 卷第 321—323页和拙著《禅宗师承记》第 222—230 页。

洞山于 63 岁时圆寂。他有许多弟子，其中有：

曹山本寂（840—901）	云居道膺（？—902）
九峰普满	龙牙居遁（835—923）
日本瓦屋能光（？—933）	洞山道全（？—894）
青林师虔（？—904）	华严休静
幽栖道幽	白马遁儒
天童咸启	白水本仁
疏山匡仁	钦山文邃
京兆蚬子	

Tsao-shan Pen-chi (Sōzan Honjaku, 840-901) was a native of Pu-tien of Chuan-chou (present Fukien Province). At the age of nineteen he left home to become a monk at Mount Ling-shih (Reiseki San) in Foochow. At the age of twenty-three, he was ordained. He was among the famous disciples of Tōzan. In fact, Tōzan and Sōzan were the co-founders of the Tsao-tung (Sōtō) School.

When Sōzan arrived at Tōzan's monastery, the Master (Tōzan) asked: "What is your name?" He replied, "My name is Pen-chi (Honjaku)." The name means "originally silent." Tōzan said: "Say something toward the Ultimate Reality." Sōzan replied: "I will not say anything." Tōzan further asked: "Why don't you speak?" Sōzan replied: "If I say more, my name is not called Pen-chi." Hence Tōzan regarded him highly as a priest with great capacity for Zen Buddhism.

The following conversation was taken from Professor Chang Chung-yuan's *Original Teachings of Ch'an Buddhism*, pages 72-73. (The Chinese original version appeared in the *Lamp Records*, Vol. 17, *Daishō Daizōkyō*, Vol. 51, pages 336-337; Y. H. Ku, *History of Chinese Zen Masters*, pages 231-236.)

A monk asked Master Sōzan, "Who is he that is not accompanied by ten thousand things?"

The Master replied, "There are many people in the city of Hung-chou. Can you tell me where they disappear?"

Monk: "Do eyes and eyebrows know each other?"

Master: "They do not know each other."

Monk: "Why do they not know each other?"

Master: "Because they are located in the same place."

Monk: "In such a way, then, there is no differentiation between eyes and eyebrows?"

Master: "Not so. Eyebrows certainly cannot be eyes."

Monk: "What is an eye?"

Master: "Straight ahead."

Monk: "What is an eyebrow?"

Master: "Sōzan is still in doubt about it."

Monk: "Why should you, Master, be in doubt?"

Master: "If I were not in doubt, it would be straight ahead."

Monk: "Where is the reality in appearance?"

曹山本寂（840—901）是泉州蒲田（在今福建省）人。他19岁时离家去福州灵石山为僧，23岁时受戒。他是洞山良价的著名弟子之一。事实上，洞山和曹山是曹洞宗的共同创建者。

当曹山来到洞山的寺院时，洞山问他："你叫什么名字？"他答道："我名本寂。"这个名字的意义是"本来就寂静"。洞山说："说说至高无上的道吧。"曹山回答："不说。"洞山进一步问："为什么不说？"曹山答："如果我多说，我的名字就不叫本寂了。"因此洞山很器重他，认为他是一位具有禅法智慧的僧侣。

下列谈话引自张钟元教授的《佛教禅宗之源》第72—73页（中文原文见《传灯录》卷17，《大正藏》第51卷，第336—337页和拙著《禅宗师承记》第231—236页）。

一僧人问曹山本寂禅师："不与万物为伴者是什么人？"

禅师答道："洪州城内有许多人，你能告诉我，他们藏到哪里去了？"

僧人："眼睛和眉毛互相认识吗？"

禅师："它们互相不认识。"

僧人："为何它们互相不认识？"

禅师："因为它们在同一个地方。"

僧人："这样一来，眼睛和眉毛就没有区别了？"

禅师："并非如此，眉毛当然不可能是眼睛。"

僧人："什么是眼？"

禅师："一直向前。"

僧人："什么是眉？"

禅师："曹山一直在怀疑。"

僧人："为什么大师您在怀疑？"

禅师："如果我不怀疑，那就一直向前了。"

僧人："现象中真实在哪里？"

Master: "Wherever there is appearance, there is reality."

Monk: "How does it manifest itself?"

The Master lifted the top of his tea-cup set.

Monk: "Where is the reality in illusion?"

Master: "Illusion was originally real."

Monk: "How can reality manifest itself in illusion?"

Master: "Wherever there is illusion there is the manifestation of reality."

Monk: "In such a way, then, reality can never be separated from illusion."

Master: "Where can you possibly find the appearance of illusion?"

Monk: "Who is he who is always present?"

Master: "It is the time when Sōzan happens to be out."

Monk: "Who is he who is never present?"

Master: "Impossible to achieve."

As the story went, someone asked Hsiang-yen Chih-hsien (Kyōgen Chikan): "What is Tao?" Kyōgen answered: "In the dry woods a dragon is singing." The questioner did not understand. So Kyōgen added: "The eye is in the skull." The same question was put to Master Shih-shuang Ching-chu (Sekisō Keisho, 807-888). Sekisō answered: "There is still joy there," referring to the singing of the dragon. Then what is the meaning of "The eye is in the skull"? Sekisō said: "There is consciousness there." Master Sōzan, hearing of this, composed the following gāthā:

> He who says that the dragon is singing in the dry woods
> Is he who truly sees Tao?
> The skull has no consciousness,
> But wisdom's eye begins to shine in it.
> If joy and consciousness should be eliminated,
> Then fluctuation and communication would cease.
> Those who deny this do not understand
> That purity is in the impure.

Sōzan entered nirvana at the age of sixty-two. Among his disciples, there were:

Tsao-shan Hui-hsia (Sōzan Eka)

Tung-shan Tao-yen (Tōzan Dō'en)

King-feng Chun-chih (Kinhō Jushi)

Lo-men Chi-chen (Rokumon Shoshin)

Tsao-an Fa-yee (Sōan Hōgi)

Ho-yu Kuang-hui (Kagyoku Kō'e)

禅师："哪里有现象，哪里就有真实。"

僧人："它如何显示？"

禅师举起他的茶杯盖。

僧人："幻象中的真实何在？"

禅师："幻象本真实。"

僧人："真实如何在幻象中显示自己？"

禅师："哪里有幻象，哪里就有真实显示。"

僧人："这样说来，真实是永远不会与幻象分离的。"

禅师："你从哪里能够找到幻象的表面形式？"

僧人："永远存在的人是谁？"

禅师："是曹山偶尔外出的时候。"

僧人："永远不存在的人是谁？"

禅师："不可能找到。"

接下来的故事这样说——有人问香严志闲："什么是道？"香严回答："枯木里龙吟。"问的人不懂。于是香严补充说："骷髅里眼睛。"有人用这样的问题问石霜庆诸（807—888），石霜针对"龙吟"的问题回答说："那里仍旧很快乐啊。"至于"眼睛在骷髅里"的意义，石霜说："那里仍旧有意识啊。"曹山禅师听到后，作了下列偈语：

枯木龙吟真见道，骷髅无识眼初明。

喜识尽时消息尽，当人那辨浊中清。

曹山 62 岁时进入涅槃。他的弟子中有：

曹山慧霞	洞山道延
金峰从志	鹿门处真
草庵法义	荷玉光慧

What important contributions did Tōzan and Sōzan make to Zen Buddhism and Zen philosophy? This question can be best answered by quoting Alan W. Watts in *The Way of Zen*, pages 102-103:

> Thus it should be obvious that the "naturalness" of these Tang masters is not to be taken just literally, as if Zen were merely to glory in being a completely ordinary, vulgar fellow who scatters ideals to the wind and behaves as he pleases—for this would in itself be an affectation. The "naturalness" of Zen flourishes only when one has lost affectedness and self-consciousness of every description. But a spirit of this kind comes and goes like the wind, and is the most impossible thing to institutionalize and preserve.
>
> Yet in the Tang dynasty the genius and vitality of Zen was such that it was coming to be the dominant form of Buddhism in China, though its relation to other schools was often very close. Kuei-feng Tsung-mi (Keihō Shūmitsu, 780-841) was simultaneously a Zen master and the Fifth Patriarch of the Hua-yen (Kegon) School, representing the philosophy of *Avatamsaka Sutra*. This extremely subtle and mature form of Mahayana philosophy was employed by Tung-shan (Tōzan, 807-869) in developing the doctrine of the Five Ranks (wu-wei or go'i), concerning the five-fold relationship of the absolute (cheng or shō) and the relative (p'ien or hen), and was related to the philosophy of the *I Ching* (*Book of Changes*, or *Ekikyō*) by his student (disciple) Tsao-shan (Sōzan, 840-901). Fa-yen Wen-i (Hōgen Bun'eki, 885-958) and Fen-yang Shan-chao (Funnyō Zenshō, 947-1024) were also influential masters who made a deep study of the Hua-yen (Kegon), and to this day it constitutes as it were the intellectual aspect of Zen. On the other hand, such masters as Tien-tai Te-shao (Tendai Tokushō, 891-972) and Yung-ming Yen-shou (Yōmei Enju, 904-975), maintained close relations with the Tientai (Tendai) and Pure Land (Jōdō) Schools.

The Five Ranks were originated by Tōzan Ryōkai, who constructed this doctrine upon the foundation of the Dialectic of Sekitō Kisen and other earlier Zen masters. However, it was Sōzan Honjaku who first, in the spirit of, and in accordance with the Master's (Tōzan's) teachings, arranged the Five Ranks in their transmitted form and explained them in many ways. The reader could refer to Tōzan's "Pao-ching-san-mei-ko" (Hōkyōzammai ka) and to Sōzan's commentary. In a treatise *The Development of Chinese Zen*, originally written in German by Heinrich

洞山和曹山对禅宗佛教和禅宗哲学有何重要贡献？对这一问题的最好回答可以引用艾伦·瓦茨在《禅道》第 102—103 页的评述：

显然，对于唐朝禅师们的"天然本性"，不能仅仅从字面上来认识，似乎禅宗大师们只是一些在空谈中传播思想、随心所欲行事（这本身只会是一种矫揉造作的假象）的洋洋得意的凡人。只有当一个人丢掉各种不自然的举止和自我意识之后，禅宗的天然本性才能得到发扬。但是这种灵性来去如风，极不可能归结为恒常不变而可以保存的事物……

在唐朝，禅宗虽与佛教其他宗派的关系往往非常密切，但其精神和活力却使它逐渐成为中国佛教的主导形式。圭峰宗密（780—841）既是禅宗大师，同时又是代表《华严经》哲学的华严宗的五祖。洞山良价在发展五位学说的过程中正是应用了这种大乘哲学的极其玄妙与成熟的形式，来论述关于绝对（正）与相对（偏）的五重对应关系。洞山的弟子曹山把这一学说与《易经》哲学联系起来。法眼文益（885—958）和汾阳善昭（947—1024）也都是对《华严经》有深刻研究的颇具影响的大师，并且构成了今天禅宗的唯理智方面的性质。另一方面，天台德韶（891—972）和永明延寿（904—975）这些禅师也与天台宗和净土宗保持了密切的关系。

洞山良价在石头希迁及其他早期禅宗大师的辩证语录基础上首创了五位学说。但是正是曹山本寂首先继承并按照师父洞山的精神和教导规定了五位学说的传授形式，并且对五位学说作了多方面的阐述。读者可以参考洞山的《宝镜三昧歌》和曹山的评注。在海因立希·杜慕林用德语写作的《中国禅宗的发展》

Dumoulin, S. J., translated into English by Ruth Fuller Sasaki, and published by The First Zen Institute of America, Inc., New York, in 1953, we find the excellent explanation of the doctrine of the Five Ranks. As this reference is not easily available, we quote as follows:

> The two principal term of the Five Ranks are shō (upright) and hen (slant or bent). For the meaning of shō, Tōzan Ryōkai explained: "There is one thing: Heaven is suspended from it and Earth rests upon it. It is black like lacquer, perpetually in movement and activity." Shō is also the One, the Absolute, the foundation of Heaven and Earth and all being. This Absolute corresponds to ri (reason) or an (darkness) in the speculation of Sekitō Kisen. In Buddhist terminology it is True Emptiness (shinkū). In hen (p'ien) the Absolute enters into appearances. It completely penetrates the phenomenal world, becomes the All and all things. With Sekitō Kisen this is ji (things) or myō (brightness). The two, Absolute and relative-phenomenal, are not separate, are not two, but one. The Absolute is the Absolute with regard to the relative. The relative, however, is relative with reference to the Absolute. The relative-phenomenal in Buddhist terminology is "marvelous existence" (myōu), which is inseparable from the True Emptiness. The expression is "shinkū myōu."

The Five Ranks:

1. Shōchūhen (Cheng chung p'ien): The Absolute within the relative. The movement is from the Absolute to the relative.

2. Henchūshō (P'ien chung cheng): The relative within the Absolute. The Second Rank is "to abandon phenomena and enter the Principle."

3. Shōchūrai (Cheng chung lai): The Third Rank shows the Absolute before any unfoldment or externalization, but pregnant with all possibilities for development.

4. Henchūshi (P'ien chung chih): The Fourth Rank signifies the relative-phenomenal alone is stark relativily. Phenomena are viewed in their respective individual forms. Thus the Absoluteness of the relative as such becomes evident.

5. Kenchūtō (Chien chung tao): The Fifth Rank signifies the highest rank, undifferentiated oneness.

With regard to the Fourth Rank, Ruth Fuller Sasaki had a footnote on page 28: "In the Rinzai School this fourth rank is termed Kenchūshi (Chien chung chih); the meaning is the same, however."

Sōzan Honjaku used the famous "Lord and Vassal" as parallel:

（罗丝·富勒·佐佐木英译，美国第一禅堂出版，1953 年纽约版）中，我们找到了关于五位学说的精彩阐述。由于该参考材料不易看到，故特引述如下：

五位的主要术语是"正"和"偏"。洞山解释"正"的意义说："有一物焉，天浮其上，地息其下。其黑如漆，永恒运转。""正"就是一，是绝对，是天地万物之基础。在石头希迁的思辨中，绝对对应于"理"或"暗"。在佛教术语中它是真空。在"偏"中绝对开始出现。它完全渗入现象世界，成为一切和一切事物。用石头希迁的话来说，偏是"事"或"明"。绝对的理念和相对的现象不可分离，不是二，而是一。绝对是对应于相对而言的绝对，相对则是对应于绝对而言的相对。这种相对现象在佛教术语中是"妙有"，它同"真空"不可分隔，即"真空妙有"。

五位：

1. 正中偏：相对中的绝对。运动从绝对走向相对。

2. 偏中正：绝对中的相对。第二位是"抛弃现象，进入本原"。

3. 正中来：第三位指的是绝对尚未有任何显露或表现形态，但已孕育着一切发展可能。

4. 偏中至：第四位标志着相对现象本身是相对明显的，现象是从它们有关的各别形态来观察的，因此，这种相对中的绝对性就变得非常清楚。

5. 兼中到：第五位标志着最高的等位，是毫无差别的统一。

罗丝·富勒·佐佐木在介绍第四位时，曾在第 28 页有一脚注："临济宗把第四位称为兼中至，意义相同。"

曹山本寂使用了内涵相同的著名的"五位君臣"名称：

1. The lord sees the vassal.

2. The vassal turns toward the lord.

3. The lord (alone).

4. The vassal (alone).

5. Lord and vassal in union.

In the Rinzai School in Japan, Dōkyō Etan (1641-1721), better known as Shōju Rōjin, gave secret transmission to Hakuin Ekaku (1685-1768) concerning the "Five Ranks." Forty years later Hakuin confided to his followers that "it was only after he (Shōju Rōjin) had completed his investigation of Tōzan's Verses that Shōju gave his acknowledgement to the Five Ranks."

We shall quote from Ruth Fuller Sasaki's translation in *Zen Dust*, pages 66-72.

> Shōju Rōjin has said: "In order to provide a means whereby students might directly experience the Four Wisdoms, the patriarchs, in their compassion and with their skill in devising expedients, first instituted the Five Ranks." What are the so-called Four Wisdoms? They are the Great Perfect Mirror Wisdom, the Universal Nature Wisdom, the Marvelous Observing Wisdom, and the Perfecting-of-Action Wisdom.
>
> ...
>
> ... But, strange to say, the light of the Great Perfect Mirror Wisdom is black like lacquer. This is what is called the rank of "The Apparent within the Real" (Shōchūhen).
>
> Having attained the Great Perfect Mirror Wisdom, you now enter the rank of "The Real within the Apparent" (Henchūshō). When you have accomplished your long practice of the Jeweled-mirror Samadhi, you directly realize the Universal Nature Wisdom and for the first time enter the state of the unobstructed interpenetration of Noumenon and phenomena (riji muge hōkkai).
>
> But the disciple must not be satisfied here. He himself must enter into intimate acquaintance with the rank of "The Coming from within

the Real" (Shōchūrai). After that, by depending upon the rank of "The Arrival at Mutual Integration" (Kenchūshi), he will completely prove the Marvelous Observing Wisdom and the Perfecting-of-Action Wisdom. At last he reaches the rank of "Unity Attained" (Kenchūtō), and, "after all, comes back to sit among the coals and ashes."

Tōzan Ryōkai's verses on the Five Ranks:

1. 主中宾　　2. 宾中主　　　　3. 主中来

4. 宾中至　　5. 兼中到

在日本的临济宗中，道镜慧端（1641—1721），号"正受老人"，曾对白隐慧鹤（1685—1768）秘密传授有关"五位"学说。四十年后白隐向其弟子吐露说：正是在他（正受老人）对洞山的诗偈作了完整的研究之后，老人才承认了"五位"。

我们现在从罗丝·富勒·佐佐木的《禅尘》第66—72页中引录下文：

正受老人曾说："为了向学禅者提供可以直接体验四智的手段，世祖们以他们的满腔热忱和智慧本领设计出权宜的方法，首先提出了五位。"什么是四智？它们是大圆镜智、平等性智、妙观察智、成所作智。

……但是，说也奇怪，广大无瑕的大圆镜智却是其黑如漆。这就是所谓的"在真实中的表象"（正中偏）。已经获得广大无瑕的大圆镜智后，现在你们可以进入"表象中的真实"（偏中正）了。

当你们已经完成三昧宝镜的长期实践，你们就直接认识到普遍存在的平等性智，并且首次进入本体和现象的了无阻碍的相互渗透（理事无碍法界）。

但是弟子不可满足于此，必须进入"从真实中来"（正中来）之位。之后，依靠到达相互结合（兼中至），就可完全证实妙观察智和成所作智，最后达到"取得一致"（兼中到）。

洞山良价的"五位"诗：

(1) The Apparent within the Real:

> In the third watch of the night
>
> Before the moon appears,
>
> No wonder when we meet
>
> There is no recognition!
>
> Still cherished in my heart
>
> Is the beauty of earlier days.

(2) The Real within the Apparent:

> A sleepy-eyed grandma
>
> Encounters herself in an old mirror.
>
> Clearly she sees a face,
>
> But it doesn't resemble hers at all.
>
> Too bad, with a muddled head,
>
> She tries to recognize her reflection.

(3) The Coming from within the Real:

> Within nothingness there is a path
>
> Leading away from the dusts of the world.
>
> Even if you observe the taboo
>
> On the present emperor's name,
>
> You will surpass that eloquent one of yore
>
> Who silenced every tongue.

(4) The Arrival at Mutual Integration:

> When two blades cross points,
>
> There's no need to withdraw.
>
> The master swordsman
>
> Is like the lotus blooming in the fire.
>
> Such a man has in and of himself
>
> A heaven-soaring spirit.

(5) Unity Attained:

Who dares to equal him
Who falls into neither being nor non-being!
All men want to leave
The current of ordinary life,
But he, after all, comes back
To sit among the coals and ashes.

Hakuin Ekaku quoted a poem by Setchō Jūken (980-1052) as a comment on Tōzan's verses:

How many times has Tokuun, the idle old gimlet,
Not come down from the Marvelous Peak!
He hires foolish wise men to bring snow,
And he and they together fill up the well.

（1）正中偏
三更初夜月明前，
莫怪相逢不相识，
隐隐犹怀旧日嫌。

（2）偏中正
失晓老婆逢古镜，
分明觌面别无真，
休向迷头犹认影。

（3）正中来
无中有路隔尘埃，
但能不触当今讳，
也胜前朝断舌才。

（4）兼中至
两刃交锋不须避，
好手犹如火里莲，
宛然自有冲天志。

（5）兼中到
不落有无谁敢和，
人人尽欲出常流，
折合还归炭里坐。

白隐慧鹤引用雪窦重显（980—1052）的一首诗作为对上述洞山诗偈的评注：

空转老钻是秃髭，
几度妙峰不归来。
雇来贤愚齐搬雪，
共同填满那水井。

Note: *Zen Dust* was based on *The Zen Koan* by Isshu Miura and Ruth Fuller Sasaki with detailed notes and other important material added, including genealogical charts and maps.

Before we trace the lineage from Tung-shan (Tōzan) to Fu-yung Tao-kai (Fuyō Dōkai, 1043-1118), Tōzan's important disciples need to be briefly presented. Yun-chu Tao-ying (Ungo Dōyō, d. 902) was a native of Yu-tien (Gyokuda), Yu-chou (Yūshu), in Northern China. At the age of twenty-five, he became a monk at the Yen-shu Temple (Enju-ji), Fanyang. He was not satisfied with learning the Vinaya (Rissui) rules and ceremonies. So he went up Mount Tsui-wei (Suiba San) to seek Tao and spent three years there. A monk who came from Kiangsi told Ungo that Tōzan was a great Zen Master. So he went to visit Tōzan. Tōzan asked him: "What is your name?" Ungo replied: "My name is Tao-ying (Dōyō)." Tōzan said: "Say something toward the Ultimate Reality." Dōyō replied: "If I say more, my name is not called Tao-ying (Dōyō)." Tozan said: "Your reply is just like what I replied to Yun-yen (Ungan), when Ungan asked me the same question." Dōyō said: "It is my fault." Note that Tōzan asked Sōzan the same question, and Sōzan gave exactly the same answer. For other anecdotes, see the *Lamp Records*, Vol. 17. (*Daishō Daizōkyō*, Vol. 51, pages 334-336; Y. H. Ku, *History of Chinese Zen Masters*, pages 237-242).

Ungo passed away in 902 A.D. His dharma heirs were: Tung-an Tao-pei (Dōan Dōhai, 889-955), Yun-chu Huai-yueh (Ungo Egaku), Kuei-tsung Huai-hui (Kisū Eki), Kuei-tsung Tan-chuan (Kisū Tangon), and Yun-chu Tao-chien (Ungo Dōken).

Master Chiu-feng Pu-man (Kyūhō Fuman Daishi) was recorded in the *Lamp Records*, Vol. 17 (*Daishō Daizōkyō*, Vol. 51, page 338; Y. H. Ku, *History of Chinese Zen Masters*, page 243) with the following:

Master Fuman asked a monk: "Where did you come from?" The monk answered: "From Fukien." Master said: "You have traveled far. The journey was not easy." The monk said: "The journey was not difficult. Once you moved your feet, you can arrive here." Master: "Was there a journey that you need not move your feet?" The monk did not answer.

According to the *Lamp Records*, Vol. 20 (*Daishō Daizōkyō*, Vol. 51, page 361; Y. H. Ku, *History of Chinese Zen Masters,* page 243), Kyūho Fuman's dharma-heir was Tung-an Wei (Dōan I) of Hung-chou (now Kiangsi), whose disciples were Shih-ching Ho-shan (Sekikyō oshō) of Chen-chou, and Chung Tung-an Kuan-chih (Chū Dōan Kanshi).

按:《禅尘》是根据伊苏·缪拉和罗丝·富勒·佐佐木的《禅宗公案》撰写而成,并增加了详细的注解和其他重要材料,包括世系表和图。

在我们追溯洞山到芙蓉道楷(1043—1118)这一世系之前,有必要简略介绍一下洞山的若干重要弟子。云居道膺(?—902)是华北幽州玉田人,25 岁时在范阳延寿寺出家为僧。他不满足于学习律宗的戒规和仪式,因而登翠微山求道,在此度过三年。有一来自江西的僧人告诉云居,洞山乃是禅宗大师。于是云居前去参谒洞山。洞山问他:"你叫何名?"云居答:"我名道膺。"洞山说:"说说至高无上之道。"云居答:"如果我再说,我就不叫'道膺'了。"洞山说:"你的回答与我回答云岩(昙晟)一样,当时云岩也问我这样的问题。"道膺说:"那就是我的过错了。"按:洞山也曾对曹山问过这一问题,而曹山也恰恰给予同样的回答。至于其他轶事,可阅《传灯录》卷 17(《大正藏》第 51 卷,第 334—336 页和拙著《禅宗师承记》第 237—242 页)。

云居于公元 902 年圆寂。他的法嗣有:同安道丕(889—955),云居怀岳,归宗怀恽,归宗澹权,云居道简。

《传灯录》卷 17(《大正藏》第 51 卷,第 338 页和拙著《禅宗师承记》第 243 页),都载有九峰普满禅师的下列轶事:

九峰普满大师问一僧人:"你从何处来?"僧人答:"福建。"大师说:"你来处很远,远行不易。"僧人说:"远行不难,只要动脚,就能到此。"大师说:"有没有你无需动脚的远行?"僧人无言。

根据《传灯录》卷 20(《大正藏》第 51 卷,第 361 页和拙著《禅宗师承记》第 243 页),九峰普满的法嗣是洪州同安威,后者的弟子有陈州石镜和尚和中同安观志。

According to the *Lamp Records*, Vol. 20 (*Daishō Daizōkyō*, Vol. 51, page 365; Y. H. Ku, *History of Chinese Zen Masters*, page 244), Dōan I left the following anecdote:

> A monk asked Dōan I: "Before Niu-tou Fa-yung (Gyūtō Hōyū) met the Fourth Patriarch, how is it?" Dōan I said: "By the roadside there was a small shrine; those who saw it raised their fists." The monk asked: "How is it after Fa-yung (Hōyū) met with the Fourth Patriarch?" The Master said: "There was no deceased person's bed in the room, hence there was no need to wear mourning clothing." The monk asked: "What is the meaning of the Patriarch's teaching?" The Master replied: "The jade rabbit (moon) did not understand the meaning of early morning; The golden crow (sun) did not wish to shine bright in the night."
>
> The monk asked: "What is the music of Tungan (Dōan)?" The Master answered:
>
> "The holy guitar does not play the worldly music;
> Only the expert in music trespasses Pai-Ya's door."

The lineage from Dōan I to Tung-an Kuan-chih (Dōan Kanshi) and Shih-ching Ho-shan (Sekikyō oshō) was recorded in the *Lamp Records*, Vol. 23 (*Daishō Daizōkyō*, Vol. 51, page 388; Y. H. Ku, *History of Chinese Zen Masters*, page 244).

The dharma heirs of Dōan Kanshi were Liang-shan Yuan-kuan (Ryōsan Enkan) and Ling-tung Ho-shan (Reisū oshō) of Chen-chou, as recorded in the *Lamp Records*, Vol. 24 (*Daishō Daizōkyō*, Vol. 51, page 398; Y. H. Ku, *History of Chinese Zen Masters*, page 244). For a long time, the dharma teacher of Tung-an Kuan-chih (Dōan Kanshi) was attributed to Tung-an Tao-pei (Dōan Dōhai, 889-955), who was a disciple of Yun-chu Tao-ying (Ungo Dōyō). From the *Lamp Records*, the present author established the lineage of the Tsao-tung School (Sōtō shū) from Tōzan to Ta-yang Ching-yuan (Daiyō Keigen, 943-1027) as follows:

(1) Tōzan Ryōkai (807-869)

(2) Kyūhō Fuman (Daishi)

(3) Dōan I

(4) Dōan Kanshi

(5) Ryōsan Enkan

(6) Daiyō Keigen (943-1027)

Liang-shan Yuan-kuan (Ryōsan Enkan) was recorded in the *Lamp Records*, Vol. 24 (*Daishō Daizōkyō*, Vol. 51, page 406; Y. H. Ku, *History of Chinese Zen Masters*, page 245). Ta-yang Ching-yuan (Daiyō Keigen) was

根据《传灯录》卷 20（《大正藏》第 51 卷，第 365 页和拙著《禅宗师承记》第 244 页），同安威留有下列轶事：

一僧人问同安威："牛头法融未见四祖之前，则如何？"同安威说："路边神庙子，见者尽擎拳。"僧人问："法融见了四祖后如何？"同安威说："室内无灵床，浑家不著孝。"僧人问："什么是四祖教导的意义？"同安威答道："玉兔不曾知晓意，金乌争肯夜头明。"僧人问："如何是同安一曲？"同安威答："灵琴不引人间韵，知音岂度伯牙门。"

从同安威到同安观志和石镜和尚的世系记载在《传灯录》卷 23（《大正藏》第 51 卷，第 388 页和拙著《禅宗师承记》第 244 页）中。

正如《传灯录》卷 24（《大正藏》第 51 卷，第 398 页和拙著《禅宗师承记》第 244 页）所载，同安观志的法嗣有梁山缘观和陈州灵通和尚。长期以来，一直把同安观志禅师认作同安道丕（889—955）的法嗣，而后者则是云居道膺的弟子。根据《传灯录》，本书作者确证了从洞山到大阳警玄（943—1027）的曹洞宗的下列世系：

（1）洞山良价（807—869）

（2）九峰普满

（3）同安威

（4）同安观志

（5）梁山缘观

（6）大阳警玄（943—1027）

梁山缘观事迹载于《传灯录》卷 24（《大正藏》第 51 卷，第 406 页和拙著《禅宗师承记》第 245 页）。大阳警玄事迹载于《传

recorded in the *Lamp Records*, Vol. 26 (*Daishō Daizōkyō*, Vol. 51, page 421; Y. H. Ku, *History of Chinese Zen Masters*, page 246). Daiyō could not find a dharma-heir during his lifetime. So he entrusted the task of finding a dharma-heir for him to Master Fu-shan Fa-yuan (Fusan Hō'en, 991-1067) of the Lin-chi School. Fu-shan had the honorary title of Yuan-chien Zen Master (Enkan Zenji) and was the dharma-heir of Yeh-hsien Kuei-sheng (Yōken Kisei). According to the *Lamp Records*, 2nd Series (*Zoku Dentō Roku*), Vol. 6 (*Daishō Daizōkyō*, Vol. 51, pages 499-500; Y. H. Ku, *History of Chinese Zen Masters*, pages 247-249), Enkan was residing at Hui-shen-yen (Ishōgan), and one night he dreamed of a blue eagle. Tou-tzu I-ching (Tōsu Gisei, 1032-1083) came to visit Master Enkan the next morning. The Master invited him to stay on, as "Gisei" implied the colour blue or green. After three years, Enkan asked him something. Gisei was about to answer. But Master Enkan used his hand to close Gisei's mouth. Another three years had passed. Enkan examined him about his understanding of Tōzan's teachings. After Tōsu Gisei showed perfect understanding, Enkan bestowed upon him Daiyō's robe, shoes, etc., such that he was to be Daiyō's dharma-heir. This was a unique instance. So Tōsu Gisei was later honored by the title Master "Miao-shu" (Myō-zoku Daishi), meaning "marvelous continuation." After telling this story (history), the lineage of the Sōtō School continues as follows:

(6) Daiyō Keigen (943-1027)

(7) Tōsu Gisei (1032-1083)

(8) Fuyō Dōkai (1043-1118)

Fu-yung Tao-kai (Fuyō Dōkai, 1043-1118) was recorded in the *Lamp Records*, 2nd Series (*Zoku Dentō Roku*), Vol. 10 (*Daishō Daizōkyō*, Vol. 51, pages 523-524; Y. H. Ku, *History of Chinese Zen Masters*, pages 250-253).

After Fuyō Dōkai, there were two branches:

(9a) Tan-hsia Tzu-zing (Tanka Shijun, 1064-1119)

(10a) Chen-hsieh Ching-liao (Shinketsu Seiryō, 1090-1151)

(11a) Tien-tung Tsung-chueh (Tendō Sōkaku, 1091-1162)

(12a) Cho-an Chih-chien (Soku'an Chikan, 1105-1192)

(13a) Tien-tung Ju-zing (Tendō Nyojō, 1162-1228)

(14a) Tao-yuan Hsi-hsuan (Dōgen Kigen, 1200-1253)

Note that Dōgen Kigen was the founder of the Sōtō School in Japan.

灯录》卷 26 (《大正藏》第 51 卷，第 421 页和拙著《禅宗师承记》第 246 页）。大阳毕生未能找到一位法嗣，因而就将为他寻找法嗣的任务委托临济宗的浮山法远（991—1067）。浮山敕号圆鉴禅师，是叶县归省的法嗣，根据《续传灯录》卷 6 (《大正藏》第 51 卷，第 499—500 页和拙著《禅宗师承记》第 247—249 页），圆鉴禅师居住会圣岩时，一晚梦见一青鹰。翌日早晨，投子义青（1032—1083）来谒。禅师邀请他留下，因为义青含有青色之意。三年后，圆鉴问投子义青某事，义青正要回答，圆鉴禅师却用手掩住义青的口。又过了三年，圆鉴考查义青对洞山教义的悟解。当投子义青显示出卓越的理解后，圆鉴就将大阳的袍鞋等赐给他，使他成为大阳的法嗣。这是一个仅有的事例。因而投子义青后来被授予"妙续"（意为"绝妙的继续"）大师的称号。在叙述了这段故事后，现将曹洞宗的世系继续序列如下：

（6）大阳警玄（943—1027）

（7）投子义青（1032—1083）

（8）芙蓉道楷（1043—1118）

有关芙蓉道楷的事迹，载于《续传灯录》卷 10 (《大正藏》第 51 卷，第 523—524 页和拙著《禅宗师承记》第 250—253 页）。

在芙蓉道楷之后，有两个分支：

（9a）丹霞子淳（1064—1119）

（10a）真歇清了（1090—1151）

（11a）天童宗珏（1091—1162）

（12a）足庵智鉴（1105—1192）

（13a）天童如净（1162—1228）

（14a）道元希玄（1200—1253）

按：道元希玄是日本曹洞宗的创建者。

Now Tanka Shijun had another disciple: Hung-chih Cheng-chueh (Wanshi Shōkaku, 1091-1157), whose dharma descendants started two sects in Japan. We started to designate Wanshi Shōkaku as (10b).

(10b) Hung-chih Cheng-chueh (Wanshi Shōkaku, 1091-1157)

(11b) Zing-tzu Hui-hui (Jōji Eki, 1097-1183)

(12b) Ming-chi Hui-tsu (Myōkyoku Eso)

(13b) Tung-ko Miao-kuang (Tōkoku Myōkō, d. 1251)

(14b) Chih-won Te-chu (Jiki'ō Tokukyo)

(15b) Tung-ming Hui-ji (Tōmyō Enichi, 1272-1340)

Tōmyō Enichi went to Japan and became the founder of the Tōmyō Sect.

Jiki'ō had another disciple Yun-wai Yun-hsu (Ungai Unshū), whose dharma-heir Tung-ling Yun-yu (Tōryō Eisho, d. 1365) went to Japan and became the founder of the Tōryō Sect. Wanshi Shōkaku was the author of *Chun-yung-lu* (*Shōyō-roku*).

Now we designate the second branch of Fuyō Dōkai's dharma heirs as the (c) line, starting with Lo-men Tzu-chueh (Rokumon Jikaku, d. 1117).

(9c) Lo-men Tzu-chueh (Rokumon Jikaku, d. 1117)

(10c) Pu-chao Hsi-p'ien (Fushō Kiben, 1081-1149)

(11c) Ling-yen Seng-pao (Reigan Sōhō, 1114-1173)

(12c) Wang-shan Ssu-ti (Ōsan Shitei)

(13c) Hsueh-yen Hui-man (Seggan Eman, d. 1206)

Rokumon had another disciple: Chen-yi Hui-lan (Jin'itsu Eran). Now we continue on the (c) line:

(14c) Wan-sung Hsing-hsiu (Manshō Kōshū, 1166-1246)

(15c) Shao-shih Fu-yu (Shōshitsu Fukuyū, 1203-1275)

(16c) Shao-shih Wen-tai (Shōshitsu Buntai, d. 1289)

(17c) Pao-yin Fu-yu (Hō'ō Fukugū, 1245-1313)

(18c) Shao-shih Wen-tsai (Shōshitsu Bunsai, 1273-1352)

(19c) Wan-an Tzu-yen (Man'an Shigen)

(20c) Nin-jan Liao-kai (Gyōnen Ryōkai, 1335-1421)

(21c) Chu-kung Chi-ping (Gukū Keihyō, 1383-1452)

(22c) Wu-fang Ke-chun (Muhō Kashō, 1420-1483)

(23c) Yueh-chou Wen-tsai (Gesshū Bunsai, 1452-1524)

　　丹霞子淳还有另一位弟子：宏智正觉（1091—1157），宏智正觉的法嗣后人在日本开创了两个支派。我们先把宏智正觉一支标明为（10b）。

　　（10b）宏智正觉（1091—1157）

　　（11b）净慈慧晖（1097—1183）

　　（12b）明极慧祚

　　（13b）东谷妙光（？—1251）

　　（14b）直翁德举

　　（15b）东明慧日（1272—1340）

东明慧日到了日本，成为东明派的创建者。

　　直翁德举还有一位弟子云外云岫，后者的法嗣东陵永屿（？—1365）也去日本成为东陵派的创建者。宏智正觉是《从容录》的作者。

　　现在我们把芙蓉道楷的第二支法嗣标明为从鹿门自觉开始的C支。

　　（9c）鹿门自觉（？—1117）　　　（10c）普照希辩（1081—1149）

　　（11c）灵岩僧宝（1114—1173）　（12c）王山师体

　　（13c）雪岩慧满（？—1206）

鹿门还有一位弟子真懿慧兰。现在我们继续叙述C支：

　　（14c）万松行秀（1166—1246）

　　（15c）少室福裕（1203—1275）

　　（16c）少室文泰（？—1289）

　　（17c）宝应福遇（1245—1313）

　　（18c）少室文才（1273—1352）

　　（19c）万安子严

　　（20c）凝然了改（1335—1421）

　　（21c）俱空契斌（1383—1452）

　　（22c）无方可从（1420—1483）

　　（23c）月舟文载（1452—1524）

(24c) Tsung-chin Tsung-shu (Sōkyō Sōsho, 1500-1567)

(25c) Yun-kung Chang-chung (Unkū Shōchū, 1514-1588)

(26c) Wu-ming Hui-chin (Mumyō Ekei, 1548-1618)

(27c) Tung-yuan Yuan-chin (Tō'en Genkyō, 1577-1630)

(28c) Chueh-lang Tao-sheng (Kakurō Dōshō, 1592-1659)

(29c) Kuan-tang Ta-wen (Katsudō Daibun)

(30c) Hsin-yueh Hsing-chiu (Shinetsu Kōchū, 1642-1696)

Note that Hsin-yueh Hsing-chiu was invited to Japan and he was the founder of the Shinetsu Sect.

Tung-yuan Yuan-chin (Tō'en Genkyō) had three dharma brothers:

(27e) Po-shan Yuan-lai (Bakusan Genrai, 1575-1630)

(27f) Shou-chang Yuan-nin (Jushō Gennei, 1579-1649)

(27g) Ku-shan Yuan-hsien (Kozan Genken, 1578-1657)

Ku-shan (Kozan) had several disciples, among them Wei-ling Tao-pai was prominent.

(28g) Wei-ling Tao-pai (Irin Dōhai, 1615-1702)

Yun-kung (Unkū) had a dharma brother:

(25d) Shao-shih Chang-ren (Shōshitsu Shōjun, d. 1585)

Shao-shih Chang-ren had the following dharma descendants:

(26d) Ta-chueh Fang-nien (Daikaku Hōnen, d. 1594)

(27d) Yun-men Yuan-cheng (Ummon Enchō, 1561-1626)

Yun-men had many disciples, among them was the following line:

(28d) Shui-po Ming-hsueh (Zuihaku Myōsetsu, 1584-1641)

(29d) Po-an Zing-teng (Ha'an Jōtō, 1603-1659)

(30d) Ku-chiao Chih-sien (Koshō Chisen)

The author is indebted to Reverend Sheng-yen, Litt.D., (Ekū Shōgen, 1930-) for supplying the information concerning the Koshō or Shōzan line as follows. (See Chart X A).

(1) Koshō Chisen

(2) Kandō Tokukyō

(3) Seki'an Gyōsai

(4) Minshū Fukuki (d. 1790)

(5) Hekigan Shōketsu (1703-1765)

(6) Saishū Chōtō (d. 1737)

（24c）宗镜宗书（1500—1567）

（25c）蕴空常忠（1514 1588）

（26c）无明慧经（1548—1618）

（27c）东苑元镜（1577—1630）

（28c）觉浪道盛（1592—1659）

（29c）阔堂大文

（30c）心越兴俦（1642—1696）

按：心越兴俦被邀赴日本，成为心越派的创建者。

东苑元镜有三位同门师兄弟：

（27e）博山元来（无异）（1575—1630）

（27f）寿昌元谧（1579—1649）

（27g）鼓山元贤（1578—1657）

鼓山有几位弟子，其中以为霖道霈最为著名：

（28g）为霖道霈（1615—1702）

蕴空常忠有一位同门法嗣兄弟：

（25d）少室常润（？—1585）

少室常润有下列法嗣传人：

（26d）大觉方念（？—1594）

（27d）云门圆澄（1561—1626）

云门有许多弟子，其中有下列几位：

（28d）瑞白明雪（1584—1641）

（29d）破阇净灯（1603—1659）

（30d）古樵智先

作者在此感谢文学博士圣严法师（1930—   ），承蒙他提供了焦山系的资料（参见附表ⅩA）：

（1）古樵智先

（2）鉴堂德镜

（3）硕庵行载

（4）敏修福毅（？—1790）

（5）碧岩祥洁（1703—1765）

（6）济舟澄洮（？—1737）

(7) Tan'un Seikyō

(8) Kyo'etsu Seikō

(9) Shūhei Seikō

(10) Shōgen Kakusen

(11) Mukkei Kai'in

(12) Getsuki Ryōzen

(13) Ryūchō Goshun

(14) Kaikō Daishu

(15) Unhan Shōdō

(16)

(17) Tokushun

(18) Kitsudō

(19) Chikō Mishō (1888-1963)

(20) Tōsho Tōrō (1908-1977)

(21) Ekū Shōgen (1930-)

Chikō Mishō had a dharma brother, Jōgen.

Chikō had another disciple, Setsuhan, who was older than Tōsho.

Tōsho had another disciple, Shōkai (1918-).

Tōsho was Founder of Chinese Buddhist Cultural Institute, Pei-tou, Taiwan. Shōgen was installed as the Second Abbot of Chinese Buddhist Cultural Institute, Pei-tou, on March 24, 1978. Shōgen was formerly Abbot of Daikaku-ji, New York, N.Y., U.S.A. The author is deeply indebted to Reverend Sheng-yen, Litt.D. for supplying the lineage of the Shōzan line from Ku-chiao Chi-sien to Tung-chu Ten-lang.

In this book, one photograph was taken when Abbot Tung-chu (Tōsho, 1908-1977) of the Shōzan line visited the United States with Reverend Sheng-yen (Shōgen) at the invitation of Dr. C. T. Shen.

According to *Dharma Records of Abbot Hsu Yun*, Vol. 9, pages 266-297, a list of the Abbots of Yung-chuan Temple (Yōsen-ji) at Ku-shan (Kozan), Foochow, was given. The Founder was Reverend Ling-chiao (Reikyō), a disciple of Ma-tsu (Baso). The First Abbot was Ku-shan Shen-yen (Kozan

Jin'an, Kokushi, 863-939), a disciple of Seppō Gizon (822-908). The 24th Abbot was Chikuan Shiki (1083-1146), a dharma heir of Ryūmon Sei'on. The 26th Abbot was Butsushin Honsai, a dharma heir of Reigen Isei (d. 1117). These Abbots belonged to the Rinzai School. The 31st Abbot was Boku'an An'ei, a dharma grandson of Daie Sōkō. The 41st Abbot was Kozen Jikyō, a disciple of Mittan. After more than forty successions, the 86th

（7）澹宁清镜　　　（8）巨超清恒
（9）秋屏觉灯　　　（10）性源觉诠
（11）墨溪海荫　　　（12）月辉了禅
（13）流长悟春　　　（14）芥航大须
（15）云帆昌道　　　（16）（不详）
（17）德俊　　　　　（18）吉堂
（19）智光弥性（1888—1963）
（20）东初镫朗（1908—1977）
（21）慧空圣严（1930—　　　）

智光弥性有一师兄弟静严。

智光弥性还有另一位弟子雪烦，比东初年长。

东初另有一位弟子圣开（1918—　　　）。

东初曾是台湾北投中华佛教文化馆创建者。圣严于 1978 年 3 月 24 日担任该馆第二任住持。圣严原为美国纽约大觉寺前任住持。圣严法师提供了从古樵智先到东初镫朗的焦山系世系表，对此作者深表感激。

本书有一张东初（1908—1977）受沈家祯居士邀请与圣严法师一起访美的照片。

根据《虚云和尚法汇》卷 9（第 266—297 页），下面提供福州鼓山涌泉寺《鼓山列祖联芳集》的名单。鼓山系的创建者是马祖道一的弟子灵峤法师。第一任住持是鼓山神宴（863—939），他是雪峰义存（822—908）的弟子。第二十四任住持竹庵士珪（1083—1146）是龙门清远的法嗣。第二十六任住持佛心本才是灵源惟清（？—1117）的法嗣。这些住持都属于临济宗。第三十一任住持木庵安永是大慧宗果的法孙。第四十一任住持枯禅自镜是弥潭的弟子。再经过四十多位传人，第八十六

Abbot was Kōan Ensei, who was to lead the Kōan line or the Kozan line to Abbot Hsu Yun (Kiun, 1840-1959) as shown in Chart VI A.

However, the 92nd Abbot was Bokusan Genrai (1575-1630), a dharma heir of Mumyō Ekei (1548-1618), who belonged to the Sōtō School. The 93rd Abbot was Sekkan Dōgin (1585-1637), Bokusan's disciple. The 94th Abbot was Eikaku Genken (1578-1657), another dharma heir of Mumyō Ekei. The 95th Abbot was Kakurō Dōshō (1592-1659), a dharma grandson of Mumyō. The 96th Abbot was Irin Dōhai (1615-1702), a dharma heir of Eikaku Genken. Irin Dōhai was to lead the Irin line to Abbot Jikō Kokai (1895-1954). (See Chart X B.) The author and his wife paid homage to Reverend Jikō's "real body" (Shinshin) enshrined at Sekishi, Taipei in the company of his brother Joseph and sister-in-law Leola.

The Irin line:

(1) Irin Dōhai (1615-1702)

(2) Kōtō Daishin

(3) Henshō Kōryū

(4) Seijun Hōkō

(5) Tōyō Kaisho

(6) Dōgen Ichishin

(7) Kei'un Teizen

(8) Zōki Shinshaku

(9) Enchi Tsūkan

(10) Nōji Tenshō

(11) Untei Kenji

(12) Jōkū Tetsuin

(13) Gogen Chihon

(14) En'ei Yōshō

(15) Jikō Kokai

(16) Genji Fukukai

Reverend Yuang-ying (En'ei) was Abbot of Tendō-ji, Ningpo. Reverend Tzu-hang (Jikō) was the Founder of Taiwan Buddhist College. The author is indebted to Reverend Yen-chih (Genji) for the above lineage. Reverend Yen-chih is at present Abbot of Hua-lien Buddhist Lotus Institute, Taiwan.

It may be noted that Abbot Hsu Yun considered himself the 47th generation dharma descendant of Tōzan in the Sōtō School of China. At Kozan, from the 92nd Abbot to the 130th Abbot, all belonged to the Sōtō School. At the same time, he was the 43rd generation dharma descendant in the Rinzai School.

任住持是高庵圆清，正如附表 VI A 所示，他领导高庵系或鼓山系一直传到虚云和尚（1840—1959）。

不过，第九十二任住持博山元来（1575—1630）即无明慧经（1548—1618）的法嗣，却属于曹洞宗。第九十三任住持雪关道闇（1585—1637）是博山的弟子。第九十四任住持永觉元贤（1578—1657）是无明慧经的另一位弟子。九十五任住持觉浪道盛（1592—1659）是无明慧经的法孙。九十六任住持为霖道霈（1615—1702）是永觉元贤的法嗣。为霖道霈领导的为霖系直至慈航古开（1895—1954）（见附表 X B）。作者夫妇曾在吾弟约瑟夫、弟媳利奥拉陪同下参拜供奉于台北汐止的慈航古开法师的真身。

为霖系：

（1）为霖道霈	（2）恒涛大心
（3）遍照兴隆	（4）清淳法源
（5）东阳界初	（6）道源一信
（7）继云鼎善	（8）增辉新灼
（9）圆智通完	（10）能持天性
（11）云程兼慈	（12）净空彻印
（13）悟源地本	（14）圆瑛耀性
（15）慈航古开	（16）严持复戒

圆瑛法师是宁波天童寺的住持。慈航古开是台湾佛学院的创建者。作者在此向提供上述世系的严持复戒法师致谢。严持复戒法师目前是台湾花莲佛教莲社的住持。

应予指出的是，虚云法师自认是中国曹洞宗洞山的第四十七代法嗣传人，而鼓山从第九十二任起到第一百三十任住持都属于曹洞宗。同时，虚云又是临济宗的第四十三代法嗣传人。

CHAPTER 8   THE UMMON SCHOOL AND THE HŌGEN SCHOOL

Yun-men Wen-yen (Ummon Bun'en, 864-929) was a native of Chia-hsin (Kiangsu Province). He first studied under Mu-chou Tao-chung (Bokujū Dōshō). Later he became a disciple of Hsueh-feng I-tsun (Seppō Gizon, 822-908). If one judges the worth of a Zen master by the number of anecdotes told of him, Ummon was at the top of the list. R. H. Blyth in his *Zen and Zen Classics*, Vol. 2, devoted Chapters XV, XVI and XVII to Ummon. Ummon was clever from a child. After he realized the significance of Huang-po (Ōbaku) as a great Zen master, Ummon went to visit Ōbaku's disciple, Bokujū Dōshō, who was also known as Chen the Elder (Chin-son-shuku). Ummon knocked at his gate. Bokujū asked: "Who is it?" Ummon answered: "Bun'en." "What is it you want?" asked Bokujū. Ummon said: "I want to understand myself. Please teach me!" Bokujū opened the gate, looked at him, and shut the gate. This went on for three days. On the third day, when the door opened, Bun'en pushed his way in. Bokujū seized him and said: "Say something!" Ummon didn't know what to say, and Bokujū pushed him out. As the Master shut the gate in a hurry, Ummon's leg was caught in it and broken. With the intense pain, Ummon came to a realization suddenly. Many anecdotes concerning Ummon appeared in the *Lamp Records*, Vol. 19 (*Daishō Daizōkyō*, Vol. 51, pages 356-359; Y. H. Ku, *History of Chinese Zen Masters*, pages 285-295).

Master Ju-min (Nyomyō) presided in the Ling-shu Monastery (Reiju-ji), at Shao-chou (Shōshū); Ummon was taking the first seat. When Ju-min was about to pass away, he recommended Bun'en to succeed him. Ummon did not forget his old teacher, Seppō Gizon, and esteemed Seppō as his master. Ummon addressed the assembly:

> Please do not think that I am trying to deceive you with words today. I can hardly help talking, that is, making a mess of it. If a clear-sighted man saw me doing this, I would be an object of ridicule. How can I avoid this ridicule now? Let me ask you all: what do you lack

at the very beginning? Even though I tell you that there is nothing lacking within you, this too is deceit. Unless your understanding has reached this stage, you are not yet on the right path. Do not ask questions carelessly and hurriedly when your mind is completely dark.

捌 云门宗和法眼宗

　　云门文偃（864—929），嘉兴（在今浙江，原隶属江苏）人。最先在睦舟道踪门下学习，后成为雪峰义存（822—908）的弟子。如果按照述及人物的轶事数来判定禅宗大师的地位，那么云门文偃应名列其首。布莱思在其《禅与禅宗经典》卷2中，用十五、十六和十七这三章来介绍云门宗。云门文偃从小聪慧。当他认识到黄檗希运作为一位禅宗大师的重要性后，即去谒见黄檗希运弟子睦舟道踪，后者也以"陈尊宿"而闻名。云门去叩他的门，睦舟道踪问："谁？"云门说："文偃。"道踪问："你要什么？"云门说："我要了解我自己。请指点！"道踪打开大门，看看他，又关了门。这样连续三天。到第三天，当门刚开，云门文偃就推门进去，道踪抓住他说："说话！"云门不知道该说什么，道踪就推他出去。由于道踪关门过急，云门的一条腿卡住了，造成骨折。剧痛使他豁然醒悟。有关云门的许多轶事见《传灯录》卷19（《大正藏》第51卷，第356—359页和拙著《禅宗师承记》第285—295页）。

　　如敏禅师在韶州灵树寺为住持，云门文偃为首席弟子。当如敏即将圆寂时，他推荐云门文偃继任己位。云门不忘原来的老师雪峰义存，尊雪峰为自己的禅门宗师。云门曾在全寺长老集会时说：

　　请别以为我今天是想用许多话来哄骗你们。不过我又不得不说，而会把事情说得很糟。如果一个眼睛明亮的人看见我做这种事，那么我就是一个被嘲笑的对象。但现在我又怎么能避免呢？我来问你们大家：你们在本源上缺乏什么？如果我告诉你们，你们心中不缺乏什么，这也是欺骗。除非你们的领悟已经达到这一阶段，否则你们就还没有走上正确的道路。当你们的心头还是黑漫漫的，别随随便便、急急忙忙地提出问题。

Tomorrow and the days thereafter, you will have the most important work to do in order to achieve enlightenment. Those whose grasp is poor and fumbling should go to the well-established schools of the great ancients and search on every side for Truth. Should you gain some inner awareness, all this is due to what is within yourself. When you are drifting in the endless *kalpa*, your mind is full of illusion. The moment you hear others talk about Tao (the Way), you will immediately want to know about it and start asking what the Buddha and the Patriarchs are. Thus you will seek high and low for understanding, but in doing so you will get even further away from Ch'an (Zen), because the searching mind is a deviation and talking about it is even worse. Is it not then true that not searching for it is the correct way? Well, what other alternatives are there, besides these two? Take good care of your own lives!

The teachings of the Three Vehicles, and of the Twelve Divisions of the Canon, expounded Buddhism in this way and that. The old masters of the present-day world give talks on Ch'an (Zen) everywhere. Compared with my approach, which concentrates on the needle point, their methods are like the medicine given by clumsy doctors, who often kill the animals. However, there are a few who can attain to Ch'an (Zen) by such methods. How can you expect there to be roaring thunder in speech and the sharpness of swords in words? In the twinkling of an eye a thousand changes can take place. When the wind ceases, the waves become calm. I beg you to accept my offer! Be Careful!

... To grasp Ch'an (Zen), you must experience it. If you have not experienced it, do not pretend to know. You should withdraw inwardly and search for the ground upon which you stand; thereby you will find out what Truth is. Outwardly not even the slightest explanation can be used to reveal your inner awareness. Every one of you should devote himself to the task of self-realization. When the Great Function (Tay-yung or Daiyō) takes place, no effort will be required of you. You will immediately be no different from the Patriarch and the Buddha.

The above English translations were taken from Professor Chang Chung-yuan's *Original Teachings of Ch'an Buddhism*, pages 283-286. Another quotation follows:

You must be cautious! Do not waste your time wandering thousands of *li* (Chinese measure of distance, about 1/3 of a mile), through this town and that, with your staff on your shoulder, wintering in one

在明天和今后的日子里，为了达到顿悟，你们会有最重要的事去做。领会既差又笨拙的人，应该向古代大师们建立的完善的教派去探索真谛的方方面面。要是你们得到一些内心的觉醒，这完全是由于你们本身内在的缘故。当你们在无边劫难中漂泊时，你们的心中充满幻象。当你们听到旁人说到大道时，就立刻想知道什么是大道并且开始询问佛陀和祖师是什么人。于是你们就到处寻求解释。但是这样做，你们只会离开禅法更远，因为探索心灵正是偏离，谈论心灵更加糟糕。那么，不去探索它才是正确的方法，这是否对呢？除了上面两种方法，还有没有其他方法呢？请你们多加珍重！

三乘和十二分教，横说竖说，天下老和尚纵横十字说，如果与我捻准针锋的道理相比，他们的方法就像害死牲畜的庸医所提供的药物。虽然如此，也有几个人能够用这些方法达到禅的境界。你们怎么可以期望言中有雷鸣、句里藏剑锋呢？眼睛一霎间会有千差万别，而风平则浪静。请接受我的献言！务须慎重！

……要掌握禅法，必须体会禅法。如果你们没有体会它，别去装懂。你们应该退到心灵深处来寻求你们的根基；这样一来就会找到何为真谛。外界片言只语的解释也丝毫不能用来揭示你们内心的醒悟，你们每人都应该致力于自我认识的任务。一旦大功告成，你们也无需费力，你们就会立刻与佛陀和祖师没有区别了。

上述引自张钟元教授《佛教禅宗之源》第283—286页的英语译文。下面是另一段引文：

你们必须注意，切莫浪费时间游州猎县，横担拄杖，一千二千里行走，这边经冬，那边过夏，好山好水堪取胜，多斋供应得衣钵，

place and spending the summer in another. Do not seek out beautiful mountains and rivers to contemplate, nor spend your time calculating, when sacrifice might be better. What a pity when one craves for trifles and loses the important things! Such a search for Ch'an (Zen) is useless!... Do not be idle and waste your time. Do not miss what this life has to offer, for you will never have another chance... Even a worldly man (Ummon meant Confucius) said, "To learn Tao in the morning and die at night—therein is my satisfaction." What efforts we Buddhists must put into this! We must work hard. Be careful!

Master Yun-men (Ummon) entered the assembly hall, held up the staff, pointed ahead, and said: "All Buddhas in the world, as numberless as grains of sand, are here on the point of my staff. They are disputing the teachings of Buddhism, and each of them tries to win the argument. Is there anyone who is going to testify? If no one is going to testify, I will give testimony myself." At that moment a monk came out of the group and said, "Please do so immediately." The Master remarked, "You fox!"

Other anecdotes are:

There was a question put to Ummon: "What is the fundamental idea of Buddhism?" Ummon answered: "When spring comes, the grass turns green of itself."

Monk: "What was Niu-tou Fa-yung before he saw the Fourth Patriarch?"

Ummon: "The Goddess of Mercy (Kuan-yin or Kannon) is worshiped in every family."

Monk: "What was Niu-tou Fa-yung after he saw the Fourth Patriarch?"

Ummon: "The moth in the flame swallows the tiger."

Monk: "What is the song of Ummon?"

Ummon: "The twenty-fifth day of the twelfth month."

Monk: "What is the roar of the earthen ox on top of the snow ridge?"

Ummon: "Heaven and earth darkened *black*." ("red" in Chang's version)

Monk: "What is the neighing of the wooden horse of Ummon?"

Ummon: "Mountains and rivers are running."

Monk: "Please give me a basic principle for our pursuit of the ultimate."

Ummon: "Look to the southeast in the morning and to the northwest in the evening."

Monk: "What would it be like if one reached an understanding in accordance with your remarks?"

苦就苦在图他一粒米，失却半年粮。这样寻求禅法是毫无用处的！……别这样虚度年华，浪费时间。别错过这一生向你提供的机会，因为你不可能再有另一个机会……即使是一位凡人（云门文偃在这里指的是孔子）也说："朝闻道，夕死可矣。"我们沙门更须努力！我们必须努力，珍重！

云门禅师上堂，大众云集，禅师举杖指向前面说："世上一切佛徒，犹如无量沙，都在我杖头所指处。他们正在辩论佛教旨意，每人都想辩出胜负。是否有人准备作证？如果无人，我来作证。"当时有一僧人走出人群说："请立刻作证。"大师即说："你这野狐精！"

其他轶事还有：

有人向云门文偃提一个问题："如何是佛法大意？"云门答："春来草自青。"

一僧人说："牛头法融未见四祖时如何？"

云门："家家观世音。"

僧人："牛头法融见过四祖后又如何？"

云门："火里蝤蟮吞大虫。"

僧人："如何是云门一曲？"

云门："腊月二十五。"

僧人："如何是雪岭泥牛吼？"

云门："天地黑。"

僧人："如何是云门木马嘶？"

云门："山河走。"

僧人："请指示我辈追求的最高真谛。"

云门："朝看东南，暮看西北。"

僧人："如果按照您的教导领会了则如何？"

Ummon: "Light the lamp in the eastern house and sit in the darkness of the western house."

Ummon lived to eighty-six years old. Once he made the following gāthā:

How steep is Yun-men's Mountain!

How low the white clouds hang!

The mountain stream rushes so swiftly

That fish cannot venture to stay.

One's coming is well understood,

From the moment one steps in the door.

Why should I speak of the *mud* ("dust" in Chang's version)

On the track that is worn by the wheel?

Ummon had a number of disciples, among them:

(1) Tung-shan Shou-chu (Tōzan Shusho, 910-990)

(2) Hsiang-lin Cheng-yuan (Kōrin Chō'on, d. 987)

(3) Shuang-feng Hui-chen (Sōhō Eshin Daishi)

Tōzan Shusho had a disciple Fu-yen Liang-ya (Fukugen Ryōga). Kōrin Chō'on had a large number of dharma descendants. The lineage is given as follows:

(1) Yun-men Wen-yen (Ummon Bun'en, 864-949)

(2) Hsiang-lin Cheng-yuan (Kōrin Chō'on, d. 987)

(3) Chih-men Kuang-tsu (Chimon Kōso)

(4) Hsueh-tou Chung-hsien (Setchō Jūken, 980-1052)

(5) Tien-i I-huai (Ten'i Gikai, 993-1064)

(6) Yuan-chao Tsung-pen (Enshō Sōhon, 1020-1099)

(7) Fa-yun Shan-pen (Hōun Zenhon)

(8) Hsueh-feng Ssu-hui (Seppō Shi'e)

(9) Zing-tzu Tao-chang (Jōji Doshō)

(10) Lei-an Cheng-shou (Raian Shōju, 1146-1208)

Note that Raian Shōju (1146-1208) was the author of *Pu-teng-lu* (*Fu-to-*

roku), dated 1204.

Yuan-chao Tsung-pen was also known as Hui-lin Tsung-pen (Erin Sōhon). Erin had several dharma brothers, among them:

(6a) Yuan-tung Fa-hsiu (Enzū Hōshū, 1027-1090)

(6b) Kuang-chao Yin-fu (Kōshō Ōfu)

云门："东屋里点灯，西屋里暗坐。"

云门文偃寿至 86 岁。有一次他作了下列诗偈（见《五灯会元》卷 15）：

云门耸峻白云低，水急游鱼不敢栖，
入户已知来见解，何劳再举轳中泥。

云门有许多弟子，其中有：

（1）洞山守初（910—990）

（2）香林澄远（？—987）

（3）双峰慧真

洞山守初有一位弟子福严良雅。香林澄远则有一大批禅法传人。现将云门世系列举如下：

（1）云门文偃（864—949）

（2）香林澄远（？—987）

（3）智门光祚

（4）雪窦重显（980—1052）

（5）天衣义怀（993—1064）

（6）圆照宗本（1020—1099）

（7）法云善本

（8）雪峰思慧

（9）净慈道昌

（10）雷庵正受（1146—1208）

按：雷庵正受是 1204 年《普灯录》的编者。

圆照宗本又名慧林宗本，他有若干位禅法兄弟，其中有：

（6a）圆通法秀（1027—1090）

（6b）广照应夫

Kōshō's disciple Hung-tsi Tsung-tsi (Kōsai Sōseki, 1009-1092) was simultaneously the Eighth Patriarch of the Pure Land School. Enzū Hōshū had sixty disciples, among them:

(7a) Fu-kuo Wei-po (Bukkoku Ibyaku)

(7b) Kai-sien Chih-shun (Kaisen Chijun)

(7c) Pao-ning In (Honin Ei)

Fu-kuo Wei-po was the author (compiler) of the Second Series of the *Lamp Records* (*Zokutō Roku*), dated 1101. Fu-kuo Wei-po had a disciple: (8a) Hui-lin Hui-hai (Erin Ekai), whose disciples were (9a) Wan-san Shu-chien [Mansan (sugi) Juken] and (9b) Wan-san Shu-lung (Mansan Juryū).

Enshō (Erin) Sōhon had some two hundred disciples. Among them were Fa-yun Shan-pen (Hōun Zenhon), Tou-tze Hsiu-yu (Tōsu Shugu), and Chang-lu Hsin (Chōro Shin). Hōun Zenhon's disciple was Hsueh-feng Ssu-hui (Seppō Shi'e), whose disciple was Zing-tzu Tao-chang (Jōji Tōshō). Jōji's disciple was Lei-an Cheng-shou (Raian Shōju, 1146-1208).

Note that Setchō Jūken (980-1052) wrote the verses for the *Blue Cliff Record* (*Pi-yen-lu*) or *Hekigan-roku*. Setchō collected one hundred *kung an* (kōan) —"public cases" of ancient events, and pointed out the import of each story with verses and additional remarks. About sixty years after Setchō's passing, Yuan-wu Ko-chin (Engo Kokugon, 1063-1135) of the Rinzai School added introductions, remarks, and commentaries all together to form the *Blue Cliff Record*, named after the abode on Mt. Chia in Hunan where Engo delivered his talks. It was Dōgen Kigen (1200-1253) who brought the *Blue Cliff Record* to Japan. (An English translation by Thomas and J. C. Cleary is now available in three volumes, published by Shambhala Publications Inc., Boulder, Colorado, in 1977.)

Take the fourteenth case of the *Blue Cliff Record*, as chosen by Setchō Jūken and interpreted by Engo Kokugon. We are indebted to Thomas & J. C. Cleary for their excellent English translation given below:

Ummon's Appropriate Statement

Case:

A monk asked Ummon: "What are the teachings of a Buddha in a whole lifetime?"

Ummon answered: "An appropriate statement."

Commentary:

Members of the Ch'an (Zen) family, if you want to know the meaning

广照应夫的弟子洪济宗赜（1009—1092），同时又是净土宗的八祖。圆通法秀有六十位弟子，其中有：

（7a）佛国惟白

（7b）开先智珣

（7c）保宁英

佛国惟白是 1101 年的《续灯录》的编者。佛国惟白有一位弟子（8a）慧林慧海，后者的弟子有（9a）万杉寿坚和（9b）万杉寿隆。

慧林宗本约有两百位弟子，其中有法云善本、投子修颙和长芦信。法云善本的弟子是雪峰思慧，后者的弟子是净慈道昌，净慈的弟子是雷庵正受（1146—1208）。

按：雪窦重显（980—1052）收集了一百则公案——古代禅林事件的公开案例，用诗句和注解指出各个故事的重要含义。雪窦去世后大约六十年，临济宗的圆悟克勤（1063—1135）增补了介绍、论述和评注，采用圆悟讲法的湖南夹山住地碧岩之名，汇总编成《碧岩集》。道元希玄（1200—1253）将《碧岩集》带到日本（其英译本为托马斯和 J. C. 克利里所译，三卷本，沙姆巴拉出版公司，科罗拉多博尔德，1977 年出版）。

作者在此谨向翻译了杰出英译文的托马斯和克利里致谢。现举《碧岩集》中的第十四则公案如下：

云门的对一说

公案：

一僧人问云门："如何是一代时教？"

云门答："对一说。"

评注：

禅家流，欲知佛性义，当观时节因缘，谓之教外别传，单传

of Buddha-nature, you must observe times and seasons, causes and conditions. This is called the special transmission outside the (written) teachings, the sole transmission of the mind seal, directly pointing to the human mind for the perception of nature and realization of Buddhahood.

For forty-nine years old Shakyamuni stayed in the world: at three hundred and sixty assemblies he expounded the sudden and the gradual, the temporary and the true. These are what are called the teachings of a whole lifetime. The monk (in this case) picked this out to ask, "What are the teachings of a whole lifetime?" Why didn't Ummon explain for him in full detail, but instead said to him, "An appropriate statement?" As usual, within one sentence of Ummon three sentences are bound to be present. These are called the sentence that encloses heaven and earth, the sentence that follows the waves, and the sentence that cuts off the myriad streams. He lets go and gathers up; he's naturally extraordinary, like cutting nails or shearing through iron. He makes people unable to comprehend him or figure him out. The whole great treasure-house of the teachings just comes down to three words "An appropriate statement"; there is no facet or aspect in which you can rationalize this.

People often misunderstand and say, "Buddha's preaching was appropriate to the conditions of one time." Or they say, "The multitude of appearances and myriad forms are all the impressions of a single truth," and call this "an appropriate statement." Then there are those who say, "It's just talking about that one truth." What connection is there? Not only do they not understand, they also enter hell as fast as an arrow flies. They are far from knowing that the meaning of that man of old is not like this.

Therefore it is said, "Shattering one's bones and crushing one's body is still not sufficient recompense; when a single phrase is understood, you transcend ten billion." Undeniably extraordinary: "What are the teachings of a whole lifetime?" Just boil down to his saying, "An appropriate statement." If you can grasp this immediately, then you can return home and sit in peace. If you can't get it, then listen humbly to the verdict.

Verse (by Setchō Jūken):

An appropriate statement;

How utterly unique!

He wedges a stake into the iron hammerhead with no hole.

Under the Jambu Tree I'm laughing: ha, ha!

Last night the black dragon had his horn wrenched off:

Exceptional, exceptional—

The old man of Shao Yang got one horn.

Commentary:

"An appropriate statement; how utterly unique!" Setchō cannot praise him enough. These words of Ummon are independent and free,

心印，直指人心，见性成佛。释迦老子，四十九年住世，三百六十会，开谈顿渐权实，谓之一代时教。这僧拈来问云："如何是一代时教？"云门何不与他纷纷解说，却向他道个"对一说"？云门寻常一句中，须具三句，谓之函盖乾坤句、随波逐浪句、截断众流句，放去收来，自然奇特，如斩钉截铁，教人义解卜度他底不得。一大藏教，只消三个字，四方八面，无尔穿凿处。人多错会，却道对一时机宜之事故说。又道，森罗及万象，皆是一法之所印，谓之对一说。更有道，只是说那个一法，有什么交涉，非唯不会，更入地狱如箭。殊不知，古人意不如此，所以道"粉骨碎身未足酬，一句了然超百亿"，不妨奇特。"如何是一代时教？"只消道个"对一说"，若当头荐得，便可归家稳坐；若荐不得，且伏听处分。

雪窦的诗颂：

对一说，太孤绝，无孔铁锤重下楔。

阎浮树下笑呵呵，昨夜骊龙拗角折。

别别，韶阳老人得一橛！

评注：

"对一说，太孤绝。"雪窦赞之不及。此语独脱孤危，光前

unique and lofty, prior to light and after annihilation. They are like an overhanging cliff ten thousand fathoms high. Then, too, they are like a million-man battleline; there is no place for you to get in. It's just that it's too solitary and perilous.

An ancient said, "If you want to attain intimacy, don't use a question to ask a question; the question is in the answer and the answer is in the point of the question." Of course it's solitary and steep, but tell me, where is it that it's solitary and steep? No one on earth can do anything about it. The monk (in the case) was also an adept, and that is why he could question like this. And Ummon too answered this way, much like "wedging a stake into the iron hammerhead with no hole." Setchō employs literary language so artfully! "Under the Jambu Tree I'm laughing: ha, ha!" In the *Scripture on the Creation of the World* it says, "On the southside of Sumeru (Mt. Himalaya) a crystal tree shines over the continent of Jambu, making all in between a clear blue color. The continent takes its name from the great tree; hence it is called Jambudvipa. This tree is seven thousand leagues high; beneath it are the golden mounds of the Jambu altar, which is twenty leagues high. Since gold is produced from beneath the tree, it is called the Jambu Tree."

Thus Hsueh-tou (Setchō) says of himself that it is under the Jambu Tree laughing out loud. But tell me, what is he laughing at? He's laughing at the black dragon who last night got this horn wrenched off. He's just looking up respectfully; he can only praise Ummon. When Ummon says, "An appropriate statement," what's it like? It's like breaking off one of the black dragon's horns. At this point, if there were no such thing, how could he have spoken as he did?

Setchō has finished his verse all at once, but he still has something to say at the very end: "Exceptional, exceptional—The old man of Shao Yang got one horn." Why doesn't Setchō say he got them both? How is it that he just got one horn? Tell me, where is the other horn?

Tung-shan Shou-chu (Tōzan Shusho, 910-990) was a disciple of

Ummon. (See the *Lamp Records*, Vol. 23, *Daishō Daizōkyō*, Vol. 51, page 389; Y. H. Ku, *History of Chinese Zen Masters*, pages 299-301.) He visited Ummon, who asked him: "Where have you come from recently?" Tōzan answered: "From Ch'a-tu." "Where were you during the summer?" asked Ummon. Tōzan answered: "I was at the Pao-tzu Monastery in Hunan." "When did you leave there?" asked Ummon. Tōzan said: "In the eighth month of last year." The Master said: "I absolve you from thirty blows!" The next day Tōzan went to ask the Master: "Yesterday you were pleased to release me from thirty blows, but I do not know what my fault was." The Master said: "Oh, you rice-bag! This is the way you wander from the

绝后，如万丈悬崖相似，亦如百万军阵，无尔入处，只是忒煞孤危。古人道："欲得亲切，莫将问来问，问在答处，答在问端。"直是孤峻。且道什么处是孤峻处，天下人奈何不得。这僧也是个作家，所以如此问，云门又怎么答，大似"无孔铁锤重下楔"相似。雪窦使文言，用得甚巧。

"阎浮树下笑呵呵"，《起世经》中说，须弥南畔吠琉璃树，映阎浮洲中皆青色。此洲乃大树为名，名阎浮提，其树纵广七千由旬，下有阎浮坛金聚，高二十由旬，以金从树下出生故，号阎浮树。所以雪窦自说，他在"阎浮树下笑呵呵"。且道他笑个什么？笑"昨夜骊龙拗角折"，只得瞻之仰之，赞叹云门有分。云门道"对一说"，似个什么，如拗折骊龙一角相似。到这里若无恁么事，焉能恁么说话。雪窦一时颂了，末后却道："别别，韶阳老人得一橛。"何不道全得，如何只得一橛？在什么处？

洞山守初（910—990）是云门的弟子（见《传灯录》卷23，《大正藏》第51卷，第389页；拙著《禅宗师承记》第299—301页），他谒见云门，后者问他："最近你从何处来？"洞山答："楂渡。"云门问："夏天你在何处？"洞山答："我在湖南报慈寺。"云门问："你何时离开？"洞山说："去年八月。"云门大师说："我赦免你三十杖！"第二天洞山去问大师："昨天您高兴地免了我三十杖，但我不知道我错在何处。"大师说："啊，你这个饭袋子！这就是

west of the River to the south of the Lake!" At hearing this, Tōzan Shusho was suddenly enlightened. Other anecdotes appeared in Professor Chang Chung-yuan's *Original Teachings of Ch'an Buddhism*, pages 296-299.

Hsiang-lin Cheng-yuan (Kōrin Chō'on, d. 987) was also Ummon's disciple. He was the dharma grandfather of Setchō Jūken. (See the *Lamp Records*, Vol. 22, *Daishō Daizōkyō*, Vol. 51, page 387; Y. H. Ku, *History of Chinese Zen Masters*, pages 301-302.) A monk asked: "How is it, when both mind and condition (kyō) are lost?" Kōrin answered: "Open your eyes, sit and sleep." A monk asked: "What is the meaning of hiding your body in the Big Dipper?" Kōrin answered: "The crescent moon is like a bending bow, little rain and much wind." Note that when a monk asked Ummon: "What word penetrates the essence of being?" Ummon answered: "Hide your body in the Big Dipper." Compare this with: When a monk asked Tōzan Shusho: "What is the duty required of a Ch'an (Zen) monk?" Tōzan answered: "When the clouds envelop the top of Mount Ch'u, there will be plenty of wind and rain." When a monk asked Master Kōrin, "Whatever words and sentences are 'guest,' how is the host?" Kōrin answered: "Inside the City of Chang-an." A monk asked: "How to comprehend this?" Kōrin said: "There are a thousand families and ten thousand houses."

Hsuan-sha Shih-pei (Gensha Shibi, 835-908) was Seppō Gizon's disciple. (See the *Lamp Records*, Vol. 18, *Daishō Daizōkyō*, Vol. 51, pages 343-347; Y. H. Ku, *History of Chinese Zen Masters*, pages 296-298.) He became a monk at the age of thirty. He was ordained by Vinaya teacher Tao-hsuan (Dōgen Rissui) at the Kai-Yuan Temple (Kaigen-ji), Kiangsi. He was a dharma brother of Seppō Gizon, but he considered Seppō as his teacher. (Note that Gensha was thirteen years younger than Seppō, but twenty-nine years older than Ummon.) R. H. Blyth in his *Zen and Zen Classics*, Vol. 2, Chapter 7, recorded the following story.

> When Gensha was young, his father was a fisherman, and being already an old man, one night fell from the boat into the water. Gensha

tried to save him with an oar, and at this moment saw the moon reflected in the water. He exclaimed, "I remember how the sages of old said that all things are like the moon in the water. If my father had lived, he would have only increased the pains of the Hell he would be reborn in. Instead, I will cut off my human relations and become a priest and thus fulfil my filial duties." Gensha found a teacher and took the vows,

你从江之西行脚到湖之南的路啊！"一听到这话，洞山守初突然醒悟。其他轶事见于张钟元教授的《佛教禅宗之源》第296—299页。

香林澄远（？—987）也是云门的弟子。他是雪窦重显的禅法师祖（见《传灯录》卷22，《大正藏》第51卷，第387页和拙著《禅宗师承记》第301—302页）。一僧人问："当心和境都失去时则如何？"香林答："开眼，坐睡。"一僧人问："北斗里藏身是何意？"香林答："月似弯弓，少雨多风。"按，当一僧人问云门："什么字句能穿透众生本性？"云门答："北斗里藏身。"试比较下面。一僧人问洞山守初："衲僧应有何种本分？"洞山答："云裹楚山头，决定多风雨。"当一僧人问香林禅师："一切字句皆为'客'，则主又如何？"香林答："长安城内。"一僧人问："如何理解？"香林说："千家万户。"

玄沙师备（835—908）是雪峰义存的弟子（见《传灯录》卷18，《大正藏》第51卷，第343—347页；拙著《禅宗师承记》第296—298页），他在30岁时出家为僧，在江西开元寺由道玄律师为授具足戒。玄沙本是雪峰义存的师弟，但他视雪峰如师。按：玄沙比雪峰小13岁，但比云门大29岁。布莱思在《禅与禅宗经典》第2卷第7章中载有下列故事：

玄沙师备年少时，其父是渔民，并且已是老人。一晚其父从小船上落入水中。玄沙竭力用桨救他（未果）。这时他看见水中的月影，惊呼道："我记得古代的圣贤说过一切都如水中之月。要是我父活着，他只会加重生在地狱中的苦难。反过来，我将割断尘缘成为僧侣，从而克尽我的子职了。"玄沙找到一位教师，

and the next night his father came to him gratefully in a dream, and said, "My son has become a priest, had I have been born in the Heavens, so I have come to thank him."

Gensha succeeded Seppō and then preached and taught Zen for thirty years. He had about eight hundred disciples, among them thirteen attained enlightenment.

Gensha's dharma heir was Lo-han Kuei-shen (Rakan Keijin, 867-928). Rakan's disciple was Fa-yen Wen-i (Hōgen Bun'eki, 885-958), founder of the Hōgen School. (See the *Lamp Records*, Vol. 24, *Daishō Daizōkyō*, Vol. 51, pages 398-400; Y. H. Ku, *History of Chinese Zen Masters*, pages 303-310.) The following is taken from Professor Chang Chung-yuan's *Original Teachings of Ch'an Buddhism*, pages 238-249.

Ch'an Master Wen-i (Bun'eki) of the Ch'ing-liang Monastery in Sheng-chou (now Nanking) was a native of Yu-hang (Chekiang Province). His original surname was Lu. When he was seven years old, he shaved his head and became the disciple of Ch'an Master Ch'uan-wei (Zen'i) of the Chih-tung Temple in Hsin-ting. At the age of twenty he was ordained in the Kai-Yuan Monastery in Yueh-chou (now Shao-hsing in northern Chekiang). During that time the Vinaya Master Hsi-chio (Kikaku) was expounding Buddhism in the Yu-wang Monastery in Mei-shan of Ming-chou (Ningpo). Wen-i went there to listen to his lectures and to seek the deep and abstruse meaning of Buddhism. At the same time, he also studied the Confucian classics and made friends with scholars and literary men. Master Hsi-chio thought as highly of Wen-i as Confucius had of Tzu-yu and Tsu-hsia.

However, when he suddenly had the urge to seek the truth of Ch'an (Zen), Wen-i immediately gave up all other pursuits, and taking up his staff, went traveling to the south. When he reached Fu-chou (Foochow, Fukien Province), he joined the Chang-ching Hui-leng (Chōkei Eryō, 854-932) congregation. Although his mind was not yet free from seeking, many people esteemed him highly.

Not long afterward Wen-i set out again with his friends across the Lake (Lake Pan-yang). Hardly had they started on their journey when a rainstorm began. The streams overflowed and flooded the land. Thereupon Wen-i and his companions took lodging temporarily at the Ti-tsang Monastery (Chizō-in) in the western part of the city of Fu-chou. While he was there, Wen-i took the opportunity to visit Lo-han Kuei-shen (Rakan Keijin, 867-928), who asked him: "Where are you going?" Wen-i replied: "I shall continue my foot travels along the road." Lo-han asked: "What is that which is called foot travel?" "I do not know,"

立下誓言，第二天夜晚梦见父亲来感谢说："我儿已经成为僧侣，我将一直在天堂生活，所以我来谢他。"

玄沙继承了雪峰的衣钵，并且传授禅法三十年。他约有八百位弟子，其中十三人获得顿悟。

玄沙的法嗣是罗汉桂琛（867—928），桂琛的弟子是法眼宗的创建者法眼文益（885—958）（见《传灯录》卷24，《大正藏》第51卷，第398—400页；拙著《禅宗师承记》第303—310页）。下文引自张钟元教授的《佛教禅宗之源》第238—249页。

升州（今南京）清凉院法眼文益禅师是余杭人。俗姓鲁。7岁时即从新定智通院全伟禅师落发。20岁时在越州（今浙江绍兴）开元寺受具足戒，当时知觉律师正在明州（宁波）育王寺讲经，文益前往听讲，探索佛经深义。同时，他也研习儒家经典，与学者文人为友。知觉律师高度重视文益，认为他犹如孔子门人子由和子夏。

但当文益突然强烈要求探索禅宗真谛时，便立即放弃其他追求，拿起锡杖南游。他到福州后即加入长庆慧棱（854—932）的法会。虽然他仍想继续寻求，但大众都非常尊重他。

此后不久，文益再度结伴出发横渡鄱阳湖。刚要出发，天忽然暴雨。溪水涨没田地。文益及其同伴因而暂时寄寓在福州城西地藏寺。到达该寺后，文益趁机参见罗汉桂琛（867—928），后者问文益："你到何处去？"文益答："我将一路行脚去。"罗汉桂琛问："何谓行脚？"文益答："我不懂。"

was Wen-i's reply. Lo-han said: "Not-knowing most closely approaches the Truth." Wen-i was suddenly enlightened.

...

A monk asked, "As for the finger, I will not ask you about it. But what is the moon?"

Master Wen-i said: "Where is the finger you do not ask about?"

Monk: "As for the moon, I will not ask about it. But what is the finger?"

Master: "The moon."

Monk: "I asked about the finger; why should you answer me, 'the moon'?"

Master: "Because you asked about the finger."

...

The Prince of Nan-tang esteemed the Master's teaching and invited him to stay in the Ch'an (Zen) Monastery of Pao-en (Hō'on-ji), and bestowed upon him the title of Ch'an Master Ching-hui (Jō'e Zenji).

The Master later stayed in the Ching-liang Monastery (Seiryō-ji). He came before the assembly and said:

"We Buddhists should be free to respond to whatever comes to us according to the moment and the cause. When it is cold, we respond to nothing else but cold; when it is hot, we respond to nothing else but heat. If we want to know the meaning of the Buddha-nature, we must watch the absolute moment and cause. In the past as well as at present there have been many means to enlightenment. Have you not read that when Shih-tou (Sekitō) understood what was in the *Treatise of Seng-shao*: 'To unify ten thousand things into one's self is to be a sage indeed,' he immediately said that a sage has no self, yet nothing is not himself. In his work *Contemplation on Identification and Unification (Tsan Tung Chi or Sandōkai)*, he first pointed out that the mind of the Buddha in India cannot go beyond this. In this treatise he further expounds this idea. You, monks, need to be aware that all things are identified with yourself. Why? Because in this world not one isolated thing can be seen!"

It was mentioned before that Tōzan Ryōkai took Sekitō's ideas and developed them into a doctrine that Sōzen later enunciated as the Five Ranks.

The lineage from Gensha to Hōgen and beyond is given below:

Hsuan-sha Shih-pei (Gensha Shibi, 835-908)

Lo-han Kuei-shen (Rakan Keijin, 867-928)

Fa-yen Wen-i (Hōgen Bun'eki, 885-958)

Tien-tai Te-shao (Tendai Tokushō, 891-972)

罗汉桂琛说：“不懂最接近真谛。”文益豁然开悟。……

一僧人问：“关于手指，我不想问，但什么是月亮？”文益说：“你不想问的手指在哪里？”僧人说：“关于月亮，我不想问，但什么是手指？”文益禅师说：“月亮。”僧人说：“我问的是手指，你为何回答我‘月亮’？”禅师说：“因为你问手指。”

南唐王子对文益禅师的讲经说法，甚为敬佩，请他居住报恩禅寺，并赠封为净慧禅师。禅师后住清凉寺，他来到僧众面前说：“我辈沙门应该按照时节因缘对一切来临之事作出反应。天冷时，我们感知到的只是冷；天热时，我们感知到的只是热。如果我们要理解佛性，我们必须注意绝对的时节和因缘。古往今来有许多顿悟的方法。你们有没有读过石头和尚的《参同契》，当看了《肇论》中的‘会万物为己者，其唯圣人乎？’后立即说圣人无自己，却没有一样不是自己。石头在《参同契》中首次指出：天竺佛心也不可能超越于此。在该论著中石头进一步阐述了该思想。尔等僧人，需要醒悟，万物都与你自己等同。为什么？因为世上并无单独孤立之物可以看见！”

前面曾提到洞山良价理解了石头的思想并将其发展为被曹山后来阐明的五位学说。下列为从玄沙到法眼及其后人的一支法系：

（1）玄沙师备（835—908）　　（2）罗汉桂琛（867—928）

（3）法眼文益（885—958）　　（4）天台德韶（891—972）

（5）永明延寿（904—975）

Yung-ming Yen-shou (Yōmei Enju, 904-975)

Tendai Tokushō was a National Teacher (Kokushi). He was ordained at the age of eighteen at the Kai-Yuan Temple (Kaigen-ji). He visited Tōsu Daidō (819-914) and Ryūga Koton (835-923). He also held conversations with Sosan Kōnin, a dharma brother of Ryūga. He had contacted fifty-four masters, but he could not find any spiritual affinity with any one of them. Finally he went to Ling-chuan (Rinsen) and paid his respects to Master Ching-hui (Jō'e). A monk asked Master Ching-hui: "What is a drop of water at Tsao-yuan (source of Tsao-hsi or Sōkei)?" The Master answered: "It is a drop of water at Tsao-yuan." The monk was puzzled and retreated. However, Tendai Tokushō was suddenly enlightened. When Tokushō reported what he understood to the Master, Ching-hui said: "You will later be the teachers of a King and spread widely the teachings of the Patriarchs. I cannot be compared to you."

Tokushō visited the Tendai Mountains and traced Chigi's footsteps. Tokushō came from the Chen family. People thought that Tokushō was the incarnation of the Tendai Master Chigi (531-597). The King of Wu-yueh asked Tao (the Way) from Tokushō at Tai-chou, when he was a prince. Now as King of Wu-yueh he made Tokushō the National Teacher. With the King's approval, emissaries were sent to Sila (now a part of Korea) to find the historical documents concerning Chigi. Thus the Tendai School was revived.

Tendai Tokushō's disciple was Yōmei Enju (904-975). (See the *Lamp Records*, Vol. 26, *Daishō Daizōkyō*, Vol. 51, pages 421-422; Y. H. Ku, *History of Chinese Zen Masters*, pages 311-312.) The following is taken from Professor Chang Chung-yuan's *Original Teachings of Ch'an Buddhism*, pages 250-253.

Ch'an (Zen) Master Chih-chio of the Yung-ming Monastery (Yōmei-ji) on the Hui-jih Mountain in Hangchow was a native of Yu-hang (Chekiang Province). His name was Yen-shou (Enju) and his original surname was Wang. From early childhood on he believed in the teachings of Buddhism. When he reached the age of twenty he began to abstain from meat and only took one meal a day. He read the *Lotus Sutra* at exceedingly great speed, as if he were glancing at seven columns at a time, and in about sixty days he could recite the entire text. It was said that a number of sheep were inspired by his reading and knelt down to listen to him. When he was twenty-eight he served as a military officer under the general who guarded Hua-ting. Later Master Tsui-yen (Suigan) came to stay at the Lung-tse Monastery (Ryūsaku-ji) and spread

天台德韶是国师。他 18 岁时在开元寺受戒。他参见过投子大同（819—914）和龙牙居遁（835—923），他也与疏山匡仁（龙牙居遁的法门师兄弟）有过多次交谈。他参见过五十四位禅师，却未能从任何一位处获得心灵印证。最后他去临川朝拜净慧（即法眼文益）。一僧人问净慧禅师："什么是曹源（曹溪之源）一滴水？"净慧禅师答："是曹源一滴水。"僧人迷惑不解，退下了。天台德韶却因此顿然开悟。当天台德韶把他已悟解的对净慧禅师讲了以后，净慧说："你今后会成为君王之师，广传祖师教义。我不能与你相比。"

德韶朝拜天台山，并沿着智顗走过的路走去。德韶俗姓陈。人们认为德韶是天台大师智顗（531—597）的化身。吴越王任台州刺史时曾请德韶说禅，继位后任命德韶为国师。经吴越王批准，派出使者去新罗（今朝鲜半岛的一部分）寻找有关智顗的历史文献，由此天台宗得到复兴。

天台德韶的弟子是永明延寿（904—975），见《传灯录》卷 26（《大正藏》第 51 卷，第 421—422 页，拙著《禅宗师承记》第 311—312 页）。下文引自张钟元教授的《佛教禅宗之源》第 250—253 页。

杭州慧日山永明寺智觉禅师，余杭（在今浙江省）人。名延寿，俗姓王。从小即信佛家学说。20 岁时，就开始吃素，每日一餐，他读《法华经》非常迅速，几乎一目七行，约六十天后就能背诵全文。据说他的诵经能使一群羊跪下来听经。他 28 岁时成为华亭镇守将军麾下的一名军官。后来翠岩令参禅师（雪峰

the teachings of Ch'an (Zen) far and wide. (Suigan Reisan was Seppō's disciple.) King Wen-mo of Wu-yueh realized Yōmei's devotion to Ch'an (Zen) and sympathized with the strong faith he had in Buddhism. Therefore the King released him from government service and let him become a Buddhist monk. Yōmei went to Suigan and became his disciple. In the temple he worked as a laborer and did all kinds of service for the other monks, entirely forgetting himself. He never wore silken fabrics, and when he ate he never took two dishes. He consumed only vegetables as his daily diet and covered himself with a coarse cotton robe as his regular dress. Thus he passed his days and nights.

Later he went to the Tendai Mountains and meditated under the Tien-chu Peak (meaning "column of Heaven") for ninety days. Little birds made their nests in the pleats of his robe. Later on he went to visit the National Teacher Te-shao (Tokushō), who esteemed him highly and personally transmitted the essence of Ch'an (Zen) to him. The National Teacher told him that because he had a spiritual affinity with the King he could make the works of Buddhism flourish. It was secretly foretold that Yōmei would achieve Buddhahood in the future.

Master Yōmei first stayed at Mount Hsueh-tou in Mingchou (Ningpo). Many disciples came to listen to him. One day the Master said to the assembly:

"Here in Hsueh-tou Mountain

A rapid waterfall dashes down thousands of feet.

Here nothing stays,

Not even the tiniest *grain* ("chestnut" in Chang's version).

An awesome cliff rises up thousands of feet

With no space for you to stand.

My disciples, may I ask:

'Where do you proceed?'"

A monk asked: "A path lies in the Hsueh-tou Mountain. How do you tread it?" The Master replied:

"Step by step the wintry blossom is born:

Each word is crystal clear as ice."

In 900 A.D., King Chung-i invited him to be the first Abbot of the
new monastery in the Ling-yin Mountain, and in the next year promoted
him to be Abbot of the famous Yung-ming Monastery (Yōmei-ji), as the
successor of the first Abbot Tsui-yen (Suigan). His followers numbered
more than two thousand.

A monk asked: "What is the profound essence of the teaching in the
Yung-ming Monastery (Yōmei-ji)?"

义存的弟子）来到龙册寺广传禅法。吴越文穆王知道延寿悉心参
禅，为他笃信佛法而深受感动。于是下令免除他的军职，让他成
为僧人。延寿遂去翠岩令参处成为弟子。在寺内他担任劳务，并
完全忘我地为其他僧人做各种杂役，他从不穿丝绸衣服，从不吃
两道菜，只吃蔬菜作为每日食物，披一件粗布袍作为日常衣服，
就这样度过日日夜夜。

后来他去天台山在天柱峰下静坐九十天。小鸟在他的僧袍的
衣褶中筑巢。其后他去参谒天台德韶国师，德韶高度赏识他，单
独传授他禅法要旨。德韶国师告诉他，因为他与吴越王有缘，定
能大兴佛教，暗喻延寿将来定能成佛。

延寿大师先隐居明州（宁波）雪窦山。许多弟子前来听讲。
一天，大师对大众说："雪窦山上迅瀑千寻不停纤粟，奇岩万仞，
无立足处，汝等诸人向何处进步？"一僧人问："雪窦山有一条
小路。您如何走上去？"大师回答："步步寒华结，言言彻底冰。"

公元 900 年，忠懿王请他担任灵隐山新建寺第一任住持，次
年，升任他为著名的永明寺住持，作为第一任方丈翠岩令参的继
任者。永明延寿的门人有二千余人。

一僧人问："如何是永明寺教义的精髓？"
大师答："炉内多加香。"
僧人说："请给予启迪。"

The Master answered: "Put more incense in the burner."

The questioner said: "Thank you for revealing it to me."

The Master said: "Fortunately, I have nothing to do with the matter."

The Master made the following gāthā:

"To know the essence of the teaching in the Monastery of Yung-ming,

Imagine that a lake lies in front of the door.

When the sun shines upon it, a bright light is reflected.

When the wind blows, the ripples rise."

The Master lived to seventy-two years old. His writings comprised several hundred volumes, among them one hundred volumes of *Tsung-ching-lu* (*Sōkyō-roku*) were famous.

His disciples were many, among them:

Fu-yang Tze-meng (Fuyō Shimo)

Chao-ming Yuan-tsin (Chōmyō Inshin)

Yōmei Enju was concurrently the Sixth Patriarch of the Pure Land School. The Patriarchs of the Pure Land School are listed below.

(1) Tung-lin Hui-yuan (Tōrin E'on, 334-416)

(2) Kuang-ming Shan-tao (Kōmei Zendō, 613-681)

(3) Mi-tu Cheng-yuan (Mita Jōén, 712-802)

(4) Cho-lin Wu-hui (Chikurin Go'e Kokushi)

(5) O-lung Tai-yen (Oryū Daigan, d. 805)

(6) Hui-ji Yung-ming Yen-shou (Yōmei Enju, 904-975)

(7) Yuan-zing Sheng-chang (Enjō Shinchō, 959-1020)

(8) Chang-lu Hung-tsi Tsung-chi (Kōsai Sōseki, 1009-1092)

(9) Lien-chi Chih-hung (Renchi Chikō, 1535-1615)

(10) Ngo-i Chih-hsueh (Gūéki Chikyoku, 1599-1655)

According to *Dharma Records of Abbot Hsu Yun*, Vol. 8, pages 262-265, since the Ummon School in China had its eleventh-generation dharma heir Kuang-shiao Chi-an (Kōkō Kian), Reverend Hsu Yun was urged to continue the Ummon line as its twelfth-generation dharma heir.

According to the same reference, since the Hōgen School in China had its seventh-generation dharma heir Hsiang-fu Liang-ching (Jōfu Ryōkyō), Reverend Hsu Yun was urged to continue the Hōgen line as its eighth-generation dharma heir.

As mentioned in the end of Chapter 3, since the Igyō School in China had its seventh-generation dharma heir, Reverend Hsu Yun was urged to be its eighth-generation dharma heir.

大师说："惜哉，我无能为力。"

大师作如下偈语：

欲识永明旨，门前一湖水。

日照光明生，风来波浪起。

大师享年 72 岁。其著作有数百卷，其中著名的有《宗镜录》一百卷。

其弟子很多，其中有：

富阳子蒙

朝明院津

永明延寿同时还是净土宗的六祖。现将净土宗的列祖名单序列如下：

（1）东林慧远（334—416）

（2）光明善导（613—681）

（3）弥陀承远（712—802）

（4）竹林五会

（5）乌龙台岩（？—805）

（6）永明延寿（904—975）

（7）圆净省常（959—1020）

（8）洪济宗赜（1009—1092）

（9）莲池袾宏（1535—1615）

（10）藕益智旭（1599—1655）

根据《虚云和尚法汇》卷 8（第 262—265 页），由于云门宗在中国的十一代法嗣为光孝己庵，虚云大师竭力继承云门系统成为它的十二代法嗣。根据同一资料，由于法眼宗在中国的第七代法嗣是祥符良庆，虚云大师也竭力成为法眼宗的第八代法嗣。正如本书第三章章末所述，由于沩仰宗在中国已有第七代法嗣，虚云大师就竭力成为该宗的第八代法嗣。

BIBLIOGRAPHY 参考文献

A History of Zen Buddhism, by Heinrich Dumoulin, S. J., English translation by Paul Peachey, Pantheon Books, New York, 1963.

Bodhidharma's Lüeh-pien Ta-cheng Ju-tao Ssu-hsing 菩提达摩略辨大乘入道四行 (*Bodaidaruma Ryakuben Daijō Nyudō Shigyō*), by Tan-lin 昙琳.

Bukkyō Dainen Hyō 佛教大年表, by Mōgetsu Shinkyō 望月信亨, 1st ed. 1909; 2nd ed. 1930; 3rd ed. 1937; 4th ed. 1955.

Ch'an-chi Kai-shih Lu of Abbot Lai Ko 来果禅师禅七开示录 (*Zenshichi Kaiji Roku of Raika Zenji*), recorded by Tao-chen 道真 (Dōshin), 1954.

Ch'an-tsung Chi-cheng 禅宗集成 (*Zenshū Shūsei*), Selections from *Manji Zoku Zōkyō* 卍续藏经.

Ch'an-tsung Shih-chen Chi 禅宗师承记 (*Zenshū Shijō Ki)*, by Y. H. Ku, Chen Shan Mei Publishing Co., Taipei, 1976.

Cheng-fa-yen-tsang (*Shōbōgenzō*), by Dōgen Kigen (1200-1253), recorded by Koun Ejō 孤云怀奘.

Cheng-fa-yen-tsang 正法眼藏 (*Shōbōgenzō*), by Ta-hui Tsung-kao (Daie Sōkō, 1089-1163).

Cheng-yuan Liao-chi 正源略集 (*Shōgen Ryakushū*), compiled by Pao-lun Tsi-yuan 宝轮际源 (Hōrin Saigen) and Chao-yueh Liao-chen 昭月了贞 (Shōgetsu Ryōtei, 1729-1785), supplement by Pao-lin Ta-chen 宝林达珍 (Hōrin Tatsuchin).

Chia-tai Pu-teng Lu 嘉泰普灯录 (*Katai Futō Roku*), compiled by Lei-an Cheng-shou 雷庵正受 (Raian Shōju, 1146-1208).

Chien-chung Ching-kuo Hsü-teng Lu 建中靖国续灯录 (*Kenchū Seikoku Zokutō Roku*), also known as *Hsü Teng Lu* (*Zokutō Roku*), compiled by Fu-kuo Wei-po 佛国惟白 (Bukkoku Ibyaku).

Ching-te Chuan-teng Lu 景德传灯录 (*Keitoku Dentō Roku*), compiled in 1004 A.D. by Tao-yuan 道原 (Dōgen).

Chuan-fa Cheng-tsung Chi 传法正宗记 (*Denhō Shōsō Ki*), compiled by Chi-sung 契嵩 (Kaisū, 1007-1072).

Chung-ko Ku-tsun-su Yu-lu 重刻古尊宿语录 (*Jukoku Kosonshuku Goroku*), compiled in 1267 by Chueh-hsin (Kakushin) 觉心.

Chung-kuo Ch'an-tsung Shih 中国禅宗史 (*Chūkoku Zenshū Shi*), by Reverend Yin-shun 印顺, Taipei, 1975.

Chung-kuo Fo-chiao Shih 中国佛教史 (*Chūkoku Bukkyō Shi*), by Chiang Wei-chiao 蒋维乔 , Shanghai, 1928.

Denkō Roku 传光录 (*Transmission of the Light*), by Keizan Shōkin 莹山绍瑾 (1268-1325).

Dharma Records of Abbot Hsu Yun 虚云和尚法汇, edited by Tsen Hsueh-lu 岑学吕, Hong Kong, 1953.

Essays in Zen Buddhism, by Daisets Teitarō Suzuki 铃木大拙贞太郎, Grove Press, New York (First Series, 1949, 1961).

History of Chinese Zen Buddhism 中国禅宗史 (in Chinese), by Reverend Yin-shun 印顺, Taipei, 1975.

Hsü Chuan-teng-lu 续传灯录 (*Zoku Dentō Roku*), compiled by Yuan-chi Chu-ting 圆极居顶 (Enki Kochō, d. 1404).

Hsü Tsang Ching 续藏经 (*Zoku Zōkyō*) (in Chinese), Hong Kong.

Hsü-kai Ku-tsun-su Yü-yao 续开古尊宿语要 (*Zokukai Kosonshuku Goyō*), compiled by Hui-shih Shih-ming 晦室师明 (Kaishitsu Shimei).

Jih-pen Ch'an-seng Nieh-pan Chi 日本禅僧涅槃记 (in Chinese), by Tseng Pu-hsin 曾普信.

Jih-pen Ch'an-seng Shih-chen Chi 日本禅僧师承记 (in Chinese), by Y. H. Ku, Chen Shan Mei Publishing Co., Taipei, 1977.

Kao Seng Chuan (*Kōsō Den*), Vol. I, compiled by Hui-chiao 慧皎 (Ekyō).

Kao Seng Chuan (*Kōsō Den*), Vol. II, or *Hsü Kao Seng Chuan* 续高僧传 (Zoku Kōsō Den), compiled by Tao-hsuan 道宣 (Dōsen, 596-667).

Kao Seng Chuan (*Kōsō Den*), Vol. III, compiled by Tsan-ning 赞宁 (Sannei).

Kinse Zenrin Sōhō Den 近世禅林僧宝传 (in Chinese), Vol. I, by Doku'en Jōju 独园承珠, 1890, 1973; Vols. II and III by Shōhata Buntei 小畠文鼎, 1938, 1973.

Ku-tsun-su Yü-yao 古尊宿语要 (*Kosonshuku Goyō*), compiled by Seng-ting Shou-tse 僧挺守赜 (Sōtei Shusaku) and published in 1144.

Lao Tzu: Tao Teh Ching 老子道德经 (translation), translated by John C. H. Wu 吴经熊, St. John's University Press, Jamaica, N.Y., 1961.

Lieh-dai Fa-pao Chi 列代法宝记 (*Rekidai Hōbō Ki*), reprinted in *Daishō Shinshū Daizōkyō*, Vol. 51.

Lin-chi Ch'an-shih Yü-lu 临济禅师语录 (*Rinzai Zenji Goroku*), compiled by San-sheng Hui-jan 三圣慧然 (Sanshō Enen).

Living by Zen, by D. T. Suzuki 铃木大拙, with Foreword by Christmas Humphreys, published by Samuel Weiser, Inc., New York, 2008.

Meibatsu Chūkoku Bukkyō Kenkyū 明末中国佛教研究 (in Japanese), by Chang Sheng-yen 张圣严, Tokyo, 1975.

Nippon Bukke Jinmyō Jisho 日本佛家人名辞书 (in Japanese), compiled by Jubi Jun 鹫尾顺, Tokyo Fine Arts Edition.

Original Teachings of Ch'an Buddhism: Selected from the Transmission of the Lamp, English translation by Chang Chung-yuan 张钟元, Pantheon Books, New York, 1969.

Outlines of Mahayana Buddhism, by D. T. Suzuki, Schoken Books Inc., 1963.

Pao-ching San-mei 宝镜三昧 (*Hōkyō Zammai, The Jeweled Mirror Samadhi*), by Tung-shan Liang-chieh 洞山良价 (Tōzan Ryōkai, 807-869).

Pi-yen-lu 碧岩集 (*Hekigan-roku, The Blue Cliff Record*), English translation by Thomas and J. C. Cleary, Sambhala Publications, Inc., Boulder, Colorado, 1977.

Platform Scriptures 六祖坛经, English translation by Wing-tsit Chan 陈荣捷, St. John's University Press, Jamaica, N.Y., 1963.

Rekidai Hōbō Ki 列代法宝记 (in Chinese), reprinted in *Daishō Shinshū Daizōkyō*, Vol. 51.

Shen-hui Ho-shan I-chi 神会和尚遗集, compiled by Hu Shih 胡适, "Academia Sinica," Taipei, 1970.

Shih-shih I-nien Lu 释氏疑年录 (*Shaku-shi Ginen Roku*), by Chen Yuan 陈垣, Fu-jen University, Peking.

Shōbōgenzō 正法眼藏 (*True Dharma Eye*), by Dōgen Kigen 道元希玄, 1231-1253.

Shōyō Roku 从容录, compiled by Manshō Kōshū 万松行秀 (1166-1246), based on *Juko Hyaku Soku* 颂古百则 by Wanshi Shōkaku 宏智正觉 (1091-1157).

Sōtō-shū Zenshō 曹洞宗全书, published by Sōtō-shū Office, Tokyo, new edition 1976.

Star-Lamp Records 星灯集, by Hsu Yun 虚云, reprinted in *Dharma Records of Abbot Hsu Yun*, Hong Kong, 1953.

Ta-cheng Hsin-hsiu Ta-tsang Ching 大正新修大藏经 (*Daishō Shinshū Daizōkyō*), 1924-1934.

The Development of Chinese Zen After the Sixth Patriarch in the Light of Mumonkan, English translation by Ruth Fuller Sasaki, The First Zen Institute of America, Inc., New York, 1953.

The Golden Age of Zen, by John C. H. Wu, Hwa Kang Bookstore, Taipei, 1975.

The Practice of Zen, by Garma C. C. Chang 张澄基, Perennial Library, Harper & Row Publishers, New York, 1970.

The Sound of the One Hand (translation with a Commentary), by Yoel Hoffman, Basic Books Inc., New York, 1975.

The Three Pillars of Zen, by Philip Kapleau, Beacon Press, 1967.

The Way of Zen, by Alan W. Watts, Pantheon Books, 1957.

The World of Zen, by Nancy Wilson Ross, Vintage Book, 1960.

Tien-sheng Kuang-teng Lu 天圣广灯录 (*Tenshō Kōtō Roku*), compiled by Li Tsun-hsu 李遵勖 (Ri Junkyoku, d. 1038).

Tsan-tung-chi 参同契 (Sandōkai), by Shih-tou Hsi-chien (Sekitō Kisen 石头希迁, 700-790).

Tun-wu Ju-tao Yao-men Lun 顿悟入道要门论 (*Tongo Nyūdō Yōmon Ron*), by Ta-chu Hui-hai 大珠慧海 (Daishu Ekai), edited by Miao-hsieh 妙叶 (Myōkyō) and first published in 1374.

Wu-chia Yü-lu 五家语录 (*Goke Goroku*), also known as *Wu-tsung Lu* 五宗录 (*Goshū Roku*), compiled by Yü-feng Yuan-hsin 语风圆信 (Gofū Enshin) and Kuo Ning-chih 郭凝之 (Kaku Gyōshi).

Wu-teng Yen-tung 五灯严统 (*Gotō Gontō*), compiled by Fei-yin Tung-yung 费隐通容 (Hi-in Tsuyō, 1593-1661) and Po-chih Yuan-kung 百痴愿公 (Hyakuchi Gankō).

Zen and Japanese Culture, by D. T. Suzuki, Princeton University Press.

Zen and Zen Classics, Selections from R. H. Blyth, compiled and with drawings by Frederick Franck, Vintage Books, 1978.

Zen and Zen Classics, Vols. I to V, by R. H. Blyth, The Hokuseido Press, Tokyo, 1960-1974.

Zen Buddhism and Psychoanalysis, by Erich Fromm, D. T. Suzuki, and Richard De Martino, Harper Colophon Books, Harper & Row Publishers, New York, 1960.

Zen Buddhism, Selected Writings of D. T. Suzuki, edited by William Barrett, Doubleday Anchor Books, 1956.

Zen Culture, by Thomas Hoover, Vintage Books, 1977.

Zen Dust 禅尘, by Isshu Miura 三浦一舟 and Ruth Fuller Sasaki, Harcourt Brace Jovanovich, Inc., New York, 1966.

Zen Flesh, Zen Bones, compiled by Paul Reps, Doubleday Anchor Book, 1960.

Zen is Eternal Life, by Jiyu Kennett, Dharma Publishing, Emeryville, California, 1976.

Zen Keys, by Thich Nhat Hanh, with an Introduction by Philip Kapleau, translated from the French into English by Albert and Jean Low, Doubleday Anchor Book, Garden City, N.Y., 1974.

Zen-shū Shi 禅宗史 (in Japanese), by Reverend Keidō (Kōhō) Chisan 孤峰智灿, 2nd ed. 1974.

Zen: Poems, Prayers, Sermons, Anecdotes, Interviews, edited and translated by Lucien Stryk and Takashi Ikemoto, Doubleday Anchor Book, Garden City, N.Y., 1965.

Zoku Tō Sonkō 续灯存稿, compiled by Shi Hai 施沛, reprinted in *Zoku Zōkyō* 续藏经, Vol. 145.

ADDITIONAL REFERENCES

A Dictionary of Buddhism, by T. O. Ling, Charles Scribner's Sons, New York, 1972.

A Dictionary of Chinese Buddhist Terms, compiled by William Edward Soothill and Lewis Hodous, Kegan Paul, Trench, Truber & Co., Ltd., London, 1937.

A History of the Interflow of China-Japan Buddhist Culture 中日佛教交通史, by Ven. Tungtsu, Taipei, 1970.

A History of the Interflow of Sino-India Buddhist Culture 中印佛教交通史, by Ven. Tungtsu 释东初, Taipei, 1968, 1972.

A Man of Zen: The Recorded Sayings of Layman P'ang, English translation by Ruth Fuller Sasaki, Yoshitaka Iriya, and Dana R. Fraser, John Weatherhill, Inc., New York, 1971.

A Modern History of Buddhism in China (2 Vols.) 中国佛教近代史（上下二册）, by Ven. Tungtsu, Taipei, 1974.

A Primer of Sōtō Zen, a Translation of Dōgen's Shōbōgenzō Zuimonki, by Reihō Masunaga, University of Hawai'i Press, 1975.

Manual of Zen Buddhism, by D. T. Suzuki, Grove Press, New York, 1960.

On Zen Practice, I and II, edited by Hakuyu Taizan Maezumi and Bernard Tetsugen Glassman, Zen Center of Los Angeles, 1976, 1977.

Pure Land & Ch'an Dharma Talks, by Reverend Hsuan-hua 宣化, Sino-American Buddhist Association, Inc., San Francisco, California, 1974.

Sixth Patriarch's Sutra, with Commentary of Reverend Hsuan-hua, Sino-American Buddhist Association, Inc., San Francisco, California, 1977.

Zen for Americans, including the Sutra of Forty-two Chapters, by Sōyen Shaku 释宗演, English translation by D. T. Suzuki, Open Court Publishing Co., La Salle, Illinois, 1906, 1974.

LIST OF CHARTS 附表十八种

Chart I   From Daruma to Enō   从达摩到慧能

Chart II   From Enō to Eisai and Dōgen   从慧能到荣西与道元

Chart III   From Engo Kokugon to Hakuin   从圆悟到白隐

Chart IV   From Kanzan Egen to Hakuin   从关山到白隐

Chart V   From Hakuin to Takujū Line   从白隐到卓洲系

Chart V A   From Hakuin to Inzan Line   从白隐到隐山系

Chart VI   From Engo Kokugon to Kozan, Kōmin, and Ingen Lines

从圆悟到鼓山、高旻与隐元系

Chart VI A   The Kozan Line   鼓山系

Chart VI B   The Kōmin and Zengen Lines   高旻及禅源系

Chart VI C   The Kōten and Tennei Lines   江天及天宁系

Chart VII   The Myōhō Sosetsu Line   明峰素哲系

Chart VII A   The Gasan Shōseki Line   峨山绍硕系

Chart VIII   The Keizan and Kangan Lines   莹山与寒岩系

Chart IX   From Tsūgen to Ryōan Line   从通幻到了庵系

Chart IX A   From Tsūgen to Fusai and Sekioku Lines   从通幻到普济与石
梁系

Chart X   From Rokumon to Shōzan Shinetsu and Irin Lines   从鹿门到焦
山、为霖与心越系

Chart X A   The Shōzan Line   焦山（古樵）系

Chart X B   The Irin Line   为霖系

219

Chart I   From Daruma to Enō 从达摩到慧能

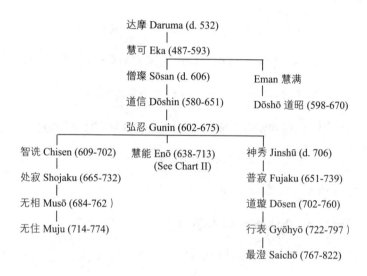

达摩 Daruma (d. 532)

慧可 Eka (487-593)

僧璨 Sōsan (d. 606)   Eman 慧满

道信 Dōshin (580-651)   Dōshō 道昭 (598-670)

弘忍 Gunin (602-675)

智诜 Chisen (609-702)   慧能 Enō (638-713)   神秀 Jinshū (d. 706)
                          (See Chart II)
处寂 Shojaku (665-732)   普寂 Fujaku (651-739)

无相 Musō (684-762）   道璇 Dōsen (702-760)

无住 Muju (714-774)   行表 Gyōhyō (722-797）

                                               最澄 Saichō (767-822)

Chart II   From Enō to Eisai and Dōgen 从慧能到荣西与道元

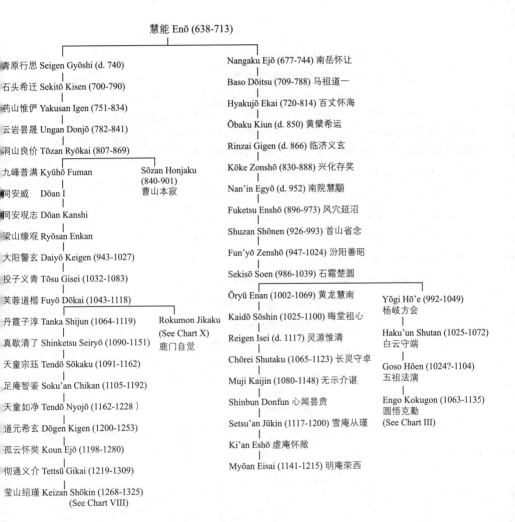

慧能 Enō (638-713)

青原行思 Seigen Gyōshi (d. 740)

石头希迁 Sekitō Kisen (700-790)

药山惟俨 Yakusan Igen (751-834)

云岩昙晟 Ungan Donjō (782-841)

洞山良价 Tōzan Ryōkai (807-869)

九峰普满 Kyūhō Fuman

同安威 Dōan I

同安观志 Dōan Kanshi

梁山缘观 Ryōsan Enkan

大阳警玄 Daiyō Keigen (943-1027)

投子义青 Tōsu Gisei (1032-1083)

芙蓉道楷 Fuyō Dōkai (1043-1118)

丹霞子淳 Tanka Shijun (1064-1119)

真歇清了 Shinketsu Seiryō (1090-1151)

天童宗珏 Tendō Sōkaku (1091-1162)

足庵智鉴 Soku'an Chikan (1105-1192)

天童如净 Tendō Nyojō (1162-1228)

道元希玄 Dōgen Kigen (1200-1253)

孤云怀奘 Koun Ejō (1198-1280)

彻通义介 Tettsū Gikai (1219-1309)

莹山绍瑾 Keizan Shōkin (1268-1325)
(See Chart VIII)

Sōzan Honjaku
(840-901)
曹山本寂

Rokumon Jikaku
(See Chart X)
鹿门自觉

Nangaku Ejō (677-744) 南岳怀让

Baso Dōitsu (709-788) 马祖道一

Hyakujō Ekai (720-814) 百丈怀海

Ōbaku Kiun (d. 850) 黄檗希运

Rinzai Gigen (d. 866) 临济义玄

Kōke Zonshō (830-888) 兴化存奖

Nan'in Egyō (d. 952) 南院慧顒

Fuketsu Enshō (896-973) 风穴延沼

Shuzan Shōnen (926-993) 首山省念

Fun'yō Zenshō (947-1024) 汾阳善昭

Sekisō Soen (986-1039) 石霜楚圆

Ōryū Enan (1002-1069) 黄龙慧南

Kaidō Sōshin (1025-1100) 晦堂祖心

Reigen Isei (d. 1117) 灵源惟清

Chōrei Shutaku (1065-1123) 长灵守卓

Muji Kaijin (1080-1148) 无示介谌

Shinbun Donfun 心闻昙贲

Setsu'an Jūkin (1117-1200) 雪庵从瑾

Ki'an Eshō 虚庵怀敞

Myōan Eisai (1141-1215) 明庵荣西

Yōgi Hō'e (992-1049)
杨岐方会

Haku'un Shutan (1025-1072)
白云守端

Goso Hōen (1024?-1104)
五祖法演

Engo Kokugon (1063-1135)
圆悟克勤
(See Chart III)

Chart III   From Engo Kokugon to Hakuin 从圆悟到白隐

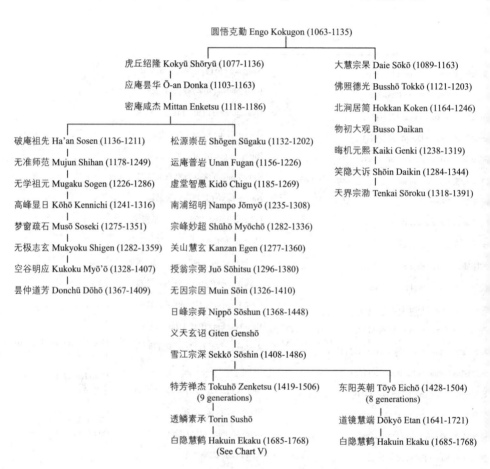

圆悟克勤 Engo Kokugon (1063-1135)

虎丘绍隆 Kokyū Shōryū (1077-1136)

应庵昙华 Ō-an Donka (1103-1163)

密庵咸杰 Mittan Enketsu (1118-1186)

大慧宗杲 Daie Sōkō (1089-1163)

佛照德光 Busshō Tokkō (1121-1203)

北涧居简 Hokkan Koken (1164-1246)

物初大观 Busso Daikan

晦机元熙 Kaiki Genki (1238-1319)

笑隐大䜣 Shōin Daikin (1284-1344)

天界宗泐 Tenkai Sōroku (1318-1391)

破庵祖先 Ha'an Sosen (1136-1211)

无准师范 Mujun Shihan (1178-1249)

无学祖元 Mugaku Sogen (1226-1286)

高峰显日 Kōhō Kennichi (1241-1316)

梦窗疏石 Musō Soseki (1275-1351)

无极志玄 Mukyoku Shigen (1282-1359)

空谷明应 Kukoku Myō'ō (1328-1407)

昙仲道芳 Donchū Dōhō (1367-1409)

松源崇岳 Shōgen Sūgaku (1132-1202)

运庵普岩 Unan Fugan (1156-1226)

虚堂智愚 Kidō Chigu (1185-1269)

南浦绍明 Nampo Jōmyō (1235-1308)

宗峰妙超 Shūhō Myōchō (1282-1336)

关山慧玄 Kanzan Egen (1277-1360)

授翁宗弼 Juō Sōhitsu (1296-1380)

无因宗因 Muin Sōin (1326-1410)

日峰宗舜 Nippō Sōshun (1368-1448)

义天玄诏 Giten Genshō

雪江宗深 Sekkō Sōshin (1408-1486)

特芳禅杰 Tokuhō Zenketsu (1419-1506)
(9 generations)

透鳞素承 Torin Sushō

白隐慧鹤 Hakuin Ekaku (1685-1768)
(See Chart V)

东阳英朝 Tōyō Eichō (1428-1504)
(8 generations)

道镜慧端 Dōkyō Etan (1641-1721)

白隐慧鹤 Hakuin Ekaku (1685-1768)

Chart IV From Kanzan Egen to Hakuin 从关山到白隐

关山慧玄 Kanzan Egen (1277-1360)

授翁宗弼 Juō Sōhitsu (1296-1380)

无因宗因 Muin Sōin (1326-1410)

日峰宗舜 Nippō Sōshun (1367-1448)

义天玄诏 Giten Genshō

雪江宗深 Sekkō Sōshin (1408-1486)

特芳禅杰 Tokuhō Zenketsu (1419-1506)　　东阳英朝 Tōyō Eichō (1428-1504)

大休宗休 Daikyū Sōkyū (1468-1549)　　大雅崇匡 Daika Senkyo

太原崇孚 Taigen Sūfu (1495-1555)　　功甫玄勋 Kofu Genkun

东谷宗杲 Tōkoku Sōkō　　先照瑞初 Senshō Zuishu

　　以安智泰 I'an Chitai

铁山宗钝 Tetsusan Sōden　　大辉祥暹 Daiki Jōsen　　东渐宗震 Tōzen Sōshin

大室祖丘 Daishitsu Sokyū　　说心宗宜 Zeishin Sōgi　　庸山景庸 Yōsan Keiyō

心岩玄精 Shingan Genshō　　龙潭元恕 Ryūtan Genjo　　愚堂东寔 Gudō Tōjitsu (1576-1661)

鳌峰道哲 Gōhō Dōtetsu　　大端宗育 Daitan Sōiku　　至道无难 Shidō Bunan (1603-1676)

节岩道圆 Setsugan Dō'en (1607-1675)　　失顺祖顺 Shitsujun Sōjun　　道镜慧端 Dōkyō Etan (1642-1721)

贤岩禅悦 Kengan Zen'etsu (1618-1696)　　单岭祖传 Tanrei Soden　　白隐慧鹤 Hakuin Ekaku (1685-1768)
　　　　　　　　　　　　　　　　　　　　　　　　　　　　　　　　　　　(See Chart V)

古月禅材 Kogetsu Zenzai (1667-1751)　　透鳞素承 Torin Sushō

月船禅慧 Gesen Zen'e (1702-1781)　　白隐慧鹤 Hakuin Ekaku (1685-1768)

Chart V　From Hakuin to Takujū Line 从白隐到卓洲系

白隐慧鹤 Hakuin Ekaku (1685-1768)
|
峨山慈棹 Gasan Jitō (1726-1797)
|
卓州胡仙 Takujū Kosen (1760-1833)

妙喜宗绩 Myōki Sōseki
(1774-1848)
|
迦陵瑞迦 Karyō Zuika
(1790-1859)
|
潭海玄昌 Tankai Genshō
(1811-1898)
|
毒湛匝三 Dokutan Sōsan
(1840-1917)
|
雾海古亮 Mukai Koryō
(1864-1935)
|
中村泰祐 Nakamura Taiyū
(1886-1954)
|
三浦一舟 Miura Isshū
(1903-)

苏山玄乔 Sozan Genkyō
(1798-1866)
|
伽山全楞 Kazan Zenryō
(1824-1893)
|
宗般玄芳 Sōhan Genhō
(1848-1922)
|
玄峰宜雄 Gempō Giyū
(1865-1961)
|
中川宗渊 Nakagawa Sō'en
(1907-)
|
岛野荣道 Shimano Eidō
(1932-)

Chart V A   From Hakuin to Inzan Line 从白隐到隐山系

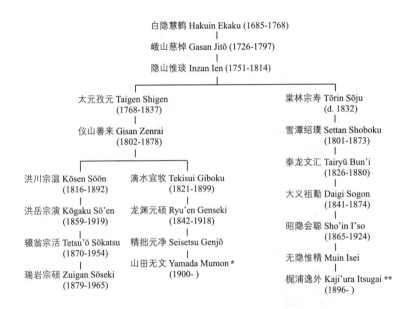

白隐慧鹤 Hakuin Ekaku (1685-1768)
|
峨山慈棹 Gasan Jitō (1726-1797)
|
隐山惟琰 Inzan Ien (1751-1814)

太元孜元 Taigen Shigen
(1768-1837)
|
仪山善来 Gisan Zenrai
(1802-1878)
|

洪川宗温 Kōsen Sōōn
(1816-1892)
|
洪岳宗演 Kōgaku Sō'en
(1859-1919)
|
辍翁宗活 Tetsu'ō Sōkatsu
(1870-1954)
|
瑞岩宗硕 Zuigan Sōseki
(1879-1965)

滴水宜牧 Tekisui Giboku
(1821-1899)
|
龙渊元硕 Ryu'en Genseki
(1842-1918)
|
精拙元净 Seisetsu Genjō
|
山田无文 Yamada Mumon *
(1900-)

棠林宗寿 Tōrin Sōju
(d. 1832)
|
雪潭绍璞 Settan Shoboku
(1801-1873)
|
泰龙文汇 Tairyū Bun'i
(1826-1880)
|
大义祖勤 Daigi Sogon
(1841-1874)
|
昭隐会聪 Sho'in I'so
(1865-1924)
|
无隐惟精 Muin Isei
|
梶浦逸外 Kaji'ura Itsugai **
(1896-)

*   Present Abbot of Myōshin-ji   妙心寺独住
** Recently retired Abbot of Myōshin-ji

Chart VI   From Engo Kokugon to Kozan, Kōmin, and Ingen Lines
从圆悟到鼓山、高旻与隐元系

圆悟克勤 Engo Kokugon (1063-1135)

虎丘绍隆 Kokyū Jōryū (1077-1136)

应庵昙华 Ō'an Donka (1103-1163)

密庵咸杰 Mittan Enketsu (1118-1186)

破庵祖先 Ha'an Sosen (1136-1211)

无准师范 Mujun Shihan (1178-1249)

雪岩祖钦 Seggan Sokin
(1216-1287)

高峰原妙 Kōhō Gemmyō
(1238-1295)

中峰明本 Chūhō Myōhon
(1263-1323)

千岩元长 Sengan Genchō
(1284-1357)

万峰时蔚 Manhō Jijō
(1303-1381)

宝藏普持 Hōzō Fuji

虚白慧岳 Kihaku Egaku
(1372-1441)

海舟永慈 Kaishū Eiji
(1393-1461)

宝峰明瑄 Hōhō Myōken
(d. 1472)

天奇本瑞 Tenki Honzui

无闻正聪 Mubun Shōsō
(1450-1512)

月心德宝 Getsushin Tokuhō
(1512-1581)

幻有正传 Genyū Shōden
(1549-1614)

净慈妙伦 Jōji Myōrin
(1201-1261)

瑞岩文宝 Zuigan Bunhō
(d. 1335)

华顶先睹 Kachō Sento
(1265-1334)

福林智度 Fukurin Chito
(1304-1370)

古拙昌俊 Kosetsu Shōshun

无际明悟 Musai Myōgo

太冈澄 Tai'oka Chō

夷峰宁 Gihō Nei
(d. 1491)

宝芳进 Hōhō Shin

野翁慧晓 Ya'ō Egyō

无趣如空 Mushu Nyokū
(1491-1580)

无幻性冲 Mugen Seichū
(1540-1611)

兴善慧广 Kōzen Ekō
(1576-1620)

普明德用 Fumyō Tokuyo
(1587-1642)

高庵圆清 Kōan Ensei
(Kozan Line) 鼓山系
(See Chart VI A)

密云圆悟 Mitsu'un Engo
(1566-1642)

费隐通容 Hi-in Tsuyō
(1593-1661)

隐元隆琦 Ingen Ryūki
(1592-1673)
（日本黄檗宗）

天隐圆修 Ten'in Enshū
(1575-1635)

玉琳通琇 Gyokurin Tsūshū
(1614-1675)
(Kōmin Line) 高旻系
(See Chart VI B)

Chart VI A   The Kozan Line 鼓山系

高庵圆清 Kōan Ensei (?-1522)
|
本智明觉 Honchi Myōkaku
|
紫柏真可 Shikaku Shinke (1543-1603)
|
端旭如弘 Tankyoku Nyokō
|
纯洁性奎 Junketsu Shōki
|
慈云海俊 Jiun Kaishun
|
质生寂文 Tetsushin Jakubun
|
端员照华 Tan'en Shōka
|
其岸普明 Chigan Fumyō
|
戣巧通圣 Taikyō Tsūshō
|
悟修心空 Goshū Shinkū
|
宏化源悟 Kōka Gengo
|
祥青广松 Shōsei Kōshō
|
守道续先 Shudō Zokusen
|
正岳本超 Shōgaku Honchō
|
永畅觉乘 Eishō Kakujō
|
方来昌远 Hōrai Shō'on
|
豁悟隆参 Katsugo Ryūsen
|
维超能灿 Ichō Nōsan
|
奇量仁繁 Kiryō Jinhan
|
妙莲圣华 Myōren Shōka
|
鼎峰果成 Teihō Kajō
|
善慈常开 Zenji Shōkai
|
演彻德清 Entetsu Tokusei (Kiun, 1840-1959) 虚云
|
宽印佛慧 Kan'in Butsu'e
|
宏妙灵源 Kōmyō Reigen (1902-)
|
惟定知生 Itei Chishin 惟柔知刚 Ijū Chigō

NOTE: Reverend Myōren Shōka, also known as Myōren Chika 妙莲地华 belonged to both the Rinzai School and the Sōtō School. (See *Dharma Records of Abbot Hsu Yun*, Vol. 8, page 265.) His dharma-teacher Kiryō Jinhan, also known as Kiryō Tetsuhan 奇量彻繁 belonged to both the Rinzai and Sōtō Schools. According to *Ku-shan Lieh-tsu Lien-fang Chi* 鼓山列祖联芳集, Kiryō, the 123rd Abbot, belonged to the 44th generation in the Sōtō School, and Myōren, the 126th Abbot at Ku-shan, belonged to the 45th generation. Tracing backward, Jōkū Ken'in (d. 1875) 净空兼印, the 118th Abbot, belonged to the 43rd generation, and Nōji Tenshō (d. 1848) 能持天性, the 116th Abbot, belonged to the 42nd generation. (See also Chart X B). Now Abbot Hsu Yun, the 130th at Ku-shan, considered himself belonging to the 47th generation in the Sōtō School. His dharma name was Kogan 虚云古岩. "Ko" was common to Enrō Kogetsu 圆朗古月, the 127th Abbot, who succeeded Myōren in 1902 and passed away in 1919, and Shinkō Koki (d. 1924) 振光古辉, the 128th Abbot.

Chart VI B   The Kōmin and Zengen Lines 高旻及禅源系

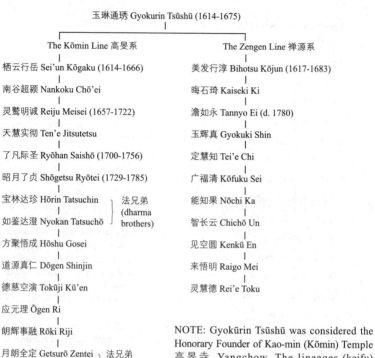

玉琳通琇 Gyokurin Tsūshū (1614-1675)

The Kōmin Line 高旻系	The Zengen Line 禅源系
栖云行岳 Sei'un Kōgaku (1614-1666)	美发行淳 Bihotsu Kōjun (1617-1683)
南谷超颖 Nankoku Chō'ei	晦石琦 Kaiseki Ki
灵鹫明诚 Reiju Meisei (1657-1722)	澹如永 Tannyo Ei (d. 1780)
天慧实彻 Ten'e Jitsutetsu	玉辉真 Gyokuki Shin
了凡际圣 Ryōhan Saishō (1700-1756)	定慧知 Tei'e Chi
昭月了贞 Shōgetsu Ryōtei (1729-1785)	广福清 Kōfuku Sei
宝林达珍 Hōrin Tatsuchin ⎫ 法兄弟	能知果 Nōchi Ka
如鉴达澄 Nyokan Tatsuchō ⎭ (dharma brothers)	智长云 Chichō Un
方聚悟成 Hōshu Gosei	见空圆 Kenkū En
道源真仁 Dōgen Shinjin	来悟明 Raigo Mei
德慈空演 Tokuji Kū'en	灵慧德 Rei'e Toku
应元理 Ōgen Ri	
朗辉事融 Rōki Riji	
月朗全定 Getsurō Zentei ⎫ 法兄弟	
楚禅全振 Sozen Zenshin ⎭ (dharma brothers)	
明轩西瑞 Meiken Saizui	
妙树来果 Myōju Raika (1881-1953)	
妙解 Myōge	

NOTE: Gyokūrin Tsūshū was considered the Honorary Founder of Kao-min (Kōmin) Temple 高旻寺, Yangchow. The lineages (keifu) of the Kao-min (Kōmin) line and the Ch'an-yuan (Zengen) line were taken from Mōgetsu Shinkyō's *Bukkyo Dainen Hyō* 望月信亨： 佛教大年表, 4th edition, page 52. The author is indebted to Reverend Lun-tsan 伦参法师 of Hong Kong and Reverend Yen-chih 严持法师 of Hua-Lien Buddhist Lotus Institute, Taiwan, for the information from Gyokūrin to Raika. Reverend Po-Yun (Haku'un) 白云上座 kindly supplied the name of Yin-yuan Li (Ōgen Ri) 应元理 between Tokūji Kū'en and Rōki Riji. Note that Shōgetsu Ryōtei 昭月了贞 and Hōrin Saigen 宝轮际源 were the compilers of *Shōgen Ryakushū* 正源略集 and Hōrin Tatsuchin 宝林达珍 was the compiler of its Supplement.

Chart VI C The Kōten and Tennei Lines 江天及天宁系

若庵通问 Jaku'an Tsūmon (1604-1655)
(Founder of Kōten Temple, Kinzan)

铁舟行海 Tetsushū Kōkai (1609-1683)

法乳超乐 Hōnyū Chōraku (1642-1702)

量闻明诠 Ryōmon Meisen
月潭明达 Getsutan Meitatsu (1665-1729)　法兄弟 (dharma brothers)

大晓实彻 Daigyō Jitsutetsu

The Kōten Line 江天系 (continued)	The Tennei Line 天宁系
天涛际云 Tentō Sai'un (d. 1766)	纳川际海 Nasen Saikai
六益了濂 Riku'eki Ryōken	净德了月 Jōtoku Ryōgetsu
沧海达慧 Sōkai Tatsu'e	恒赀达如 Kōsan Tatsunyo
不空悟圆 Bukū Go'en	雪岩悟洁 Seggan Goketsu
正一悟明 Shōichi Gomei	普能真嵩 Funō Shinsū
志学悟通 Shigaku Gotsū　法兄弟 (dharma brothers)	定念真禅 Teinen Shinzen　法兄弟 (dharma brothers)
广慈真济 Kōji Shinsai	青光清宗 Seikō Seishū
道华清登 Dōka Seito	冶净清镕 Yakai Seiyō
乐亭清耀 Rakutei Seiyō　法兄弟 (dharma brothers)	善净清如 Zenjō Seinyo　法兄弟 (dharma brothers)
月溪显谛 Getsukei Kentei	琢如显泉 Takunyo Kensen
观心显慧 Kanshin Ken'e	明镜显宽 Meikyō Kenkan
惟章显然 Ishō Kennen　法兄弟 (dharma brothers)	惟宽显彻 Ikan Kentetsu　法兄弟 (dharma brothers)
浑容显镜 Konyō Kenkyō	证莲密源 Shōren Mitsugen (1893–1967)
大定密圆 Daitei Mitsu'en	慧轮密诠 Erin Mitsusen　法兄弟 (dharma brothers)
常净密传 Shōjō Mitsuden	永培密华 Eibai Mitsuka
性莲密法 Seiren Mitsuhō　法兄弟 (dharma brothers)	敏智 Binchi
隐儒密藏 Inju Mitsuzō	[Reverend Ming-chih (Binchi) is the dharma-heir of Reverend Cheng-lien (Shōren)]
慈本印观 Jihon Inkan	
青权印开 Seigon Inkai	
梅村印修 Baison Inshū　法兄弟 (dharma brothers)	
融通印彻 Yūtsū Intetsu	
宗仰印楞 Shugyō Inryō (1865-1921) (Founder of Seika-ji) 栖霞寺开山	

NOTE: Jaku'an (Rian) Tsūmon, dharma-heir of Ten'in Enshū 天隐圆修 (1575-1635) and co-complier of *Zokutō Sonkō* 续灯存稿, was the Honorary Founder of Kiang-tien (Kōten) Temple 江天寺, Chinshan (Kinzan) 金山. Five generations later, Nansen Saikai became the Founder of Tien-ning (Tennei) Temple 天宁寺, Changchow (Kiangsu). The lineage from Tetsushū Kōkai to Inju Mitsuzō and the lineage from Nansen Saikai to Yakai Seiyō were taken from Mōgetsu Shinkyō's *Bukkyō Dainen Hyō* 望月信亨: 佛教大年表, 4th edition, page 52. The author wishes to thank Reverend Yen-chih 严持法师 of Hua-lien Buddhist Lotus Institute for supplying additional names. (In the Kōten line, Daigyō Jitsutetsu 大晓实彻 had other disciples: Tokukō Sai'en 德宏际圆, Sōkō Saichū 沧洪际注, Fukō Saimei 扶功际明 and Saikaku 际觉. In the Tennei line, Jōtoku Ryōgetsu 净德了月 had other disciples: Teisei Tatsuden 鼎成达传, Sekisen Tatsutei 石泉达鼎, Ekyo Tatsurin 慧炬达轮, Kōsan Tatsumei 广参达明, Rōshō Tatsu'iku 朗照达昱 and Ryōtō Tatsu'u 染栋达宇.)

Chart VII　The Myōhō Sosetsu Line 明峰素哲系

明峰素哲 Myōhō Sosetsu
(1277-1350)

珠岩道珍 Shugan Dōchin
(d. 1387)

彻山旨廓 Tetsuzan Shikaku

桂岩英昌 Keigan Eishō

筹山了运 Chuzan Ryōun (1350-1432)

义山等仁 Gisan Tonin (1386-1462)

绍岳坚隆 Shōgaku Kenryū (d. 1485)

几年丰隆 Kinen Hōryū (d. 1506)

提室智阐 Teishitsu Chisen (1461-1536)

虎溪正淳 Kokei Shōjun (d. 1555)

雪窗祐补 Sessō Yūho (d. 1576)

海天玄聚 Kaiten Genshu

州山春昌 Shūzan Shunshō

超山阁越 Chōzan Gin'etsu (1581-1672)

福州光智 Fukushū Kōchi

明堂雄暾 Meidō Yūton

白峰玄滴 Hakuhō Genteki (1594-1670)

月舟宗胡 Gesshū Sōko (1618-1696)

卍山道白 Manzan Dohaku (1635-1714)

月涧义光 Gekkan Gikō
(1653-1702)

大用慧照 Daiyō Esshō

华严曹海 Kegon Sōkai

祥云太瑞 Shōun Taizui

日轮当午 Nichirin Tōgō

尊应教堂 Sonnō Kyodō

祖岳灵道 Sogaku Reidō

大俊鞭牛 Daishun Bengyū

孤峰白岩 Kohō Hakugan

莹堂智灿 Keidō Chisan *
(1879-1967)

明洲珠心 Meishū Shushin

密山道显 Mitsuzan Dōken

达岩寂玄 Tatsugan Jakugen

北宗良潭 Hokushū Ryōtan

一峰觉专 Ichihō Kakusen

台山千丈 Daizan Senjō

通山哲俊 Tsuzan Tetsushun

象山来道 Zōzan Raidō

大哲俊乘 Daitetsu Shunjō

英蕴文雄 Ei'un Bunyū

禅海文山 Zenkai Bunzan

药栏文狮 Yakuran Bunshi

形山瑾映 Gyōzan (Keizan) Kin'ei **

庆屋定绍 Kei'oku Teishō
(1339-1407)

柏岩树庭 Hakugan Jutei

玄室智玄 Genshitsu Chigen

东林暾 Tōrin Ton

茂林善荣 Morin Zen'ei

竹堂慧严 Chikudō Egen

学海性文 Gakukai Shōbun

天怡道悦 Ten'i Dō'etsu

怡山文悦 I'san Mon'etsu

育翁道养 IKu'ō Dōyō

通山慧馨 Tsuzan Ekei

快寿山悦 Gaiju San'etsu

朝山永暾 Chōzan Eiton

谦岩寂英 Kengan Jaku'ei

玉岩懒牛 Gyokugan Raigyū

朝云喝宗 Chō'un Katsusō

雷洲大震 Raishū Daishin

单山良传 Tanzan Ryōden

机外默禅 Kigai Mokuzen

默渊慧安 Mokuen E'an

太梅慧方 Taibai Ehō

默道慧昭 Mōkudō Essho

明峰慧玉 Myōhō Egyoku ***

* 　Former Abbot of Sōji-ji
　　前总持寺独住
** 　Present Abbot of Sōji-ji
　　总持寺独住
*** Present Abbot of Eihei-ji
　　永平寺住持

Chart VII A   The Gasan Shōseki Line 峨山绍硕系

峨山绍硕 Gasan Shōseki
(1274-1365)

太原宗真 Taigen Soshin
(d. 1370)

梅山闻本 Baisan Bunhon
(d. 1417)

如仲天阎 Nyochū Tengin
(1363-1442)

喜山性赞 Kisan Shōsan (1377-1442)	真岩道空 Shingan Dōkū (1374-1449)
茂林芝繁 Morin Shihan (1393-1487)	川僧慧济 Sensō Esai (d. 1475)
崇芝性岱 Sūshi Shōtai	大年祥椿 Dainen Jōchin (1434-1513)
贤仲繁喆 Kenchu Hantetsu (1438-1512)	大路一遵 Dairo Ichijun (1399-1518)
大树宗光 Daiju Sōkō	林英宗甫 Rin'ei Sofū (d. 1531)
琴峰寿泉 Kimpō Jusen	大阳一鸮 Daiyō Ichirei (d. 1569)
铁叟栖钝 Tetsusō Seidon	天阳一朝 Tenyō Ichichō (d. 1549)
舟谷长春 Shūkoku Chōshun	潜龙慧湛 Senryū Etan (d. 1566)
杰山铁英 Ketsuzan Tetsuei	天叟善长 Tensō Zenchō (d. 1572)
报资宗恩 Hōshi Sōon	凤山等膳 Hōzan Tōzen (d. 1590)
五峰海音 Gohō Kai'on	一柱禅易 Ichichū Zeneki (d. 1598)
天桂传尊 Tenkei Denson (1648-1735)	士峰宗山 Shiho Sōzan (1542-1635)
像山问厚 Zōzan Monkō	
二见石了 Niken Sekiryō	

玄楼奥龙 Genrō Ōryū (1720-1813)	灵淡鲁龙 Reitan Roryū
风外本高 Fugai Honkō (1779-1847)	觉城东际 Kakujō Tōsai
旃崖奕堂 Sengai Ekidō (1805-1879)	觉庵了愚 Kakuan Ryōgu
大休悟由 Daikyū Goyū (1833-1915)	了呆大梅 Ryōka Daibai
	云岩愚白 Ungan Guhaku
	梅庵白纯 Baian Hakujun
	太山前济 Taizan Maizumi

NOTE: The lineage from Taigen Sōshin to Sengai Ekidō was based on Mōgetsu Shinkyō's *Bukkyō Dainen Hyō*, 4th edition, page 58. Sengai Ekidō was Chief Abbot (Dokuju 独住) of Sōji-ji and concurrently Kanchō 贯长 of the Sōtō-shū Group. He was succeeded by Daioka Baisen (1825-1910) 大冈楳仙 and Mokusan Kin'ei (1821-1910) 穆山瑾英. Daikyū Goyū was Chief Abbot (Kanshu 贯首) of Eihei-ji, succeeding Rosan Takushū (1836-1897) 鲁山琢宗.

Chart VIII   The Keizan and Kangan Lines 莹山与寒岩系

寒岩义尹 Kangan Gi'in
(1217-1300)

仁叟净熙 Jinsō Jōki
(d. 1364)

能翁玄慧 Nō'ō Gen'e

泰庵了运 Tai'an Ryōun

古泉利蒙 Kosen Rimō

竺方宗仙 Jikuhō Sōsen

圆应正莹 En'ō Shō'ei

心岩元统 Shingan Gentō

清峰庆梵 Seihō Kyōbon

定林玄智 Tekirin Genchi

明山春察 Myōzan Shunsatsu

大云玄广 Daiun Genkō

龙伯广瑞 Ryūhaku Kōzui

大焉广椿 Dai'en Kōchin

万安英种 Man'an Eichū
(1591-1654)

懒禅舜融 Raizen Shunyū
(1613-1672)

龙蟠松云 Ryūban Shō'un

梅峰竺信 Baihō Jikushin
(1633-1707)

高云祖棱 Kōun Soryō
(1636-1696)

莹山绍瑾 Keizan Shōkin
(1268-1325)

峨山绍硕 Gasan Shōseki
(1274-1365)

无外圆照 Mugai Enshō
(1311-1381)

无着妙融 Muchaku Myoyū
(1332-1393)

南阳融薰 Nanyō Yūkun

的林融中 Tekirin Yūchū

月山融照 Getsusan Yūshō

大芳融真 Daihō Yūshin

玉室融椿 Gyokushitsu Yūchin

梅溪融薰 Baikei Yūkun

月春融鉴 Getsushun Yūkan

古心融镜 Koshin Yūkyō

阳室融庆 Yōshitsu Yūkyō

畅庵融悦 Chōan Yūetsu

养寂融供 Yōjaku Yūkyō

安考融察 Ankō Yūsatsu

久学融贞 Kyūgaku Yūtei

东甫融菊 Tōfu Yūkiku

一庭融顿 Ichitei Yūton
(1580-1653)

雪山鹤昙 Sessan Kakudon
(d. 1649)

月舟宗林 Gesshū Sōrin
(d. 1687)

独庵玄光 Dokuan Genkō
(1630-1689)

Chart IX　From Tsūgen to Ryōan Line 从通幻到了庵系

峨山绍硕 Gasan Shōseki
(1274-1365)

通幻寂灵 Tsūgen Jakurei
(1323-1391)

了庵慧明 Ryōan Emyō
(1337-1411)

无极慧彻 Mukyoku Etetsu
(1350-1430)

月江正文 Getsukō Shōbun
(d. 1463)

泰叟妙康 Taisō Myōkō
(1406-1485)

天庵玄彭 Ten'an Genho
(d. 1500)

云冈舜德 Unkō Shuntoku
(1438-1516)

喜州玄欣 Kishū Genkin
(d. 1536)

节庵良筠 Setsuan Ryōshin
(1458-1541)

泰翁德扬 Tai'ō Tokuyō
(1481-1555)

在天宗凤 Zeiten Sōhō
(1490-1572)

久室玄长 Kyūshitsu Genchō
(d. 1585)

瑞翁俊鸄 Zui'ō Shunzoku
(d. 1596)

头室伊天 Tōshitsu Iten
(1523-1600)

一峰麟曹 Ichihō Rinsō
(1567-1623)

心灵中道 Shinrei Chūdō
(d. 1655)

十州补道 Jūshu Hodō
(d. 1646)

高岩薫道 Kōgan Kundō
(d. 1656)

不中秀的 Fuchū Shūteki
(1621-1677)

狮岩梅腑 Shigan Baifu
(1636-1680)

如实秀本 Nyojitsu Shuhon

岭南秀恕 Reinan Shūjo
(1675-1752)

⋯

一州正伊 Ichishu Sho'itsu
(1416-1487)

贤室自超 Kenshitsu Jichō

嗽如全芳 Sonyo Zenhō

青岩周扬 Seigan Shūyō
(d. 1542)

大州安充 Daishū Anchū

兴山圭隆 Kōzan Kiryu

看荣禀阅 Kan'ei Hei'etsu

用山元照 Yōsan Genshō

仁山岭恕 Jinsan Reinyo

雪庭钝好 Setsutei Tonko

大宣碧传 Daisen Hegiden

泰道秀国 Taidō Shūkoku

临峰良极 Rinho Ryōkyoku

日信义重 Nichishin Gizon

大安良义 Dai'an Ryōgi

温山良恭 Onzan Ryōkō

寰山义邦 Kansan Gihō

洞外仙州 Tōgai Senshū

大超寅州 Daichō Inshū

大愚万拙 Daigu Mantetsu

海云真龙 Kai'un Shunryū

佛海宗国 Bukkai Sōkoku

绝海胜俊 Zekkai Shōshun *
　(Iwamoto 岩本)

* Recently retired Abbot of Sōji-ji 总持寺独住

Chart IX A From Tsūgen to Fusai and Sekioku Lines
从通幻到普济与石梁系

莹山绍瑾 Keizan Shōkin (1268-1325)

峨山绍硕 Gasan Shoseki (1274-1365)

通幻寂灵 Tsūgen Jakurei (1323-1391)

普济善救 Fusai Zengu (1347-1405)	石屋真梁 Sekioku Shinryō (1345-1423)
玉窗良珍 Gyokusō Ryōchin (d. 1498)	竹居正猷 Chikukyo Shōyu (1380-1461)
性海慈孝 Shōkai Jikō	器之为瑶 Chishi Ihan (1404-1468)
明室慧灯 Myōshitsu Etō	大庵须益 Dai'an Su'eki (1406-1473)
国岩周邦 Kokugan Shūhō	全岩东纯 Zengan Tōjun (d. 1495)
水庵圣泉 Suian Shōsen	足翁永满 Soku'ō Eiman (1435-1505)
静安性腾 Joan Shōtō	天甫存佐 Tenfu Zonsa
三应寿寅 San'ō Juin	奇伯瑞庞 Kihaku Zuibō (1463-1547)
中明全的 Chūmyō Zenteki	助翁永扶 Jo'ō Eifu (d. 1548)
大仙淳智 Daisen Junchi	龟洋宗鉴 Kiyō Sōkan (1487-1563)
不异永龙 Fui Eiryū	异雪庆珠 Isetsu Kyōju (1502-1564)
无隐永有 Muin Eiyū	繁兴存荣 Hanko Zon'ei (1514-1571)
一峰宗润 Ippō Sōjun	阅翁珠门 Estu'ō Jumon (1521-1603)
纲庵宗祝 Kōan Sōshuku	安叟珠养 Ansō Juyō (d. 1604)
功雪润作 Kōsetsu Junsa	贵云岭胤 Kiun Rei'in (d. 1619)
真庵元达 Shinan Gentatsu	铁村玄鹫 Tetsuson Genju (1567-1638)
月海宗珠 Gekkai Sōju	岭室禅鹫 Reishitsu Zenju (1579-1636)
南龙存舜 Nanryū Sonshun	国嵬宗珍 Kokugi Sōchin
卓州有暾 Takujū Uton	
悟溪狼顿 Gokei Yōton	
巨峰狼秀 Goho Yōshu	
天岩舜佐 Tengan Shunsa	
王山狼佐 Ōzan Yōsa	
白堂树林 Hakudō Jurin	
月堂海印 Getsudō Kai'in	
月江良纹 Gekkō Ryōmon	
耕堂祖耘 Kōdō Soun	
孝槃铁山 Kōhan Tesan	
苍海铁龙 Sōkai Tetsuryū	
禹门活龙 Umon Katsuryū	
守道铁关 Shudō Tekkan	
维石铁岩 Iseki Tetsugan	
碓能铁嘴 Tainō Tetshi	* Present Abbot of Saijō-ji 最乗寺住持
禅月翠岩 Zengetsu Suigan *	

Chart X   From Rokumon to Shōzan, Shinetsu and Irin Lines
从鹿门到焦山、为霖与心越系

鹿门自觉 Rokumon Jikaku (d. 1117)

普照希辩 Fushō Kiben (1081-1149)

灵岩僧宝 Reigan Sōhō (1114-1173)

王山师体 Ōsan Shitei

雪岩慧满 Seggan Eman (d. 1206)

万松行秀 Manshō Kōshū (1166-1246)

少室福裕 Shōshitsu Fukuyū (1203-1275)

少室文泰 Shōshitsu Buntai (d. 1289)

宝应福遇 Hō'ō Fukugū (1245-1313)

少室文才 Shōshitsu Bunsai (1273-1352)

万安子严 Man'an Shigen

凝然了改 Gyōnen Ryōkai (1335-1421)

俱空契斌 Gukū Keihyō (1383-1452)

无方可从 Muhō Kashō (1420-1483)

月舟文载 Gesshū Bunsai (1452-1524)

宗镜宗书 Sōkyō Sōsho (1500-1567)

少室常润 Shōshitsu Shōjun (d. 1585)	蕴空常忠 Unkū Shōchū (1514-1588)	
大觉方念 Daikaku Hōnen (d. 1594)	无明慧经 Mumyō Ekei (1548-1618)	
云门圆澄 Ummon Enchō (1561-1626)	东苑元镜 To'en Genkyō (1577-1630)	永觉元贤 Eikaku Genken (1578-1657)
瑞白明雪 Zuihaku Myōsetsu (1584-1641)	觉浪道盛 Kakurō Dōshō (1592-1659)	为霖道霈 Irin Dōhai (1615-1702) (Irin Line) 为霖系
破闇净灯 Ha'an Jōtō (1603-1659)	阔堂大文 Katsudō Daibun	
古樵智先 Koshō Chisen (Shōzan Line) 焦山系	心越兴俦 Shinetsu Kōchū (1642-1696) 心越派 (东渡)	

Chart X A The Shōzan Line 焦山（古樵）系

古樵智先 Koshō Chisen
|
鉴堂德镜 Kandō Tokukyō
|
硕庵行载 Seki'an Gyōsai
|
敏修福毅 Minshū Fukuki (d. 1790)
|
碧岩祥洁 Hekigan Shōketsu (1703-1765)
|
济舟澄洮 Saishū Chōtō (d. 1737)
|
澹宁清镜 Tan'un Seikyō
|
巨超清恒 Kyo'etsu Seikō
|
秋屏觉灯 Shūhei Seikō
|
性源觉诠 Shōgen Kakusen
|
墨溪海荫 Mukkei Kai'in
|
月辉了禅 Getsuki Ryōzen
|
流长悟春 Ryūchō Goshun
|
芥航大须 Kaikō Daishu
|
云帆昌道 Unhan Shōdō
|
德俊　　Tokushun
|
吉堂　　Kitsudō
|
智光弥性 Chikō Mishō (1888-1963)
|
东初镗朗 Tōsho Tōrō (1908-1977)
|
慧空圣严 Ekū Shōgen (1930-)

Chart X B　The Irin Line 为霖系

为霖道霈 Irin Dōhai (1615-1702)
|
恒涛大心 Kōtō Daishin (d. 1728)
|
遍照兴隆 Henshō Kōryū (d. 1775)
|
清淳法源 Seijun Hōkō
|
东阳界初 Tōyō Kaisho
|
道源一信 Dōgen Ichishin
|
继云鼎善 Kei'un Teizen
|
增辉新灼 Zōki Shinshaku
|
圆智通完 Enchi Tsūkan
|
能持天性 Nōji Tenshō (d. 1848)
|
云程兼慈 Untei Kenji
|
净空彻印 Jōkū Tetsuin
|
悟源地本 Gogen Chihon
|
圆瑛耀性 En'ei Yōshō (1877-)
|
慈航古开 Jikō Kokai (1895-1954)
|
严持复戒 Genji Fukukai (1929-)

NOTE: According to Mōgetsu Shinkyō's *Bukkyō Dainen Hyō* 望月信亨：佛教大年表, 4th edition, page 48, the Ku-shan (Kozan) line 鼓山系 started from Ku-shan Yuan-hsien [Kozan Genken 鼓山元贤 (1578-1657)], followed by Irin Dōhai (1615-1702). The next was Ijo Dōan 惟静道安. Then Kōto Daishin (d. 1728), who was Dōhai's dharma-heir, followed. Then the list gave: Engyoku Kōgō 圆玉兴五, Zōsen Hō'in 象先法印, Tannen Hōbun 淡然法文, Jōmin Hōjun 常敏法濬, before Henshō Kōryū (d. 1775), who was Kōtō's dharma-heir. So Mōgetsu's lineage was the "garan" line 伽蓝系, but not the "dharma" line. This "garan" line checked with the list of Abbots given in *Ku-shan Lieh-tsu Lien-fang Chi* 鼓山列祖联芳集, reprinted in *Dharma Records of Abbot Hsu Yun* 虚云和尚法汇, Vol. 9, pages 266–297.

　　Note that Irin Dohai was the 96th Abbot at Ku-shan, Kōtō was the 98th Abbot, Henshō was the 103rd Abbot, Seijun was the 104th Abbot, Tōyō was the 105th Abbot, Dōgen was the 106th Abbot, and Kei'un was the 107th Abbot. Now Enchi was the 111th Abbot, while his dharma-teacher Zōki was the 113th Abbot. Enchi's dharma-heir Nōji was the 116th Abbot, and Nōji's heir Untei was the 117th Abbot.

　　The author wishes to thank Reverend Yen-chih (Genji) 严持法师 for supplying the above lineage.